Praise for *Love Every Day*

"Alexandra Solomon's work is mandatory for anyone who desires a road map to improve their relationships (especially with the person in the mirror). Her thoughtful teachings make it easy to view the world with sincere humility, resulting in more confidence and peace within."

—**Kristen Bell,** actress, producer, author,
entrepreneur, and mental health advocate

"Alexandra Solomon's *Love Every Day* is like a daily taste of Belgian chocolate: rich and thoughtful musings for when you're hungry for more satisfying relationships."

—**Esther Perel,** psychotherapist, *New York Times* bestselling
author, and host of the *Where Should We Begin?* podcast

"If you're ready to deepen and revitalize your relationship, look no further than *Love Every Day*. With hundreds of reflections and lessons on topics such as trust, intimacy, communication, and commitment, this book is an essential and approachable guide to modern relationships. Solomon is sharp and compassionate, inspiring readers to cultivate the love they truly deserve."

—**Lori Gottlieb,** *New York Times* bestselling author of *Maybe You
Should Talk to Someone* and co-host of the *Dear Therapists* podcast

"Each of the daily insights that make up *Love Every Day* is a gift. Solomon's writing is a refreshing blend of clinical wisdom, life-giving empathy, and humor that will guide you to clarity and connection in your most important relationships. What are you waiting for?"

—**Terry Real,** founder of the Relational Life Institute in Massachusetts and *New York Times* bestselling author of *Us: Getting Past You and Me to Build a More Loving Relationship*

"In *Love Every Day*, Alexandra Solomon takes us on a magnificent journey of self-reflection, with each daily entry uncovering a key to creating deeper connection with the people we love. I highly recommend this book to anyone seeking to transform their relationships—and their lives—for the better."

—**Dr. Shefali Tsabary,** clinical psychologist and *New York Times* bestselling author of *The Conscious Parent*

"Have you ever wished you could have one of the wisest, kindest, most thoughtful and relationally aware therapists in the world supporting you in your daily practice of living and loving with more compassion and curiosity? *Love Every Day* is just that. Dr. Solomon perfects offering a meaningful reflection every day, while balancing the need for grace and accountability for self and other through that process. Your life and relationships will undoubtedly begin to expand and heal throughout the year."

—**Vienna Pharaon, LMFT,** author of the national bestseller *The Origins of You*

"Intimate relationships have always been hazardous terrain for me: as powerfully as they draw me in, they also have the singular ability to fog up the windshield of my self-awareness, scramble my signals, and leave me disoriented, dysregulated, and discouraged. How encouraging, then, to have Alexandra Solomon's calm, steady guidance piped in via these bite-sized daily entries, each packed full of fruitful questions and readily applicable wisdom. She understands that true closeness with another starts with making our own intimate acquaintance. In *Love Every Day*, Dr. Solomon's wise and compassionate approach is like making a daily date with those stowaway parts of us that, through no fault of their own, fear and resist the thing we most deeply desire—to be known, seen, understood, and accepted—so that they don't have to drive us or our relationships into the ditch in order to be heard."

—**Daniel Maté,** co-author of the *New York Times* bestselling *The Myth of Normal: Trauma, Illness, and Healing in a Toxic Culture*

"Another powerful relationship book by Dr. Solomon! *Love Every Day* offers you the chance to deeply reflect, question, and change relationship behaviors and patterns. This book not only offers you the opportunity to improve your relationship with a significant other, it invites you to grow into a deeper connection with yourself. Ultimately, we all long to be intimately known, and Dr. Solomon gives us 365 practices to help us thrive."

—**Dr. Tracy Dalgleish,** psychologist, couples therapist, and author of *I Didn't Sign Up for This*

"Through a theoretical lens of relational self-awareness and a digestible calendar format, Dr. Solomon offers more effective ways for the reader to heal from trauma, interrupt reactivity, and foster deeper communication in intimate relationships."

—**Resmaa Menakem,** trauma specialist, healer, and *New York Times* bestselling author of *My Grandmother's Hands*

"Dr. Alexandra Solomon brilliantly combines her extensive clinical acumen with her unique insights to create *Love Every Day*. This comprehensive guide, with its 365 thought-provoking prompts, ushers us into a new level of relational self-awareness. A must-have tool for anyone seeking to enhance their relationship dynamics and create healthier love."

—**Terri Cole,** psychotherapist and author of *Boundary Boss*

"This book is a must-have for anyone wanting to learn more about themselves, love, and how to cultivate incredible relationships—and in turn, an incredible life. There is no one more qualified to write this book and guide us toward this beautiful destination than Dr. Alexandra Solomon. She is not only a prolific writer but also an incredible teacher. I have never witnessed anyone distill easy daily steps to creating better relationships better than Dr. Solomon does in this book. If I could give this book a million stars, I would, because it's written by one of the most thoughtful and brilliant relationship luminaries of our time."

—**Mark Groves,** relationship expert, author, speaker, coach, and founder of Create The Love

ALEXANDRA H. SOLOMON, PHD

LOVE
EVERY
DAY

365 RELATIONAL SELF-AWARENESS PRACTICES TO HELP YOUR RELATIONSHIP HEAL, GROW, AND THRIVE

LOVE EVERY DAY
Copyright © 2023 by Alexandra Solomon

Published by
PESI Publishing, Inc.
3839 White Ave
Eau Claire, WI 54703

Cover and interior design by Amy Rubenzer
Editing by Chelsea Thompson
Photo credit: Sam Hardy Portraits

ISBN: 9781683736530 (print)
ISBN: 9781683736547 (ePUB)
ISBN: 9781683736554 (ePDF)

To my incredible family:
Todd, Brian, and Courtney

You are my strength and my joy.

TABLE OF CONTENTS

WELCOME

I like to say that falling in love is like shaking a snow globe: old stuff (from previous relationships and even from childhood) gets activated, swirling up from where it all settled at the bottom. This does not happen because people are silly or broken. *This is simply the nature of romantic love.* Rather than fear the storm or succumb to it, our work in love is to grab our hat and mittens and face it with our partner.

Over the past two decades, I've had the privilege of teaching thousands of students, working with hundreds of couples in my therapy practice, and sharing my relationship insights with millions on social media. I'm thrilled to compile many of these reflections all in one place in this volume to help us explore the most profound and pressing relationship challenges of our time. This book, and my work more broadly, is here to help you cultivate what I call **Relational Self-Awareness**, an ongoing curious and compassionate relationship we each have *with ourselves*. By helping us take responsibility for how we "show up" in our relationships, Relational Self-Awareness provides the foundation for thriving intimate relationships.

The journey of developing Relational Self-Awareness is not about striving for perfection—it's about becoming humble and curious about our inner world and the way we relate to others. In this book, you will be invited to cultivate and improve skills such as listening with empathy, understanding and interrupting unhealthy patterns, advocating for your needs, offering heartfelt apologies, tending to your inner child (or what I call **Little You**), practicing self-compassion, and so much more. In addition, one of the pillars of Relational Self-Awareness is the practice of adjusting our lens to understand how our inner world, our relationship patterns, and our larger cultural context all affect and influence each other. You will find a number of entries in this book that explore how various influences on our relationships—the micro (individual and couple dynamics) and the macro (cultural factors)—mirror each other.

Introspection and intimacy are inextricably linked. When we truly love and allow ourselves to receive love, especially over the long term, our tender spots, emotional wounds, deepest fears, and insecurities are revealed. Though this can be scary, it creates the possibility for us to be seen and loved as our most authentic selves . . . and to heal from the times when we weren't.

If you are currently in an intimate relationship, this book can help you and your partner ensure that your partnership becomes a "classroom," where all your experiences (joyful, frustrating, confusing, poignant) become lessons that help you understand yourselves and each other more deeply. You will learn to coauthor a love story with the power to heal your past and help you celebrate your individual and collective potential.

And if you are currently single or between relationships, this book can help you understand your past (both in the family you grew up with and your prior intimate relationships) so you can make wise and conscious choices in your present and build toward a thriving future.

When compiling my essays and adding new ones to create this collection, I had readers of all relationship statuses in mind. This book is for the person who married their high school sweetheart and is still in love with them fifty years later. It's for the young adult who has just started their dating journey and is both bewildered and excited to find someone special. It's for the person who is healing from heartbreak or a difficult childhood. And it is for the couple who is beginning a new chapter in the wake of a major life event, growing their family, or facing a relational challenge. No matter who you are, the journey of Relational Self-Awareness is for you. By picking up this book, you are making a brave and meaningful investment in yourself and your relationships.

Intimacy is a journey, not a destination. My hope is that Relational Self-Awareness can become your trusty internal compass, guiding you toward relationships that nourish you and away from relationships that replicate old pain, and help you hold the beautiful complexity of being both whole as you are and forever a work in progress. I'm so glad you're here.

HOW TO USE THIS BOOK

This book offers 365 entries designed to help you heal, grow, and thrive. It doesn't matter which day of the year your journey begins. Just find today's date and dive in.

Each entry in this book aligns with one of the nine central themes of Relational Self-Awareness: **Healing from the Past, Practicing Self-Compassion, Honoring Your Feelings, Understanding Relationship Dynamics, Getting Your Needs Met, Transforming Conflict, Addressing Relationship Problems, Developing Sexual Self-Awareness,** and **Navigating Love's Stages**. Each of these themes corresponds to a specific color, noted in the following table, to make them easier to find. Based on your history, it is possible that certain themes become more prominent at different times, so anytime your relationship feels upsetting or perplexing, you can flip through the book to find an entry that addresses what you need in that moment. However, it's important to explore each of the nine themes and how they relate to each other so that your journey to Relational Self-Awareness is holistic and complete.

THEMES	DESCRIPTION
Healing from the Past	Make connections between your family dynamics, traumatic experiences, and other emotional "baggage" and your current relationship dynamics to better understand how the past shows up in your relationships today.
Practicing Self-Compassion	Rest more comfortably in self-worth and understand the powerful connection between self-love and intimacy with a partner.
Honoring Your Feelings	Understand and interpret the "data" within your internal world and work more effectively with emotional triggers (your own and your partner's).
Understanding Relationship Dynamics	Lose the "me versus you" mindset and move into an "us versus the problem" mindset that deepens intimacy.
Getting Your Needs Met	Learn strategies for creating healthy boundaries and setting expectations in ways that create respect and prevent resentment.
Transforming Conflict	Learn what it means to fight against disconnection rather than against each other.
Addressing Relationship Problems	Understand the issues behind common but complex relationship problems (trust, infidelity, betrayal, jealousy, ambivalence).
Developing Sexual Self-Awareness	Find reasons to feel good in your skin and connect with a partner in ways that feel wonderful for both of you.
Navigating Love's Stages	Celebrate the narrative arc of an intimate relationship and gain insight into what it takes to make love last.

Toward the back of the book, you will find a glossary of terms (these words appear capitalized throughout the entries) and additional resources for continued support on your journey of Relational Self-Awareness.

To get the most out of this book, I recommend setting aside some time each day to read an entry. You can then work with the entry in any or all of the following ways:

1. **Write in your journal.** Many of the entries offer Relational Self-Awareness questions that promote reflection, which can be done by writing—or simply considering—your thoughts. For those entries without reflection questions, you can use the following general questions:

    ◦ What does this entry remind you of or make you think about?

    ◦ How does this entry leave you feeling?

    ◦ What does this entry make you want to embody or practice in your life? How might you begin to do this?

2. **Meditate on a word or phrase from the entry.** Set a timer for 5 to 10 minutes. Sit quietly and let the message of the entry settle inside you.

3. **Share the entry with someone you love and trust and use it to spark a conversation.** For this option, remember to initiate the conversation with a loved one (your intimate partner, a friend, a family member) in a curious and open-hearted way. Do not lead with a guilt trip ("The least you could do is read this entry for me!") or a criticism ("You really need this entry!"). This will likely activate a defensive response in the other person, and the conversation will go poorly as a result. Instead, try something like, "It means so much to me when you read these entries with me"

or "I love it when we use these entries as a conversation starter. I learn so much from it!"

4. **Form a reading circle with friends or loved ones.** Use the entries as a jumping-off point for conversation and collective care.

There are no wrong ways to use this book. See what works best for you!

A NOTE ABOUT GENDER

This book is designed to serve readers of all sexual and gender identities in all stages of relationship development. However, research shows that gender role norms tend to occur most rigidly and narrowly within the realms of intimate relationships. With this in mind, some entries address the specific and harmful impacts of heteronormativity on these types of partnerships. I've done my best to include ideas about how a particular dynamic may play out for readers who belong to the LGBTQIA+ community. However, as all people and partnerships are distinct, there may be some instances where a certain experience is not as well represented. I hope that you feel seen, supported, and valued in these pages.

WELCOME TO CLASS

Love is a classroom where we learn about ourselves, others, and the world around us in the most profound and humbling ways imaginable. Since none of us received an instruction manual for intimate relationships, learning to love others well and receive love ourselves is a lifelong journey, one that therapy, community, and books like this can support. Seeking out resources to improve your relationship is a sign of strength and emotional maturity, and an investment that will pay off for years to come. I hope this book can serve as a textbook of sorts for your relationship, sparking inquiry and self-reflection in that beautiful space of learning. I am grateful to be on this journey with you.

CAVEAT ABOUT ABUSE AND ADDITIONAL RESOURCES

Throughout this book, we will address a wide range of common relationship dynamics, and I will offer language, tools, and guidance for how to manage your thoughts and emotions so you can advocate in positive and effective ways with your intimate partner. However, these essays are *not* applicable for readers who are in an abusive relationship.

The National Domestic Violence Hotline (http://thehotline.org) defines relationship abuse as a pattern of coercive behavior used to maintain power and control over a current or former intimate partner. Relationships like these can include some or all of the following:

- Emotional abuse (name-calling, belittling)

- Physical abuse (grabbing, hitting, shoving)

- Sexual abuse (forcing or coercing sexual activity)

- Threats and intimidation intended to gain or maintain power

- Isolation (limiting, monitoring, or preventing access to family and friends)

- Financial abuse (preventing someone from getting a job, controlling access to money)

- Using children to gain power (telling children lies about the partner, threatening to take children away)

For more resources regarding domestic violence, please see the crisis support section at the end of this book.

Healing isn't a straight line.

Early in our healing journey, we tend to talk about the changes we crave in a way that unwittingly puts an immense amount of pressure on ourselves. We tend to say things like:

- "I want to stop acting like this."
- "I hate this part of me."
- "I want to fix this problem."

The trouble with this language is that it ends up creating a binary:

- Bad behavior versus good behavior
- Unacceptable versus acceptable parts of the self
- Broken versus fixed

Binaries can be incredibly limiting, as we have been blessed to learn from those of us who are finding infinite ways to live beyond the gender binary. For example:

- **Binaries put us in boxes.** I am either *this* or I am *that*.

- **Binaries create the conditions for self-flagellation.** If I am not *this* it means I am *that*, and now I'm "effed" because I told myself and everyone else that I'm no longer *that*.

- **Binaries are too perfectionist and static.** If I am *this*, I can/will/ must never be *that*.

Healing is not an on/off switch. The human condition demands a path of profound gentleness. See what shifts for you emotionally when you use these phrases to talk about the changes you want to make:

- "I'm working on being less like *this* and more like *that* . . ."
- "I am letting go of *this* and beginning to practice *that* . . ."
- "I'm committed to moving away from *this* and embracing *that* . . ."

JANUARY 2

Be brave enough to ask yourself
What's it like to be with me right now?

It can be so easy to be oblivious to the impact we are having on the people around us because most of us have an **Origin Story**—the experiences we went through that shaped our current relationship to relationships—that creates a tendency for us to hyper-focus on what *someone else* (our parent, our partner, our kid) is doing. For example:

- **You were highly sensitive as a kid.** Being hyper-focused on the mood of the grown-ups around you may have helped you prepare yourself for being hit with big and unpredictable emotions.

- **You occupy one or more marginalized identities.** Being hyper-focused on those who have more power is a survival strategy.

- **You were the "golden child" in your family dynamic.** As a result, nobody held you accountable for how your behavior affected others.

- **You occupy one or more privileged identities.** This can make you more accustomed to setting the tone rather than responding to it.

The first two bullets represent powerlessness, while the last two denote a false sense of power. Neither of them lays the foundation for healthy relationships.

Life may not have given you many opportunities to get curious about how the people around you experience you. But even when we have a **Growing Edge** (something we are currently working on trying to improve upon or master in our life) that isn't our "fault," it is nonetheless ours to remedy—recognizing this deficit is the first step to resolving it.

Develop a practice of imagining how other people feel in your presence:

- *Am I making it safe to speak vulnerably to me?*

- *How gentle is my tone?*

- *To what degree is my energy opening dialogue up or shutting it down?*

If you don't like your answers to the previous questions, don't use them as fuel for self-flagellation. Instead, take this as an opportunity to get insight on yourself and guide new choices:

- Do you need more sleep?

- Do you need some space?

- Are you being hard on them because you're hard on yourself?

- What are you afraid will happen if you become more approachable?

When the models of intimate partnership that you saw growing up leave you with a clearer sense of what you do not want than what you do want, you get to fill in the blanks for yourself.

The luckiest among us grew up surrounded by healthy models of intimate partnership. Others witnessed conflict, distance, or worse. We were left to figure it out as we fumble along, patching together an image of love from fairy tales, rom-coms, porn, and song lyrics. But to experience true intimacy, you have to (and get to) burn down these templates and build something real from the ashes.

Relational Self-Awareness Prompts
In my intimate relationship:

- I want to feel . . .
- I want my partner to feel . . .
- I want to be seen as . . .
- I want to be trusted to . . .
- I want to know . . .
- I want my partner to know . . .
- I want my partner to be able to . . .
- I want to be able to . . .

These are not demands. These are intentions, guiding principles, and invitations for the kind of love you want. Define it. Describe it. Declare it.

When you catch yourself wondering why your reaction in the present moment seems bigger than it "should" be, remind yourself that new pain connects itself to old pain.

Today's grief calls forth the grief of long ago. Feelings you have known before visit you again, amplified by their familiarity. Grief demands that you work with it, not against it. You must meet it, not push it away. If you feel tears pressing behind your eyes, I hope you let yourself cry. Resist the urge to tell yourself that you should feel some other kind of way. Feel how you feel.

Because grief echoes through time, it must be carried with great gentleness. When everything feels so big, focus on what is real, here and now. For example:

- Your child's laugh
- The evening crickets
- A nighttime sweet treat
- The blanket on your lap
- An absorbing show that allows you to "escape" for a while

When you allow grief to move through you, you create the possibility for something new to arise. Perhaps presence. Perhaps tenderness. Perhaps a reminder that to be alive is to sit with strong and difficult emotions while striving to remain engaged and kind.

We can be tender with our Core Wounds even as we address our Coping Strategies.

Core Wound: The pain left by an experience or a dynamic we had to deal with when we were too young to understand, control, or change it. Core Wounds stem from experiences that are too much for us to handle, happen too soon in our lives, and/or that we're left to deal with all alone.

Examples of Core Wounds include:

- *I am not a priority.*
- *I am not protected.*
- *I don't belong.*
- *I am not worthy.*

Coping Strategy: The thing(s) we started doing to make our too-big feelings feel manageable. They are "where we go" when we get upset.

Examples of Coping Strategies include:

- People-pleasing
- Numbing out with drugs or alcohol
- Demanding perfection or overworking
- Needing to be needed
- Being hyper-independent
- Leaving before you can be left

In my many years of doing therapy, I have never met a Core Wound that doesn't evoke deep compassion inside me. In contrast, I have met many Coping Strategies that are troubling and intimacy-eroding. Core

Wounds and Coping Strategies originate in our early years and travel with us into adulthood.

The work of Relational Self-Awareness is to understand how your past shapes your present and to cultivate relationships in which it is safe enough to share your story with your partner, not as an excuse for "bad" behavior but as a context for understanding and intimacy.

Instead of asking, "Why didn't you do X?" try asking, "What kept you from doing X?"

Partner A makes a request of Partner B. Partner B doesn't deliver. Partner A feels some mix of hurt, confusion, and anger. When Partner A approaches Partner B to figure out why stuff went off the rails, Partner A needs to ask what we in the world of family therapy call a *constraint question*.

A constraint question is founded in a belief that our loved one *wants* to give us what we want, but something is getting in the way. To quietly invite the loving response we crave and plant the seed of intimacy, a constraint question starts with the words: "What kept you from . . ."

- Instead of "Why did you lie?" ask, "What kept you from telling the truth?"
- Instead of "Why didn't you call?" ask, "What kept you from calling?"

When you ask a constraint question, you are inviting your partner to look together at what's blocking their loving/connecting/adaptive response. Rather than looking only at their mistakes, inadequacies, and

Core Wounds, asking a constraint question is courageous because it puts the relationship itself under the microscope.

Here's a heads-up, though: asking a constraint question means taking a risk. You may hear something tender from your partner, like, "Your responses are loud and unpredictable. I'm afraid to be honest with you." This does not mean their lying is your fault. But it does mean you are invited to look at the kind of relational climate you *both* are creating. You get to explore how to break the cycle together—you can work on emotion regulation in order to invite more truth, and they can be more truthful so you get less mad. A constraint question repositions you and your partner on the same side of the problem.

The marriage you need at age 30 is different from the marriage you need at age 50, and both are different from the marriage you need at age 70. If you're very lucky (and very skilled), you'll have all of those marriages with the same person.

One of the beautiful things about intimate relationships today is that we place such a high value on intimacy—that is, truly seeing each other. We strive to get beyond the *role* of boyfriend/girlfriend/partner/husband/wife/ spouse and to really treasure the *soul* of the person we are partnered with.

Our souls are not bound by linearity, time, or role. To love another's soul is to love an essence that transcends the wet towel on the floor, the cranky attitude at dinner, and the miscommunication about money. Through this lens, an intimate relationship is about shepherding the journey of our beloved's soul. Through this lens, the contexts change, the bodies change, the energy levels change, the dramas change, but what is constant is the gift of staying near someone we treasure.

Let me draw your attention to the **Both/And** of luck and skill: *both* are required for a relationship to succeed *and* I don't know the exact mix a given couple needs to thrive—every relationship is different after all! Skill helps . . . but so does luck. Burdens and privileges are far from equally distributed among us, and that goes for couples as well. Remember that despite being at the whims of the universe, the work you do on yourself and within your relationship makes a real difference.

Our relationships tend to need *less* problem-solving and advice and *more* space-holding and empathy.

Discernment is about assessing a situation well and selecting the response that best serves the relationship. When someone opens up to us, our responses can be divided into two broad categories:

- **A problem-solving response:** This response is about fixing or advising, and it sounds like this:

  - "You should . . ."

  - "You need to . . ."

  - "You have to . . ."

- **An empathy-based response:** This response is about holding space, and it sounds like this:

  - "This is complicated."

- "I can see why you're struggling here."
- "I think I'd feel the same way if I was in your shoes."

It's safe to say that most of our relationships would be improved if we offered more empathy and less advice. Empathy is empowering—it helps the other person clarify how they feel and decide for themselves how to solve the problem. Their next step will feel more authentic and aligned because they felt their way into it rather than being directed into it. This allows us to get closer to our partner as we establish ourselves as a compassionate listener in their lives.

"Overreacting" may mean that you buried your feelings about earlier slights.

My first clinical supervisor, Dr. Bill Pinsof, used to say, "God is in the sequence." He meant that one of the most important things a couples therapist can do is track the familiar patterns—the "choreography," if you will—of their interactions. For example:

- Partner A did not shovel the driveway despite it being "their job."
- Partner B feels really upset about this.
- Partner B approaches Partner A with tears in their eyes and deep upset in their voice.
- Partner A says, "You're totally overreacting. I'll go do it now."

First of all, if you want a happy and peaceful relationship, strike the word *overreacting* from your vocabulary forever. It's invalidating and invites defensiveness. But second, let's understand the force of Partner B's response to Partner A's seemingly minor infraction:

- Perhaps Partner B has bitten their tongue over a prolonged series of painful moments with Partner A, and the shoveling incident is the final straw.

- Perhaps Partner A is hard to approach with problems/concerns.

- It may be that Partner B grew up in a family that didn't do emotional attunement, and thus got very good at saying, "It's fine/I'm fine."

Healing is about learning to notice all the shades of feelings. When you get better at tracking sequences and get curious about what sets them off, you can intervene in your customary choreography and create a new set of steps with your partner.

JANUARY 10

Everyone brings baggage into their intimate relationships. The brave ones open up their bags so they can explore and share what's inside.

We cannot be held responsible for our temperaments. We cannot be held responsible for the families we're born into. In fact, we cannot be held responsible for *many* of life's curveballs, disappointments, and losses. Still, these factors shape our behavior and our expectations of ourselves and each other. Some of us resist looking at what love stirs within and between us because:

- It makes us feel vulnerable.

- We think it's tantamount to blaming our grown-ups or letting ourselves off the hook.

- Looking forward, not back, is the only way we've known how to survive.

Intimacy is not about holding out for some fairy tale moment when your baggage is finally fixed. It's not about discovering a "twin flame" who travels unencumbered by any of their own stuff. It's about finding someone who can be real with you—who can care for you and receive your care and for whom you can do the same. Understanding yourself helps you deepen your commitment, share and receive appreciation, stay present and connected for lovemaking, and navigate the inevitable bumps in the road. The more willing each of you are to understand and be responsible for what you're bringing into the relationship, the healthier the dynamic will be.

JANUARY 11

Relational Self-Awareness is a marathon, not a sprint.

The one thing I have heard most often from people who are learning to practice Relational Self-Awareness? "I wish I had discovered your work years ago!" In fact, it's common for self-reflection to bring about many different realizations. For example:

- Learning how to pay attention to what is happening inside of you highlights the years you spent not knowing how to listen to yourself.

- Learning how to communicate more effectively with your partner highlights the years when fear, not love, was in the driver's seat.

- Learning how to enact healthier boundaries highlights all the times when your boundaries created pain inside you and/or the people around you.

Insights can create impatience. Our thinking can start to sound like this: *I have to work really hard at Relational Self-Awareness; I want to figure it all out right now.* There are two problems with this:

1. **There is no final destination.** You will not "arrive" at Relational Self-Awareness. Instead, you will develop a set of tools that help you relate to painful and frustrating moments with more patience and compassion.

2. **Faster doesn't mean better.** Healing has a pace of its own, and forcing yourself to do more can backfire by creating burnout and numbness.

It's why I love the structure of this book—it creates opportunities for bite-sized reflections. Create an insight, hold it, work with it, integrate it. Then create another insight. This intimacy within yourself, born of insight and reflection, helps you create intimacy with your partner.

JANUARY 12

We are forever changed by love. Our work is to be expanded, rather than diminished, by it.

Fear of losing yourself in an intimate relationship arises from the awareness that love changes you. If you sense the change will be a diminishment rather than an expansion, it's time for self-reflection. You may carry this fear for any number of reasons, including (but not limited to):

- Seeing one parent chronically accommodate another parent

- Having a past relationship in which your needs and concerns were ignored

- Occupying one or more marginalized identities, so the world has given you the message that you are less important than others

Love does not leave us where it finds us. We must open ourselves to let another person in. We must decenter our own wants/needs/opinions in order to make space for someone else's. Do not conflate *change* with *loss*. In a healthy intimate relationship, we get to become *more* of ourselves.

An intimate relationship will always require some amount of shift from *me* to *we*. The process of moving toward interdependence is more intuitive than logical, more qualitative than quantitative. If you start keeping track of how often you accommodated them versus how often they accommodated you, you're going to end up exhausted. Furthermore, you won't feel particularly sexually engaged with each other, as the transactional and the erotic don't pair so well together.

Stepping into the bewildering experience of love is a brave act. Therefore, paradoxically, a fear of losing yourself can be a sign of progress toward intimacy!

Relational Self-Awareness Questions

- What, specifically, are you afraid of losing?

- Who are you afraid of becoming?

- What signs could you see to show you are in fact losing yourself?

- What do you want your partner to understand about your fear of losing yourself?

Self-compassion benefits you *and* your partner.

We can be nicer to our partner than we are to ourselves, at least for a while. But that plan is unsustainable—it sets us up to resent our partner long-term. If we're giving up all the goodies and saving none for ourselves, we will likely end up completely depleted. The practice of self-compassion helps us in our intimate relationships by nourishing our soul and readying us for intimacy with another person. How amazing that a practice designed to heal us as individuals is wildly helpful for us as couples!

According to Dr. Kristin Neff, self-compassion consists of three elements:

1. **Self-kindness:** Talking to yourself the way you would talk to a dear friend

2. **Common humanity:** Remembering that you're not the first, last, or only person to struggle with whatever you're struggling with

3. **Mindfulness:** Bringing your attention to the present moment and dropping judgment

When you know you are suffering, that's your cue to practice self-compassion. The goal isn't to reduce your suffering but instead to meet it in a different way. Rather than focusing on how you shouldn't have gotten yourself into this spot in the first place, or how someone smarter/cooler/savvier would figure this out, or how this shouldn't hurt as badly as it does, put your hand on your heart and offer kindness to yourself. Slow down. Breathe deep. Create safety inside.

Anxiety invites us to hone our ability to find peace in a storm.

Anxiety is wildly seductive. It whispers that you'll be able to exhale once you reach a finish line. For example:

- "I'll feel less anxious once I reach 20 weeks in this pregnancy."
- "I'll be able to relax when this batch of papers is graded."
- "I'll love my body after I lose five pounds."

Breaking big things into littler things helps us tap into our resilience. (It's why my Peloton® instructors tell me there's only 20 seconds left in a tough interval.) But it also feeds the beast. The promise of a finish line postpones the vital work of learning to cultivate peace/power/calm/joy/comfort while we're *inside* the storm.

Life offers no guarantees or promises. Instead, it invites us again and again to be present within the unfolding mystery. It is in the uncertainty that we find our resilience—but only if we accept the challenge.

Relational Self-Awareness Questions

- What finish lines have you created for yourself?
- What bit of peace might you claim now, instead of making it contingent on something in the future?
- Is there someone in your life that holds space for you and helps you process anxieties? Can you also be that person for someone else?

A "fear of commitment" might be a misunderstanding of what's being asked.

There are two reasons I am going to talk about fear of commitment in a gendered way. First, when I get asked about this, it's usually by a woman who is partnered with a man. Second, I want to address gender role-based scripts that can create constraints to commitment:

- Do all men fear commitment? No.

- Do some women who love men fear commitment? Yes!

- Do same-sex couples and couples who live beyond the gender binary fear commitment too? Of course!

When someone is avoiding commitment, it can be immensely helpful to do some **Ghostbusting**—working together to explore how pain from the past is compromising connection and ease in the present. Is there a childhood wound, a past trauma, or a previously broken heart blocking the path to deeper intimacy? Or could it perhaps be a *projection* that is getting in the way?

Our traditional (and still dominant) relational model states that when a man commits, he takes on a responsibility to provide. Even if a woman is clear about wanting to co-create an interdependent model that suits each of them financially, emotionally, and pragmatically, her words may not impact what he *imagines* she wants and will expect of him. She also may be blind to her male partner's belief because it feels tremendously personal when someone pulls back. She may understandably get lost in a story that he would commit if she were different/better/worthier.

The work for a couple in this position is to stand shoulder to shoulder and deconstruct the cultural baggage they both have inherited. This process holds the promise of liberating them from others' expectations so they can create their own.

JANUARY 16

You are a story. Who you were, who you are, and who you will be are a part of a series of unfolding chapters.

The particular challenges you face today are shaped by things like where you live, what you do for work, and whom you are surrounded by. But if you dig deeper, you find ways that your current challenges activate and are activated by old stuff. Exploring the connection between your current stressor and the old stuff it kicks up is helpful—you give yourself an opportunity to attend to old pain and give the people around you the chance to understand you more deeply.

Relational Self-Awareness Questions

- How does your current challenge remind you of an earlier chapter in your life?
- What might you be able to ask for now that was not available to you back then?
- What might you be able to do for yourself now that you were not able to do for yourself back then?

When you're bridging a self-awareness difference in your intimate relationship, be careful not to confuse inexperience with contempt.

One of the most confusing differences some couples bridge is a contrast in Relational Self-Awareness. However, sameness is not a prerequisite for intimacy. In fact, curiously exploring the nature of your differences side by side is a powerful way to promote intimacy.

I am not telling you to stay or go if you're facing a Relational Self-Awareness difference. However, I *am* saying that there are a lot of reasons people may differ in their level of self-awareness. Your partner's **Family of Origin** dynamics or gender and cultural barriers may have kept them from leaning into resources. Likewise, your partner's prior relationships may not have asked for the kind of depth you are craving. As a result, they may have thought the "kiddie pool" was the limit, and perhaps you are inviting them to swim in the deep end.

Inexperience with Relational Self-Awareness sounds like:

- "I am not sure what you're asking of me, but I want to understand."

- "I don't have a ton of language for my experience, but I want to try."

- "I value how you can talk about your feelings like this, and I want to get better at doing that too."

- "Let's keep talking like this."

Contempt for Relational Self-Awareness sounds like:

- "I don't believe in therapy."

- "You're too emotional."
- "What happened in my childhood is irrelevant."
- "I don't want to talk about this stuff."

Can you feel the difference? If your partner is inexperienced but willing, your patience is loving, not foolhardy. As your partner steps into this lifetime journey of Relational Self-Awareness, can you learn to celebrate their progress rather than focus on their deficiencies?

Some of us need to practice replacing "I'm sorry" with "Thank you."

As a kid, we may have been told:

- "You should be seen and not heard."
- "Don't make a fuss."
- "Don't take the biggest piece."

. . . and we were very good listeners! We internalized those messages and learned how to shrink down, blend in, or go without. This tendency followed us into adulthood, and it can be accompanied by a difficulty with being accommodated—if someone else changes what they were going to do in order to take our needs into account, we respond with an apology:

- "I'm sorry we went to this restaurant to accommodate my gluten allergy."
- "I'm sorry you started the meeting five minutes late because my train was delayed."

- "I'm sorry we weren't able to try this sexual position because of my injury."

In each instance, the apology arises from a belief that you *ought not* require accommodation. Let's go through each example again, replacing the "I'm sorry" with a "Thank you":

- "Thank you for trying this restaurant with me. The gluten-free pasta is so good!"
- "Thank you for starting the meeting a bit late because of my train delay. I'm so excited about this project!"
- "Thank you for your erotic creativity tonight. My injury has been dragging me down, and it felt so good to feel good with you!"

How does your body feel as you read these alternative responses?

Try replacing your next few "I'm sorries" with "Thank yous." As you do, take note of your internal response. How does the shift feel inside of you? How does it change the dynamic between you and the other person?

JANUARY 19

Explaining before empathizing blocks connection.

As I wrote in the introduction, falling in love is like shaking a snow globe: old stuff (from previous relationships, childhood, etc.) that you thought had settled inside of you gets stirred back up. This is not because you are silly or broken—this is the nature of romantic love. I would even say that the activation of Core Wounds is how you know you've let someone matter to you. But let's be crystal clear: the activation of a Core Wound is NOT a free pass to say or do whatever you want. There's a world of difference between *rationalization* and *contextualization*.

Let's say your partner tells you they're going out with friends, and you proceed to spend the day sulking. They ask why you refuse to talk with them, and you respond, "I am doing this because I have a fear of abandonment!" Presenting your Core Wound as a *rationalization* for your behavior is a relational dead end. Where does the relationship go from here? Your partner cancels their plans with friends? You silently communicate your hurt? There are not a lot of moves available.

In contrast, the path of Relational Self-Awareness guides you to pause and check in with yourself when your partner asks about your silence. You can:

- **Rewind the tape.** Identify that you went from open to closed-off when they made plans.

- **Own your response.** "Yeah, I really did shut down, didn't I?"

- **Offer empathy.** "I can imagine that felt confusing and upsetting for you."

- **Offer some *contextualization*.** "In my self-awareness work, it has become clear that some stuff I endured in my childhood set me up to be really sensitive to disconnection. I am continuing to tend to my 'scared little girl' so I can talk with you when I feel worried, rather than communicate it with my behavior. I have a lot of compassion for myself for what I went through as a kid, and I hope you do too. And I know I have a chance to do this differently here with you in our relationship."

explanation before empathy =
a *rationalization* that yields relational disconnection

empathy before explanation =
a *contextualization* that yields relational connection

The same quality in your partner is often a source of attraction in the easy moments and a source of distress in the difficult moments.

The scientist is drawn to the artist because the artist reminds the scientist that the irrational is sacred. The introvert is drawn to the extrovert because the extrovert moves the introvert out of their comfort zone. The feeler is drawn to the thinker because the thinker shows the feeler that sometimes the shortest distance between two points is, in fact, a straight line.

But during moments of frustration and stress, the scientist wishes the artist could make a plan and stick to it, the introvert wishes the extrovert could feel content at home, and the feeler wishes the thinker could let down and cry sometimes.

It is one of love's unshakable truths: the same quality that attracts us to a partner holds the power to repel us as well. This double-edged sword of differences is puzzling. But there's a hidden beauty in how this paradox reminds us:

- **To be humble:** The complexities of love are to be navigated rather than solved.

- **To practice grace:** When we can love multifaceted truths about our partner, we can tolerate the same within ourselves.

Loving someone can provide the motivation needed to shed old ways of coping that were born of necessity when you were young.

All of us learn ways of managing pain. For some of us, our early years were full of hurt: feeling unseen and misunderstood, being mistreated physically and emotionally, dealing with stressors that far outpaced our ability to cope. The Coping Strategies we developed to protect ourselves from pain—finger-pointing, blaming, criticizing, running away, going numb, shutting down, going silent, placating, appeasing, reflexively apologizing—were necessary, maybe even lifesaving.

But then we grew up and fell in love. Falling in love requires shifting from a protected stance to an open one. It threatens old Coping Strategies by moving us toward vulnerability.

To the kid who dwells within us, opening up and trusting is scary. Downright terrifying, in fact. That little kid is scared that vulnerability will leave them feeling unsafe and unseen.

For this reason, it makes sense to go slowly when building an intimate relationship. It also makes sense to let your partner know when you feel shaky and unsure: "My instinct is to escape this tender/confusing/ upsetting moment by relying on an old Coping Strategy. But I love you. I love me. I love us. I want to stay present."

Neutrality is not a condition of healing.

Feeling neutral about a former partner is neither a condition of our healing nor proof that we're ready to move on. We do not need to wait for the total absence of feelings about our former partners to entertain the idea of loving again. Because love never leaves us where it finds us, we may carry a "forever pang" when we think of them. And that is okay.

We place perfectionistic expectations on our visions of how we think our healing "should" look. For example:

- "I must have closure." (As if love plays by the rules of linearity and simplicity.)

- "I must be able to think about my former partner without experiencing any level of upset." (As if there aren't 50 shades of emotional gray between a freshly broken heart and a wistful pang about what once was.)

- "I must be able to talk about my former partner with a voice that is nothing but calm and clear." (As if we can't occupy a place of both wholeness and humanness.)

Here's what I know for sure: You have an infinite capacity to love and be loved. Your past experiences take nothing from your present. Love is a renewable resource.

The strongest couples are Ghostbusters.

When we fall in love, our past gets stirred up from within us. The only question is what you will *do* when ghosts from long ago threaten to shift you from open to closed, from loving to afraid, or from calm to controlling. The answer: partner with a Ghostbuster! This is someone who is ready, willing, and able to recognize when their past takes the wheel and begins to drive.

You'll ask her to please pick her wet towel off the floor; you'll watch her bristle, and you won't know why. But she is courageous enough to *pause*, turn her attention inward, and figure out why your request triggers her. Then she says some version of this: "I think we're dealing with a ghost. I'm getting lost in an old story and it's getting in our way. In moments like this, it feels like you're my demanding father. In his eyes, I could never measure up. But that's not what you're doing, is it? You're stressed out and bringing order to chaos helps you feel calm."

With that, the little girl who felt like she never measured up recedes into the background, and the empowered adult reaches for her partner in the service of love. You both exhale, followed by a fist bump because you're badass Ghostbusters. With connection restored, you say, "Thank you for owning your piece of our dance. I commit to doing the same when Little Me gets stirred."

The best you can do is work to liberate yourself and your partners from wounds you didn't ask for but are called to heal.

JANUARY 24

A healthy intimate relationship is marked by the degree to which you get to show up as your *you-est* expression of you.

A healthy intimate relationship is not marked by perfection but by the degree to which you get to show up as your *you-est* expression of yourself. In a healthy intimate relationship, you will not get all of your needs met, but you also will not be criticized for having them. In a healthy intimate relationship, you get to bring all of you to the table: the silly you, the tender you, the brave you, the sassy you, the confused you, the jagged you, the lazy you, the passionate you. A healthy intimate relationship consists of two people figuring it out together, refining and reimagining as they go.

Healing shame is about your relationship with you.

Research shows that a healthy intimate relationship has the power to:

- Make a skeptical partner believe once again in the power of love
- Help an anxiously attached partner develop secure attachment strategies
- Embolden partners to take risks and try things that scare them

Unfortunately, a healthy relationship alone cannot heal shame. Shame has less to do with what your partner thinks of you and more to do with what *you* think of you. Your partner can offer comfort and nearness as you ride a wave of shame, but they cannot move you from shame to worthiness. This is simultaneously sad and liberating. It is sad to realize that someone else cannot rescue or fix you. It is liberating to know that you have the power to gently and lovingly offer compassion to yourself— you do not need to wait for anyone else!

Creating and maintaining a happy and healthy intimate relationship does not require being 100 percent shame-free 100 percent of the time. You must simply be able to remember that tending to your shame is *your* job.

It's well past time to liberate ourselves and each other from the idea that there is a right age and a wrong age to accomplish anything in life.

We inherit a ton of messages about timing and sequencing. We believe we have to go in the right order: *do this before you do that*. We believe we have to meet thresholds: *don't do this until age whatever*. These messages seduce us into thinking there are hard and fast secrets to success. Decision-making is stressful, so it's understandable that we seek a "recipe" to create comfort on the inside and connectedness between ourselves and others. But the truth is, life is unpredictable in the way it unfolds, and no one timeline is superior to another.

The hidden advantage of departing from a prescribed timeline is you get to feel deeply rooted in your choices and the experiences that follow from them. By trusting the timing of your own life, you can show up for others and for yourself with compassion and curiosity, and even be a model for those who are doing it differently. You never know what will happen when you divert from the norm. For example:

- Someone who finishes college at age 48 will have magnificent stories about what they learned in higher education with their additional maturity. Plus, professors and classmates love older students, so there's that!

- Someone who starts their family at age 22, years before their peers, may lose out on some experiences or early career milestones, but they may climb a fabulous career ladder in midlife.

- Someone who signs up for hip-hop dance classes at age 64 gets to have wonderful new rhythm and movement and inspires the people around them to follow their exuberance.

When you free yourself from a self-imposed (or society-imposed) timeline, you open yourself up to far more opportunities and experiences than you could have ever imagined. Relationships are vastly more valuable and affirming when they are made up of people who have had different journeys.

JANUARY 27

Saying to your partner, "If you loved me, you would . . ." invites your partner to say to you, "If you loved me, you wouldn't ask me to . . ."

> When I mention these words, I am talking broadly about
> someone saying it as a stance or a mindset during conflict. Using
> these exact words as a threat is a sign of abuse.

The parts of our brain that take over when we are upset are not famous for holding nuance or occupying shades of gray. This is why slipping into binaries is a hallmark of conflict. *Either I win or you win. Either my needs count or yours do.* This type of thinking only creates a power struggle.

You cannot change a pattern until you can identify a pattern. Learn to notice when you and your partner get locked into this binary stance. (Just noticing is a huge step forward!)

The next order of business is to shift your stance:

- The binary stance = *You* versus *Me*

- The relational stance = *You and Me* versus *The Problem*

When you and your partner look together at the problem, you will start to see new paths from disconnection to connection and new possibilities for how you can help each other balance acceptance and change.

Relational Self-Awareness Questions

Explore the following questions together with your partner:

- To the partner who wants change:
  - What do you worry will happen if you accept the status quo?
  - What do you want your partner to understand about why this change matters to you?
  - When have you experienced this worry before? In other words, how does this fear of the status quo connect to your Core Wound?

- To the partner resisting change:
  - What do you worry will happen if you make this change?
  - How can your partner help you feel safer and prouder about making this change?
  - When have you experienced this worry before? In other words, how does this resistance to change connect to your Core Wound?

- When it comes to the issue at hand, what is the overarching value (freedom, flexibility, trust, affirmation, commitment, comfort, etc.) that you both agree on?

Understanding that someone's harmful behavior originates from their Core Wounds or unfinished business neither absolves them of their responsibility nor necessitates your tolerance.

The journey of Relational Self-Awareness will widen your perspective:

- You will move from simplistic either/or answers to descriptions that hold shades of gray.
- You will do less finger-pointing and more self-reflecting.
- You won't need quick fixes and will instead tolerate uncertainty.

And just when you think you've got it all figured out, you will be confronted with the challenge of *feeling* compassion that is big and wide while *enacting* boundaries that are grounded and empowered. But just because you *can* does *not* mean you must:

- Just because you can see that terrible behavior is nearly always a reflection of pain does *not* mean you need to be a doormat.
- Just because you can feel a deep well of love inside of you does *not* mean you need to keep trying to love someone into their own recovery.

Repeatedly tolerating the fallout of another person's terrible behavior (because you know it's driven by their Core Wound) may actually prevent *them* from the reckoning that can motivate their transformation. Here's some language to use:

- "When I stay silent about how your behavior affects me, I am depriving you of information."

- "I know you are not trying to hurt me, *and* I am feeling hurt by your behavior. If/when you are ready to talk about it together, please let me know."

- "I am trying really hard to figure out how to advocate for you while protecting me."

Sometimes your only choice is to love from a distance. At least for a time.

Romantic love invariably stirs the old yearnings and stories that reside within us, awakening the possibility that we will be hurt once again in our most tender of places.

Falling in love reawakens vulnerability that parallels the vulnerability we experienced as kids in relation to our grown-ups. This is unavoidable. If what we received from our caregivers was inadequate, unpredictable, or hurtful, we may be very afraid to take the risk of being hurt like that ever again. Falling in love is truly an act of courage. Even as the kid within us is afraid to let someone get close, our adult self can be brave enough to take the lead. Romantic love *also* brings the possibility of healing:

- Our adult self can manage boundaries in ways a child cannot.

- Our adult self can ask for what we need in ways a child cannot.

- Our adult self can take responsibility for our thoughts, feelings, and behavior in ways a child cannot.

It can be different now. However, in order for our adult self to take the lead in love, we must first acknowledge the kid that lives within each of us. We must listen to their fear and anger, offering our comfort and reassurance: "I feel you, Little Me. I know you're scared. You're here with me and you are safe." As we are able to do that, romantic love becomes a profoundly powerful vehicle for healing. As we parent ourselves from within, we can connect deeply with our beloved and create a relationship of recovery.

Just because something is hard, it does not mean you're doing it wrong.

Picture yourself in the following scenarios (and having those pesky thoughts we all have at one point or another):

- You're at the park and your child is melting down. You look around at all the other kids who are *not* melting down.
  - Sneaky thought: *I must be doing this parenting thing wrong.*
- You and your partner are in a rough patch (sexual dry spell, bickering, etc.). You scroll through social media looking at all those "happy" couples.
  - Sneaky thought: *We are doing this relationship thing wrong.*
- You are busting your ass at work or school. You look around at your colleagues or classmates who appear to be coasting along.
  - Sneaky thought: *I must be doing this work thing wrong.*

What I want to highlight is *not* the comparison aspect. That's certainly brutal and will quickly drain you of joy and gratitude. But here, I want to highlight the subtle error of logic: *If I'm having a hard time, it must be because I'm doing it wrong.* It voices that nagging sense that someone else in this set of conditions would be able to meet the moment with a kind of grace and clarity you could only dream of.

If this resonates with you, the first step is to *notice* when that belief is sneaking up on you. Noticing grants you the power of choice:

- **Path 1:** Follow the belief down the rabbit hole of shame, costing you emotional health and the ability to connect with those around you. Shame takes you out of connection, making you unreachable.

- **Path 2:** Meet the belief with self-compassion: "This is hard because it's hard." Self-compassion quiets the criticism and attendant shame, freeing you up to meet the moment as it is.

When you opt for Path 2, you practice gentleness with yourself and model it for those you love.

JANUARY 31

In our relationships, we must keep a lookout for the times when a familiar scenario plays out differently. These moments remind us that change is possible.

When therapists are getting to know a couple in therapy, our job is to dissect the anatomy of their conflict. We ask questions like:

- How often do you fight?

- About what topics?

- How does the fight begin?

- What do each of you do during a typical fight?

- What has been your worst fight?
- How do you repair the relationship?

We ask these questions so we can learn the dimension, the texture, and the tone of their moments of frustration and misunderstanding. Most couples have a choreography they can tell you about. Themes. Variations on themes. Typical moves.

But we also ask about the *alternative adaptive sequence*, which is a deviation in their rehearsed choreography. It might sound like this: "Tell me about a time when the conditions were ripe for you to have a fight (that same tender topic, that tricky time of the day, that past due bill) but the sequence played out differently and you bypassed the fight."

How can asking about an alternative adaptive sequence help a relationship?

- **It can instill hope.** You and your partner are likely feeling pretty hopeless and overwhelmed. It can be a real pick-me-up for you to think about a time that was a win.

- **It highlights your agency.** You were—and are—able to do things that change the course of a tough moment.

- **It points you in the direction of your transformation.** Understanding what both of you can do to stay engaged and empathic helps you begin to imagine the path forward.

When was the last time you and your partner handled a conflict with more care, patience, and attention? How can you create the conditions for that awesome response to happen again? The two of you already have the power in your hands. Keep an eye out for that alternative adaptive sequence!

When your partner is struggling in their relationship with your Family of Origin, you are caught between people you love, but you are also called upon to become a relational leader, helping everyone understand each other more deeply.

There's an old saying that goes, "When you marry someone, you marry their family." Although this admittedly sounds a little enmeshed, there's no denying that becoming a couple means creating a bridge between two family systems. This also marks a life stage transition in the life of a family system:

- It's so *cool* in so many ways, bringing new opportunities for relationships and rituals.

- It's so *challenging* in so many ways, presenting new opportunities for divisiveness, factions, and boundary violations.

So many of the roles we end up playing in a family system (son-in-law, mother-in-law, etc.) are roles we've received no training or preparation for, and every new role has a way of kicking up dust inside of us. Therefore, it is our responsibility to use the tools of Relational Self-Awareness to get curious about what this new role is stirring up.

Each partner must differentiate themselves from their Families of Origin in the service of their relationship while *also* being grateful to and respectful of the attachment figures who likely did their very best. When working toward this dichotomy, the goals are:

- For all members of the relationship matrix (the couple, the parents, etc.) to feel like they are on the same team: Team Family

- For partners to feel prioritized by each other
- For everyone to practice walking around in each other's shoes

Learn how to recognize and work with your defensiveness so others can feel safe around you.

Defensiveness *feels* like:

- A tightening in your chest
- A quickening of your heart rate
- A flush in your cheeks

Defensiveness *sounds* like:

- "Yes, but . . ."
- "That's not what I meant."
- "You're wrong."

Defensiveness *looks* like:

- Rolling your eyes
- Crossing your arms
- Sighing deeply

Defensiveness is less a personality trait and more a pattern that arises in a relational context. Some of us have a hair trigger, perceiving a criticism/threat/judgment (and getting defensive) where there actually isn't any. This may come from:

- Being raised by people who seemed to be waiting for us to screw up
- A past relationship with a highly critical partner
- Having a very self-critical nature—we imagine others are doing to us what we do to ourselves

When you feel the rise of defensiveness, shift yourself toward empathy. Remember that the person giving you feedback wants to be heard and understood. They have a problem, and your presence is the solution.

Relational Self-Awareness Questions

- How does defensiveness feel inside your body?
- What is so painful about feeling misunderstood or criticized?
- Does this misunderstood feeling remind you of similar feelings you've had in the past?

FEBRUARY 3

When someone you love gives you feedback about how your tone of voice impacts them, see if you can get curious rather than defensive.

In a world that prioritizes thought, what we sense and feel has been systematically disregarded. But our body's intelligence matters. Your tone of voice lands inside your partner's and has the power to create constriction or ease inside of them.

- **On the one hand, tone policing is something that folks with privilege often do when in conversation with marginalized folks.** "It's hard to listen when you're so angry!" This declaration from a person with more culturally ascribed power puts additional labor on the person with less power to modulate tone so they can be palatable.

- **On the other hand, *both* partners in an intimate relationship need to be curious about their tone and its impact on their**

partner. To keep communication flowing, you need to ensure that your tone helps your partner stay present, open, and engaged versus distant or defensive.

If your partner gives you feedback that they are having a hard time with your tone, get curious by asking them:

- Does my tone remind you of someone from your past? Who?

- What happens inside of you when you hear this tone in my voice?

> We will continue this topic in tomorrow's entry.

When there's misalignment between words and tone, tone will carry the day.

"It wasn't *what* you said. It was *how* you said it!"

I cannot tell you how many times I have heard some version of this in couples therapy! Tone matters. When you need to give your partner feedback about their tone, instead of criticizing ("Your tone is so harsh"), see what happens if you:

- **Describe what you're hearing.** "To me, your volume is going up, and your tone is becoming sharp and urgent."

- **Talk about what happens inside of you.** "I am beginning to feel tense and self-protective, which makes it hard to listen to you the way I want to."

- **Ask for what you want instead.** "I really do want to keep working on this together. Could you please try a gentler tone?"

Let's stop elevating some sexual behaviors above other ones.

The fact that our dominant sexual script is a heterosexual sexual script is problematic—it "otherizes" anyone and everyone who is not heterosexual. Additionally, normalizing a heterosexual sexual script means that we end up internalizing a sexual hierarchy in which penetrative sex is elevated above all other sexual behaviors. Penetrative sex ends up being viewed as the most intimate or most important sexual behavior.

Recognizing this is an invitation to *all* of us to shift our mindset in a way that is good for everyone. Let's move away from a hierarchical view of sex in which we value some behaviors over others. Let's move toward viewing sex more like an artist's palette. No color is better than any other color, and no matter which colors you use, you get to create something beautiful together.

Marriage is: Thrill and also boredom. Ease and also challenge. Predictability and also surprise.

As a culture, we are far more obsessed with *falling* in love than *living* in love. We value romance over commitment. We idealize the chase and demean the cultivation. The result? A whole lot of us struggle when lust becomes love. A single woman shared with me that her married friend told her, "I think you keep feeling disappointed by your boyfriends because you think love is more exciting than it actually is." Honestly, who can blame her?! Rom-coms never show us a random Wednesday night during year eight of a couple's relationship. The result? If our love story has lost some of its breathless-make-out-in-the-rain vibes, we feel like we're doing it wrong. We say something like, "Maybe this isn't the right person for me." Or we ask, "What is wrong with me?"

If you feel disappointed, shut down, or ashamed of your relationship, you must approach it as a "we" problem. Turn toward your partner, lead with love, and enlist their help: "I am feeling disconnected lately. I miss how we used to behave. How about you?" Work together to figure out what helps each of you move from withdrawn to engaged.

FEBRUARY 7

Sexual challenges will happen. It's how we cope that matters.

Research indicates 43 percent of women and 31 percent of men report some degree of sexual difficulty. 1 in 4 premenopausal women and 1 in 2 menopausal women struggle with low libido, while as many as 1 in 2 men over 40 report erectile dysfunction and 1 in 3 men report premature ejaculation. According to the National Center for Injury Prevention and Control, as many as 1 in 2 women and 1 in 3 men are survivors of physical sexual violence of some kind. Survivors of sexual violence often struggle with longer-term sexual concerns such as avoiding, fearing, or lacking interest in sex, feeling emotionally distant during sex, and difficulties with orgasm.

When it comes to sex, vulnerability is inescapable, which means shame is an ever-present possibility. We may be able to skirt these tender feelings when our sexuality is clicking on all cylinders: desire is steady, erections are reliable, orgasms are consistent. But when we hit a bump in the road, shame may keep us from tending to the problem, asking for help, and/or talking about it with our partner. In other words, we are at risk of making a difficult thing even more difficult.

If you are single, remember that your sexual challenges don't compromise your worth or desirability. If you are partnered, make a point to cultivate emotional safety, curiosity, and care in the space between both partners so you can stay on the same team.

Go to couples therapy with your partner the first time they ask you to go.

The longer the gap between your first conversation about couples therapy and your first session of couples therapy, the more work the three of you will need to do together. If you've been saying to your partner, "I think we could use a third person to help us understand each other better," and your partner has been tuning you out, you get this. Another brick is added to the wall between you and your partner each time they minimize your concerns or tell you that they don't believe in therapy. Couples therapy isn't Santa Claus; it isn't something to believe in or not believe in.

I've been practicing for over 20 years and I get it: nobody *wants* to do couples therapy. It's not fun or easy or relaxing. But the research is clear:

- Couples therapy works.
- The problems couples bring to therapy tend *not* to resolve on their own.

It's never too early to go. I love when dating couples reach out for therapy. You don't have to wait until you're cohabitating or engaged or married. And I certainly don't want you waiting until you're on the brink of a breakup.

So how do you know when it's time to go to couples therapy? Consider the following questions, exploring them with your partner when you are ready:

- Are we having the same fight/misunderstanding over and over?
- Do I feel confused about how my partner processes things?
- Do I feel misunderstood by my partner?
- Do one or both of us bring complicated relationship histories into our partnership? Do these histories seem to make our problems feel tougher to navigate?
- Do I question whether this relationship is viable?

FEBRUARY 9

Your sexuality is a dynamic and unfolding story that you get to write.

We bring into the bedroom our deeply human stuff: our yearnings, our Core Wounds, our hopes, our fears. Our best and bravest work is to turn toward the meaning and the emotion that accompany the behavior with nothing short of total self-compassion and curiosity. The sexual self is an essential yet often misunderstood and even abandoned part of who we are as human beings.

It's well past time for us to relate to our sexuality in a wholehearted way. Your sexuality is yours. Always has been, always will be. Yours to get to know again and again. Yours to embody in ways that leave you feeling connected to yourself, to your partner, to life in general. Sex is a powerful channel for connection and healing, but we must empower ourselves with information and self-compassion.

You get to decide who has the privilege of weighing in on your choices.

Opinions and advice tend to be the primary modes of communication of those who cannot tolerate sitting with another person's feelings. (Or their own feelings, for that matter.) If you are struggling and invite me to come hang out in your muck with you, it is both kind and strategic for you to offer me some "rules of engagement":

- **You might tell me that you would love a sounding board, but not instructions.** I then get to decide whether I can (or want to) provide that. If I decide I can provide that, I deserve to feel proud of myself because being a sounding board is one of the greatest things we can ever be! It is powerful beyond measure to be a space-holder, a deep listener, a soul-resonator.

- **You might tell me that you would love to hear what I would do in your shoes.** It is a special honor when someone gives us that kind of access. But I also must remember that I have neither a crystal ball nor a magic wand—I'm just making my best guess, based on an understanding that is framed through the lens of *my* experience, *my* identity, *my* personality, *my* cultural location…not yours.

Knowing how to listen and being able to voice how you'd like to be listened to are both foundational relational skills. Each starts with an understanding that one partner's view of the other's situation will always be slightly limited, and vice versa.

When your words or actions hurt someone else, offer an apology: Even if you've had a terrible day. Even if you didn't mean to hurt them. Even if you wouldn't be hurt if the roles were reversed. Offer an apology.

I know so much about apologies—I've been teaching them for decades—yet they remain my kryptonite. Why? I'm glad you asked. It's because the messes I make in my relationship with my husband usually come from projecting how I feel about *me* onto *him*. In other words, I tend to get nasty with him when I'm feeling critical of myself! (It turns out that it's very hard to be kinder to others than we are to ourselves.) Then, when I realize that I have been mean to him because I am feeling bad about me, I feel even worse about myself.

Shame blocks connection, and an apology is a relational process. We have to be connected to someone else to apologize to them. Initiating a repair has to start with forgiving *ourselves* for hurting someone who matters deeply to us. Once we are standing on solid ground internally, we must reach out and repair—no matter how we feel about the situation:

- **"But I didn't mean to hurt them!"** It doesn't matter. You can have both *innocent intent* and *harmful impact.*

- **"But I think they are overreacting."** It doesn't matter. Also, ban the word *overreacting* from your vocabulary—you are not the Actuary of Emotional Responses.

- **"But I've had such a bad day."** It doesn't matter. Of course, a bad day makes it harder to be sweet, patient, or playful with the people in our lives. But a bad day is not a free pass to act any old kind of way.

When your words or actions hurt the people you love, you need to say "I'm sorry." It's a complete sentence.

There's a big difference between being emotionally unavailable and being mindful of emotional dysregulation.

Having a short fuse isn't a character flaw, but it is a call to action. If you are at risk of saying things that hurt the people you love when you get triggered, it is *your* responsibility to practice prevention, not *their* responsibility to act like it didn't happen.

Real empowerment requires ownership and responsibility. Your irritability beckons you for attention and care to two matters:

1. The root cause of the short fuse

2. The impact of the short fuse

Committing to working on your short fuse is brave. Apologizing after the fact is all well and good, but your real work lies in prevention. How might you inoculate yourself against the tendency to blow up? By learning to pause and step away in the service of the relationship.

Of course, there are healthy and unhealthy ways to step away. If you grew up in a family where you saw people storm off and slam doors or move through time and space in icy silence, you may not have had a model for how to take an intimacy-promoting time-out. Being prone to yelling or shutting down is nothing to feel ashamed of, but you need and deserve to learn new ways to proceed with care. When you're feeling too upset to keep talking, try saying one of the following:

- "I'm having a hard time with this conversation right now."
- "I'm worried I'm going to say something that I'll regret later."
- "I'm going to need to take a break for a bit."

Accepting our imperfections isn't a free pass. Rather, it's the first step in the journey of empowerment and growth. When you choose silence over snark and take a time-out in service of your relationship, make sure you celebrate the eff out of yourself. Change isn't easy, but it's so worth it!

When you sweep your loved one's harsh words under the rug, you deprive them of the opportunity for the growth that accompanies ownership.

Hurtful words can linger in the air long after the tense moment passes. When repair doesn't happen, trust—the central tenet of our relationships—is at stake. The person on the receiving end of the sharp words risks the erosion of their self-worth. The one on the speaking end risks the heart-closing that occurs when we defend the indefensible, as well as the shame that results from not being committed to recovery.

People end up with a short fuse for all kinds of reasons:

- Some folks are born fiery. Temperament is no joke!
- Stress compromises the ability to hold a space of grace and patience.

47

- Trauma is embodied, and when unhealed, it can make it hard to distinguish between a minor irritation and a five-alarm fire.

- Relational distress can lead to a short fuse by creating a "victim mentality" that leads people to feel entitled to say what they want, when they want, how they want.

We must hold both *empathy* and *accountability*. Can you have empathy for the root cause of your partner's short fuse without giving your loved one a free pass to say whatever they want when they are frustrated or overwhelmed?

Valentine's Day reminder: Romance is defined in the space between the two of you.

My mom is an elite giver of gifts. She invented a concept called "The Birthday Table" (an elaborate display of beautifully wrapped gifts), and our Christmas tree was always chock full of presents. I married someone who is, well, the opposite. My one-year anniversary gift from him was a half-eaten Burger King burger. For Valentine's Day 2019, he gave me a fun-size Snickers bar left over from Halloween and a dollar bill tucked into a small plastic bag.

I used to get confused and hurt about this "character flaw," which is understandable, given:

- My experience growing up (We had a full *table* of gifts!)

- Our respective genders (The heteronormative romance script involves *him* pampering *her*, especially on Valentine's Day.)

- The Valentine's Day industrial complex (I don't think it's really called that, but you know what I mean.)

Over time, I've learned to anchor into my deep truth: I feel loved by this man. Enduringly. Robustly. Truly. It's not the exchange of gifts that creates or reflects the spirit of romance in our marriage.

Love makes us feel so darned vulnerable. I think sometimes we want to receive a gift or a specially planned event because the gesture serves as reassurance that it is safe for us to be vulnerable, that all the risk we are taking by opening our hearts is reciprocated, and therefore worth it.

What's tricky about giving and receiving gifts is that it involves surprise and surrender. There's a lot going on in the space between giver and recipient: expectations, opinions, and beliefs about how much to get; how much to spend; what counts as a "good" gift and what doesn't. If we have expectations, we ought to communicate them. I get that this is tough because sometimes we don't even know we have an expectation until our partner doesn't meet it. When that happens, use the experience to understand more deeply what it is that you were craving (and why) so you can set your partner up for success next time.

Be careful not to judge the quality of the relationship by how you spend Valentine's Day—it's just a single day out of the entire year. Oh, and remember that asking for what you want does not take the fun out of receiving it.

FEBRUARY 15

Love will grow your ass up.

Romantic love evokes the past, shining a light on wounds that may have been dormant for years or decades. Romantic love invites us to work and rework ourselves in the presence of another person. This work is both difficult and sacred, personal and relational, expanding us and affirming us. This work is the seat of intimacy. And it's never done.

Relational Self-Awareness is the through-line of my work, whether I'm teaching, writing, doing therapy, or connecting with my husband. At its heart is a commitment to growth. Relational Self-Awareness is about accepting and embracing that we are forever evolving. We get to (and must) meet ourselves and each other again and again. We learn about ourselves and each other in the sweet moments—the laughter, the gifts, the gestures, the inside jokes, the ordinary nights.

We learn about ourselves and each other in the painful moments as well. Your reactivity to your partner is a teacher. The question is whether you will show up for the lesson or play hooky. If you decide to play hooky by blaming or shutting down, you will be presented with the very same lesson again. (And again.) If you decide to show up for the lesson, you can become a student of your reactivity.

Your intimate partnerships offer you ceaseless opportunities to be re-wounded or healed. You must be willing to study your reactions and choose your responses.

Relational Self-Awareness Questions
When you feel triggered by something that's happening with a partner:

- What are you wanting/needing in this moment?
- How is your partner experiencing you in this moment?
- What does this dynamic remind you of from when you were younger?
- Who are you afraid of "becoming" in this moment?

FEBRUARY 16

A boundary is healthy when: You feel protected and connected. You feel empowered

**and authentic. You can hear yourself
and listen to the other person. Your feet
are planted and your heart is open.**

A boundary marks the space between you and another person. Boundaries vary based on a variety of factors:

- **Relational boundaries are dynamic, not static.** A healthy boundary on a first date looks very different from a healthy boundary after marriage.

- **Relational boundaries are culturally bound.** What is considered appropriate to talk about in one part of the world is considered "airing dirty laundry" in another.

- **Relational boundaries are relationship-specific.** A healthy boundary with my therapy client looks very different compared to a healthy boundary with my best friend.

Rather than seek external validation of whether a boundary is healthy or not, you need to use Relational Self-Awareness as your guide. You need to *feel* your way into healthy boundaries. The point of creating a healthy boundary is so you can love another person with gusto. Heart open. Fully present.

FEBRUARY 17

**Sometimes it's so hard to resist the
urge to give advice when someone we
love is standing at a crossroads.**

When your partner is struggling, it can feel automatic to go into problem-solving mode. But this is not always what they need. Here's what you can do instead:

- **Offer empathy.** Empathy means feeling *with* another person. It looks like an open body posture and a concerned and present face. It sounds like reflecting back how you imagine the other person feels: "That sounds so painful" or "I can imagine how heavy this must feel for you." Or it may sound like inviting them to share more: "Mmhmm" or "Say more about that." When we attune ourselves to another person through empathy, it changes their experience of their problem: They are no longer alone with it. The burden may feel lighter; new avenues may open. Empathy creates change.

- **Go Meta.** *Going Meta* means going "up a level" in your discussions—talk *about* talking. Say something like, "I want to be clear on what you're asking of me. What would help you feel supported by me right now? Do you want me to hear you out? Do you want advice?" Often when we are giving advice, it is unsolicited! We don't check with the other person before we start directing them, either because we're anxious or hurried or because we're a bit full of ourselves in the moment. Ask first.

- **Ask follow-up questions.** Support your person in getting clear on why they want answers that come from outside themselves: "Why are you wanting advice from me? What is keeping you from trusting yourself?"

See how you feel if you show your support in a less directive way . . . and see how your partner responds!

Couples must continually wrestle with the following question: "In what ways does this intimate partnership nourish our individual ambitions, passions, and dreams?"

In a heterosexual relationship, the force of our culture's patriarchal narrative will tilt toward *her* accommodation of *his* ambition. Not because he's a jerk or because she's a doormat, but because both are the inheritors of an entrenched system. All too often he is told (directly or indirectly) that he's less of a man for the care he gives, and she's told (directly or indirectly) that her ambition threatens him.

When a man and a woman build an intimate relationship together, they must sit with the fundamental question: "How will this relationship support both of our ambitions?" Since the default is to support his ambition, when both partners work together to honor her ambition, the couple deserves to feel uplifted and proud.

> Queer couples must explore how gender expression
> (masculine presentation and feminine presentation)
> could create tilts toward or away from each partner's ambitions.

An intimate relationship will ask you to become *we*. The *we* must hold your dreams, your partner's dreams, and both of your dreams as a couple:

- Partner with someone who cares about your dreams.

- Care about your partner's dreams.

- Make a mutual commitment to check in on a regular basis about your individual hopes and ambitions.

Relational Self-Awareness Questions

- How do you hold onto *both* your desire to succeed *and* your desire to be loved?

- What helps you trust that your relationship can/will support your ambition?

- What helps you feel proud of supporting your partner's ambition?

When we use the word foreplay, we reinforce gender inequality.

Our words highlight what we value and reflect how we have ordered the world. I used the word *foreplay* for years, unaware of how it subtly reinforces a sexual climate that leaves a lot to be desired, especially for women. It is well established that the person least likely to experience an orgasm is a woman who is having sex with a man—far less likely than a woman with a woman, a man with a woman, or a man with a man. This finding, known as the *orgasm gap*, makes total sense when we consider that the predominant script for straight sex is one that we learned on the playground: first base, second base, third base, home run. In this model, the home run of penetrative sex is held up as the only thing that "counts." The other bases are foreplay—the stuff we do to get to the "real" thing. The problem is that the behaviors we unwittingly minimize with the word *foreplay* are the ones that tend to feel best and most reliably produce an orgasm for people with a vulva! My friend Dr. Laurie Mintz takes it a step further, pointing out that a sexual script based on what we know about female pleasure would call foreplay "sex" and penetration "post-play."

Having an orgasm isn't everything, and people can have very pleasurable experiences without doing so. But I would like us to move toward a world where everyone is set up for experiences that maximize the opportunity for orgasm.

Reflect on what separations and reunions with your partner evoke in you.

As a child of divorce, my childhood was a series of hellos and goodbyes with my parents. To my single parent, divorced, and remarried readers, there is *no* judgment heading your way! I'm simply naming an experience in my Family of Origin that created a sensitivity in me, one that my husband and I have learned to manage together.

My husband travels a lot for work. Before he heads out, I know I pull back a bit. We strive to have conversations that make space for *both* his need to go *and* my tender spot. When he gets home, I feel my inner conflict—I want him back in the flow of our family life *and* I feel a bit slow to warm up. Over time and with care, we have learned what helps us reconnect:

- Acknowledging my tender spot
- A nice long walk that lets us catch up
- My gratitude for his attention
- His gratitude for me holding down the fort

Although your adult self might fully get that what's happening is a temporary separation, Little You might be carrying a story about hellos and goodbyes that deserves to be told.

Relational Self-Awareness Questions

- What do separations and reunions stir in you?
- How do you cope with those feelings? Do you pull back, or push your partner away?
- What does Little You feel and need?
- What helps (or could help) you and your partner find your way back to each other?

Healing is about: Unlearning. Learning. Shifting. Expanding. Becoming.

Instead of working toward a magical moment in time when you stop being X and instead become Y, approach your healing like a journey during which you increasingly *become* more of X and less of Y. Processes, not decisions. Evolutions, not moments. This framing allows you to celebrate micro-moments—those little victories that happen in the ordinary and the quiet—while making space for the inevitable backsliding and lingering imperfections.

Healing is not marked by no longer falling, but by not falling down quite so far and not staying down quite so long. Healing is feeling the tug of an old Coping Strategy, meeting it with love, and saying, "Thank you. You protected me in the past, but today I have other ways of dealing with my life." Make it a practice to notice and honor the times when you choose mindfulness instead of an old Coping Strategy, a self-care behavior instead of self-abandonment. And make sure you have people in your corner who can shine on you every step of the way.

- What are you becoming less of?

- What are you becoming more of?

- What image best captures your healing journey?

FEBRUARY 22

Something can be both "normal" and emotionally challenging.

Extraordinary changes to our lives, like a breakup, a job loss, or a scary diagnosis, are bound to throw us for a loop. But we can also feel confused when the "normal" stuff feels disruptive and hard. For example:

- The first holiday we spend with our partner's family instead of our own

- The first time our baby feeds themselves

- The first time our teenager prioritizes time with friends over time with family

Intellectually, we know this is how it "should" be—this is the circle of life, blah blah blah. But emotionally, the normal stuff can be so damn hard. There's so much *allowing* that needs to happen. So much moving with, instead of against, the passage of time. It is good to remind ourselves of this with a compassionate affirmation like, "This change is normal." Do not panic. Do not fight it. This is the order of things.

However, *This change is normal* can also be a deeply invalidating judgment. When said in a critical tone, these words convey that our reaction is outsized, wrong, problematic. Speaking to ourselves or each other in this way feels deeply invalidating, so we need to be careful when we remind ourselves or others that the changes that accompany the passage of time are normal.

Things can be normal, expected, appropriate, healthy . . . and still be really hard. Remember this the next time you and/or your partner struggle with a seemingly "normal" experience.

An experience of deep intimacy with your partner may set you up to feel more sensitive to subsequent distance, impatience, or disconnection.

A couples therapy session often begins with one or both partners wanting to process a painful fight/conflict/misunderstanding. They will talk me through the difficult scenario: "I said this and then they said this and then I did this and then they did that." Before we begin to unpack the fight, I will often ask them to "rewind the tape" a bit more. Why? Because a painful moment often follows a tender one.

Conflict is often preceded by intimacy. My former supervisor and mentor, Dr. Bill Pinsof, used to call this "the rubber band theory." When a couple stretches into deeper vulnerability, they can sometimes then move into conflict. I don't think this happens because of physics or self-sabotage. I think it happens because although being intimate, close, and connected is delicious, heart-opening, and healing, it is also a wildly sensitizing experience. It can create a tendency to scan for threats: that we might lose this person who means so much, or that our sense of self is now bound up in their presence with or perception of us. All of this can understandably make us sensitive to any sign of distance, impatience, or disconnection.

Here's what you can do:

- **Name the feeling for yourself and your partner.** Rather than judging yourself and/or each other for being so sensitive, you can breathe with the feeling: "Ah. This is so understandable. Being so close feels so good but also so intense."

- **Shift your focus.** Move from your fears of loss and instead, move toward gratitude for what is present between the two of you.

- **Remember that relationships are alive and dynamic.** While you don't want to swing from one extreme to the other, you can normalize shifts in your connection. This helps you move with, not against, the dynamics of intimacy.

When a couple learns to contextualize their conflict as following from an experience of closeness, they can access relational pride, which helps them unpack the conflict from a more collaborative stance.

FEBRUARY 24

Relational betrayal comes in all kinds of textures and tones.

When we think of betrayal in relationships, we often think first about infidelity. Sexual betrayal is surely painful and seismic, shaking the entire foundation of a relationship. But sometimes betrayal is:

- Keeping vital information secret
- Making surprise financial decisions or purchases

- Being dishonest (about work, the past, friendships, health problems, family matters, etc.)

There are hundreds of other ways we deceive, disappoint, and destroy trust. At the level of the *individual*, each person has work to do. The one who has been hurt sits with questions:

- *How did I miss this?*
- *Who am I for opting to stay?*
- *How will I know whether and when I'm safe?*
- *What do I need to learn from this?*

The one who has been dishonest sits with questions:

- *How could I hurt someone I love?*
- *Will I be forgiven?*
- *How do I have empathy for their pain without drowning in my own shame?*
- *What do I need to learn from this?*

The realization of betrayal positions the couple at a crossroads: Does this destroy us, or do we try to repair? The path of recovery is rich with both landmines and opportunities.

FEBRUARY 25

We must practice discernment about whether and how we share our story.

We will use the example of disclosing a mental health diagnosis, but imagine any tender tale you want. We need to find a shade of gray between two extremes:

1. **"My mental health challenge is under lock and key. Nobody can ever know."** This scenario tends to be fueled by shame (which is understandable given the stigma around mental health), and the consequence tends to be isolation, disconnection, and a sense that nobody really knows you.

2. **"My diagnosis is the first thing I'm going to tell you about myself. I will share in detail anytime, anywhere."** This scenario leaves you unprotected. By sharing willy-nilly, you are at risk of being subject to someone else's reckless projections. If they don't really know you, their response to your share is informed largely by their own stereotypes, fears, or judgments.

A stance of Relational Self-Awareness lives somewhere in between. When a personal challenge (like a mental health diagnosis) is new, you may oscillate between these extremes until you find your way to the discernment needed to assess the situation:

- **You check in with yourself.** How ready are you for a deeper dialogue?

- **You read the other person's cues.** How open/trusting/kind do they feel to you?

From that place of awareness and observation, choose whether to disclose or not disclose. Release your attachment to the outcome, but use the outcome to determine whether you want to be more or less open next time.

Clarity is not cruelty.

I continue to be struck by how subtly women (and girls) learn to accommodate the needs/whims/preferences/insecurities of men (and boys) in a way that serves neither! Many of us have been left falsely equating *clarity* with *cruelty*:

- "I don't want to give you my phone number" = *I'm a withholding b*tch*
- "I don't want a second date" = *I think I'm better than you*
- "I don't want to continue this relationship" = *I am heartless and harmful*

Maybe this is being said explicitly. Often it isn't. The message to girls and women is that:

- Our truth does harm.
- Our preferences are a kind of violence.
- Our needs damage other people's self-esteem.

Years ago, my therapist said to me, "Say what you mean, mean what you say, but don't say it in a mean way." Clarity is not cruelty. You can be both firm and kind.

We can help heal the wounds of patriarchy by teaching our boys and men that they can be denied without it compromising their wholeness. Being told no is a gift—it gives the opportunity to learn to tolerate disappointment. Without acting out. Without retaliating. Without withering.

Far from a sign of brokenness, seeking couples therapy is a powerful way to say to yourself and your partner, "This matters. We matter."

When a couple comes to see me (especially a young or early-stage couple), we often have to spend some time offloading shame. We must transform the idea that couples therapy means they are damaged or doomed and replace it with a deeply felt courage that says, "I love us so much that I want to get this right!" Couples therapy is a powerful way to say *I believe in us.*

Here are three things to know about hiring a couples therapist:

1. **Somebody can be an awesome individual therapist but an ineffective couples therapist.** When you make the initial phone call, ask about their training in working with couples. There are specific skills designed to help a therapist hold onto what's happening both *inside* each partner and in the space *between* the partners.

2. **Give it some time.** All relationships take time to build, and your relationship with your couples therapist is no exception.

3. **Therapy works when you work.** If you and your partner go to therapy to help you decide whether or not to stay together, your therapist is likely to ask you to agree to a certain number of sessions, during which you'll roll up your sleeves and give this relationship everything you've got. Couples therapy is hard work, and you need a safe container to hold that work.

The research is clear: Couples therapy helps. Go early. Go often.

There's a world of difference between being responsible to someone's healing and being responsible for it.

We've already established that we all have baggage. You have a responsibility *to* your partner's baggage:

- To be careful with it
- To be compassionate about it
- To tread lightly when you're near it

These are the foundation of a love that heals. However, you are absolutely not responsible *for* your partner's baggage. You cannot:

- Reparent them
- Do their work for them
- Be so perfect that they never hurt

Being responsible *to* is about being gentle with your partner's tender spots. Being responsible *for* is about working overtime to ensure that you partner never feels discomfort or disappointment. Can you feel the difference?

The line between *to* and *for* may be fuzzy for those of us who grew up trying to be everything to everyone. We may fancy ourselves to be healers and givers. But scratch the surface and we may discover something that's a bit harder to sit with: our fear of feeling the limits of what we can control. Overfunctioning can be preferable to sitting with the sadness and disappointment that we cannot do it all.

If your relationship began on the false notion that you could save them from themselves, change is possible. As you learn the difference between care and codependence, you begin to step back. As you step back, they will do one of two things: step in and own their healing or punish you for not being who you used to be.

- The former option? That's the seat of relational transformation.
- The latter option? That sucks . . . but at least you have clarity.

MARCH 1

Our relationships have the power to wound us and the power to heal us.

I've been integrating attachment science into my work as a relationship educator for more than 20 years. The science of attachment is a powerful way to invite people to:

- Explore how early experiences lay the foundation for expectations, behaviors, and fears in adult intimate relationships.
- Examine how each partner's individual psychology creates relationship dynamics.

In other words, attachment science is an effective way to help people understand that the past impacts everyone, for better and for worse. Understanding our attachment style/strategy empowers us to remember that we developed these behaviors to get our needs met in our important relationships. Research shows that:

- A therapy relationship can move someone from insecure attachment to secure attachment.
- Partners in couples therapy can "earn security" and move from insecure to secure attachment.

Learning your attachment strategy is a helpful way to understand where you've been and how you've come to where you are. That said, your attachment strategy is not your relational destiny. You always have the freedom to chart a new course.

> If you'd like to discover your attachment strategy, head to
> https://www.attachedthebook.com/wordpress/compatibility-quiz.
>
> We will continue this topic in tomorrow's entry.

MARCH 2

You are more than your attachment style.

Attachment "styles" sound like set-in-stone identity variables that are the sum total of who we are. I am vigilant about calling them attachment *strategies* instead because this language reminds us that although we have particular behavioral tendencies (seeking reassurance, shutting down, etc.) in our relationships, there is more to our attachment than a label. Knowing your strategies helps you to heal more effectively:

- It's immensely helpful to know if you're prone to avoidant attachment strategies so you can learn to regulate yourself and turn toward, rather than away from, your partner. It's also helpful for your partner to know this about you! Incredibly, research shows that when someone with avoidant tendencies is given space by their partner, they become less avoidant over time.

- It's immensely helpful to know if you're prone to anxious attachment so you can co-create relational agreements that help you pace yourself so you can feel more enthusiasm than anxiety as your relationship grows.

It's most important to remember that there's a difference between what you need and who you are. Secure attachment doesn't make you perfect and problem-free; insecure attachment doesn't make you broken. Rather, your attachment strategy is an invitation to Relational Self-Awareness so you can create a relationship that heals the kid you were and celebrates the grown-up you now are.

There is a world of difference between feeling disappointed in the outcome and feeling devastated about yourself.

To look for love is to sit with uncertainty. To date is to dance with unknowns:

- *Do they like me?*
- *Do I like them?*
- *To what degree do our values align?*
- *What are they wanting and available for?*
- *What am I wanting and available for?*
- *How well would our lives entwine?*

At some point in time, you will likely want and need some clarity: "Who are we to each other? What is this? Are you feeling me the way I'm feeling you?" In other words, you want to "shoot your shot." When you reach this point, you need to roll your shoulders back, take a deep breath, and ask.

Then you will see what happens. You are in charge of the process, but you are not in charge of the outcome.

If the outcome is not the outcome you want (profound reciprocity and readiness to take this thing to the next level), promise that you will strive to feel *sadness*, not *shame*. Grieve the fact that this person does not want what you want, but do not turn against yourself. Direct your disappointment toward the outcome, not toward you as a person.

MARCH 4

Gossip is insecurity dressed up like power.

Gossip erodes relational trust: If you gossip with others, others will be wise to assume that you will gossip about them.

We gossip because it:

- Makes us feel central, relevant, necessary, powerful

- Bonds us to the person we are talking to

- Gives us a sense of control

Gossip is likely a Coping Strategy intended to alleviate a Core Wound. For example:

- **You grew up in a blended family.** Perhaps you felt powerful when transmitting information between homes. As an adult, sharing stories like this feels like the way to feel connected and valued in a relationship.

- **You grew up feeling unpopular and marginalized.** As an adult, spilling tea feels like an antidote to years of invisibility.

- **You grew up as a confidant to an unhappy parent.** As an adult, you may not even notice the line between your business and other people's.

Your urge to talk about someone who isn't there alerts you to an unmet need that lives inside you and warrants your attention.

What to do instead of gossiping:

- Ask questions of the person you're talking to.
- Share stories from your life.
- Reminisce together.
- Engage in an activity together.

Relational Self-Awareness Questions

- In what contexts are you most at risk of gossiping? Why?
- How do you feel when you are gossiping? How do you feel after the fact?
- If you view gossip as a Coping Strategy, what is the feeling you are trying to fix/allay/reduce? What makes this feeling so painful for you?

MARCH 5

Walking on eggshells is a symptom of a power imbalance.

Power imbalances (work, intimate, family, friendship, etc.) are wholly unavoidable in our relationships, and they show up in all kinds of sneaky ways. Rather than acting as if a relationship can or should be 100 percent equal, our work is to notice and address the ways that we silence ourselves or are silenced by others. Feeling like you are walking on eggshells with your partner is a blinking indicator light—it tells you that a power imbalance is compromising vulnerability, creativity, and authenticity in your relationship. Your silence further compromises intimacy because *intimacy is founded on authenticity*:

- At the macro level, power imbalances happen when people of color/LGBTQ folks/immigrants/gender minorities quiet down so as not to make cis/het/white folks feel uncomfortable.

- At the micro level, power imbalances happen when one person in a relationship repeatedly accommodates their partner.

Eggshells and authenticity cannot coexist. Leaving out parts of yourself keeps those parts invisible to your partner, and this tends to be a recipe for resentment. Shedding anything familiar requires courage. Your voice may begin as only a whisper, but a whisper holds the potential to shift an entire dynamic, a bit at a time.

If the cost of speaking up would be too great, grant yourself permission to keep quiet, at least for now. Just make sure you practice self-compassion, cultivating a sense of pride in what you are giving up for some greater good.

Relational Self-Awareness Questions

- In what way is this "eggshells" role familiar to you?

- What is the impact of your silence?

- When you silence yourself, what important information is your partner missing?

- What would you say if you weren't afraid?

A pang of regret beckons you to return your focus to your life today.

Regret leads us to put our focus on the rearview mirror instead of the road ahead. Still, it is hard to avoid, in part because it offers the illusion of control, tricking us into imagining we can redo that which has already been done. When regret grabs you in its tight embrace, ask yourself, "What is feeling out of control in my life right now?" Are you engaging in mental masturbation (yeah, I said it!) to distract yourself from something that feels unpredictable, scary, or new?

When you notice yourself being captured by regret:

- **Come back to this moment.** Focus on what is right here, right now. Five senses. This breath. Folding this shirt. Listening to this song. Focus the mind rather than chasing it down a rabbit hole.

- **Change the ending.** Instead of imagining that project would have resulted in fortunes or that relationship would have been a real-life fairy tale, imagine that it all would have crashed and burned. Since you can't know for sure, write yourself an ending that makes you feel better!

- **Trust the process.** Lean on your higher power and return yourself to a place of wonder. Trust that everything unfolds in perfect time. We cannot possibly see every variable at every moment. We do the best we can each step of the way.

Regret is an invitation to be gentle with ourselves and others.

Here's something that is both sacred and challenging about being in an intimate relationship: When you deal with a personal challenge, your partner is right there.

How you feel in your own skin powerfully impacts the space between you and your intimate partner. When you feel confident, upbeat, and energized, it's easy to feel open to connection. You can tap into playful, curious, optimistic energy, which benefits not just you but also your partner and the dynamic between you. But what about when you're in the throes of a deeply personal challenge? For example:

- *I feel insecure about my career.*
- *I feel critical of my body.*
- *I feel scared about my health.*

How beautiful that an intimate relationship can provide comfort for these feelings! Sitting in the muck with someone who loves you can be deeply comforting. At the same time, it can be really hard to be in a personal crisis *and* in an intimate relationship. Being supported during a dark night of the soul is lovely, but it's also hard because there is nowhere to hide. You know you don't feel like your normal self, and your partner can sense it too. This awareness can add a layer of shame on top of the knot of self-criticism and self-doubt. So what can you do?

- **Cultivate self-compassion.** Be gentle with yourself. Nobody ever shamed themselves out of a funk!

- **Look for resources outside of your intimate partner.** Enlist the support you need from friends, therapy, movement, a great book.

Although it may seem paradoxical, asking *less* from your partner may create more intimacy by unburdening the space between you.

- **Balance your pain with pleasure.** Ask your partner, "What can we do to nurture our connection while I'm having a hard time?" By naming the issue, versus painting on a smile, you can nudge your struggle out of the constant spotlight. Being in pain doesn't make you unworthy of pleasure.

You don't have to be perfect to be loved. But you do need to be real about the fact that your individual challenges affect your relationships.

MARCH 8

Collectively, we seem to be doing a better job raising our daughters to be leaders than raising our sons to be caregivers. Yet being fully human requires the cultivation of both ambition and connection.

Women outperform men at every level of education:

- For every 74 college diplomas earned by men, 100 are earned by women.

- In 50 percent of mixed-sex marriages in the U.S., she out-earns him (or they earn the same). That number was 3 percent in the 1960s.

- So many of today's mamas are unapologetic about teaching their daughters that their sexual comfort and pleasure are central. This next generation may well close the orgasm gap! Our foremothers' jaws would drop.

> I share this with full awareness that: Our reproductive rights are under attack, a gendered pay gap persists, rape culture persists, and systems of oppression create disproportionate harm in the lives of BIPOC, poor, and trans women.

What is abundantly clear is that cisgender heteronormative capitalist patriarchy harms the health and well-being of boys and men too. When we talk about "precarious masculinity," what we mean is that notions of what it means to be "man enough" are largely performative—that is, they are states of *doing* (leading, conquering, controlling, accomplishing, etc.) rather than qualities of *being*.

One's place in the hierarchy must be proven again and again, in relation to women and to other men. The side effect of all that competition is that what's neglected is the entire realm of experience that is about caregiving. Caregiving is non-competitive by nature:

- There's no end-goal, no score, no conquest.
- There is presence and connection.
- There is delight and simplicity.
- There is redundancy, exhaustion, and invisibility, which is why it has historically been relegated to those with less power.

But it doesn't get better for any of us until the boys and men among us can experience a sense of worthiness that isn't contingent on their paycheck, their last sexual performance, or their latest achievement. We are most whole when we feel worthy in our striving and worthy in our caregiving.

MARCH 9

How relationally nourishing it is to hold disappointment as such, without turning it into blame or shame.

My husband, Todd, and I were going to head to the city for a couple's weekend. I went to the gym before we left and tweaked my lower back. Todd had to do almost everything to get us packed and ready, and our hopes for long walks and dancing were dashed. I felt disappointed and frustrated. I also felt a tender part from my past saying, *Why would I work out like that on the morning of our couple's adventure?* That self-critical part of me holds the power to move me from disappointment to shame:

- **Disappointment:** "What a bummer that we need to reimagine our plans!"
- **Shame:** "I ruined our plans."

Although these feelings were happening inside of me, the slippery slope of moving from disappointment to shame would create relational fallout. Moving into shame pushes Todd away:

- When he offers help, I push it away—after all, it's my fault.
- When he offers empathy, my ears distort it and hear pity.
- When he shares his disappointment, I get defensive.

Staying with disappointment, on the other hand, pulls Todd close:

- When he offers help, I can express gratitude.
- When he offers empathy, I can breathe it like medicine.
- When he shares his disappointment, I can validate that I am bummed too; then, we can work together on a new plan.

Here's how I worked with that tender part of me:

- I greeted that part. All parts are welcome.
- I invited that part to have a seat. That part was allowed to watch the action but it could not take charge.

Ambivalence and grace live in tension with each other.

Research shows that happy couples wear rose-colored glasses. They pay close attention to what they adore about their partner and offer grace when faced with their partner's shortcomings, remembering that the best an imperfect person can ever do is love the daylights out of another imperfect person. Simple, but far from easy.

If you're trying to figure out whether the relationship you're in can go the distance, I hold you in warm compassion. There are no easy answers. But here is what I do know:

AMBIVALENCE ↔ GRACE

The more ambivalence you feel, the less grace you have to offer. The less ambivalence you feel, the more grace you have to offer.

- **More ambivalence:** The more you swirl around in your head about whether you and your partner are a good fit, the more their foibles and faults stand out in bold relief. The more you focus on their faults, the more ambivalent you feel about them. The more ambivalent you are, the harder it is to offer grace in the face of their inevitable humanness.

- **More grace:** The more grace you offer them, the less ambivalence you will feel about your relationship. The more you accept that they, like yourself, are a bodacious blend of strengths and Growing Edges, the more you will trust your choice of them as a partner.

See what shifts inside of you as you hold onto the bidirectional nature of this dynamic.

You are going to stumble headlong into other people's tender spots—not because you are a bad person, but because you don't know what you don't know.

Every day we are gifted an opportunity to leave people better than we found them:

- We can listen to the echoes of a pain we didn't cause.

- We can opt for humility instead of justification.

- We can pay attention to their hurt rather than prove our innocence.

All these choices help to shift the other person's narrative.

Sometimes that narrative is personal and idiosyncratic, reflective only of someone's unique history. Sometimes that narrative is collective, revealing pain that has accumulated over many generations. The latter is what we call a *microaggression*. Microaggressions are sometimes known as "death by a thousand cuts"—while not life-and-death offenses, they kick off a painful emotional sequence. Microaggressions are a source of chronic stress, particularly in the lives of BIPOC-identifying people.

When we are a perpetrator of a microaggression or other type of hurtful action and the other person takes the risk of letting us know, we face a ginormous fork in the road. We can choose the path of status quo (perpetuation of pain) by letting our defensiveness and need to be right take the lead. Or we can choose the path of healing through accountability and witnessing. In these moments, strive to be a force for good by focusing more on the repair than on your good intentions. None of us is solely responsible for the generational pain of the world, but each of us has a chance to be a force for healing.

It is infinitely easier to take responsibility for your part of an unfortunate moment when your partner is willing to take responsibility for theirs as well.

The vast majority of unfortunate moments that couples experience can be mapped onto what I call the **Golden Equation of Love**:

My Stuff + Your Stuff = Our Stuff

We know we are not honoring the Golden Equation of Love when blame or shame, the two great intimacy busters, arrives on the scene:

- **Blame says:** "This problem is happening because of Your Stuff. Your Stuff = Our Stuff."

- **Shame says:** "This problem is happening because of My Stuff. My Stuff = Our Stuff."

But honoring the Golden Equation of Love means sitting in the complexity, the nuance, the inevitability of wound activation:

- Wound activation may be happening because the two of you have been through this before in your relationship and you are upset it's happening again.

- Wound activation may be happening because this dynamic reminds you of something from your past, likely something from your Family of Origin.

It is far easier to sit in love's complexities when our partner is ready, willing, and able to sit beside us. Sitting alone in complexity can feel so demoralizing. How do we optimize the conditions for mutual accountability?

- We can remember that most crimes of the heart are misdemeanors, not felonies.

- We can remember that we are more than our mistakes or our strong reactions.

- We can commit to exploring what blocks our ability to own our part of the problem. This is like meta-accountability, if you will: Accountability for the tendency to struggle with accountability.

Relational Self-Awareness Questions

- Around what topics do you tend to have the hardest time taking responsibility for your part?

- What are you afraid will happen if you own your part?

- Is that fear based in experiences in this relationship or experiences from your past?

MARCH 13

Sometimes, by grieving who we wish our parents could have been, we can begin to embrace who they actually are.

Sometimes our parents are emotionally or physically dangerous, and we need firm, clear, immovable boundaries in order to be safe, well, and whole. Despite knowing this, we still cling to:

- The image of the mother we craved but didn't get

- The vision of the father we needed but didn't have

We hope against hope that *this* time they will validate/comfort/praise us. And when they don't, or can't, or won't, we experience that familiar despair, feeling invalidated, upset, unworthy. And sometimes we add insult to injury by turning against ourselves and saying *we* should not have gotten our hopes up.

But sometimes you can break a cycle of expectation and disappointment by letting yourself grieve that your parent was not able to be who you needed them to be. By allowing yourself to feel the length, width, and depth of the sadness, you begin to shift from stuck to pliable. When you do this, the grief opens space inside of you to feel compassion for your parent:

- For the traumas that kept them from being empathic with you

- For the relational dramas that kept them from being attuned to you

- For the busyness that kept them from being present with you

These glimpses of compassion become building blocks for a new relationship, adult to adult, in which you aren't reliant on your parent for validation, comfort, or worth. You'll practice sourcing those from within. Instead, be curious about getting to know the parent you *actually* have, right here right now—foibles, quirks, limitations, imperfections, and all.

This approach is a process. It doesn't make the grief go away, but it blends the grief with something else: grace.

Our current circumstances give us clues about our current level of self-worth.

A follower of my work once shared that his ex-girlfriend told him that she wanted to be friends. So they hung out. And snuggled . . . in just their underwear. And they sometimes kissed, but just for a minute. Then she reminded him that she *just* wanted to be friends. Feeling stuck and confused, he wanted help understanding what was going on with her. I offered empathy and encouraged him to turn the lens on *himself* with these questions:

- What might his tolerance of this situation be showing him about his relationship with himself?

- What is familiar for him about acting like he's satisfied even though he's only getting relational "scraps?"

- If he believed fully in his worthiness, how would he handle this situation?

Your relationship with yourself sets the tone for your relationships with everyone else.

Relational Self-Awareness Questions

- What might you say no to if you believed that you had nothing to prove?

- What might you say yes to if you believed that you are worthy as you are?

In a misguided effort to feel safe, we may create the conditions for our partner to feel jealous.

Feeling insecure—a little, or a lot—is par for the course in an intimate relationship. Vulnerability and intimacy are inextricably bound. If we aren't able to reckon with our inevitable insecurity (meet it tenderly, contain it, talk about it with our partner, etc.), we will act it out. One of the ways we are at risk of doing this is by projecting it onto our partner. It becomes a game of vulnerability hot potato: "I don't like feeling insecure. Here, *you* feel insecure!" We might tell a story about how the barista flirted with us or how our ex liked our photo on Instagram. Or we might do any number of other subtle things that put us just a wee bit "one-up."

Family of Origin dynamics that fostered competition (between siblings for example) or scarcity can fuel this behavior. But I'd argue that *all* of us are at risk to some degree because we live in a culture of dominance that says you either have all the power or you don't have any power.

We are all at risk of playing into the idea that relationships are one-up, one-down arrangements. I am not saying that fostering jealousy is good/ right/healthy; I am saying it's real. By owning what is real, we open up healthier ways of coping with how vulnerable love can make us feel.

One of the biggest challenges of moving in together is that your partner now has a front row seat to the daily rhythms of your life.

When you live together, your partner sees it all: the days you get up early and go for a run, and the days you struggle to get out of bed. If you've historically coped with your lows by pulling away, you will be challenged. Retreating without explanation isn't great for your relationship. Your partner can see that you're in a funk—denying it just feels invalidating and crazy-making to your partner. Remember:

- You can own your funk without feeling ashamed of it.
- You can feel your funk without making it your partner's problem.
- You can sit in it without worrying that the whole relationship is at risk.

You both deserve a relationship that is big enough to contain each of your fluctuations. When you accept each other's shifting moods, the lows tend to be briefer and not so deep because you can just feel low rather than feeling low *and* afraid of what might happen next. Let yourself be loved in all your realness.

The length of time between rupture and repair matters.

Relationships exist in cycles of connection, disconnection, and repair, but have most of us ever learned *how* to offer a heartfelt apology to someone we've hurt? The words and the tone of an apology matter tremendously, but what about the timing?

There's a Goldilocks issue when it comes to timing an apology (not too rushed, not too delayed). If you apologize one second after your partner lets you know that they're hurt, perhaps they'll feel validated. More likely though, they'll feel like you're just trying to make the problem go away. Even though your rushed "I'm sorry" may reflect your shame and fear, your partner, nonetheless, will likely feel placated—or worse—patronized. In your hurry to reconnect with them, you risk losing the lessons from the rift: the deeper understanding of what they want and need and who they are as a person, as well as the blind spot or pain point that drove your hurtful behavior.

But what about a scenario in which your partner feels like they're waiting interminably for you to heal the space between you both? In this version, you are likely drowning in shame, which blocks connection. Heartfelt apologies rest on a foundation of basic self-worth—if you can't be gentle with yourself, you can't reach for your partner. The tragic side effect of your shame spiral is that it leaves the ones you love out in the cold. Your withheld apology could be driven by something else, like the inability to look at the impact of your own behavior. But whatever is driving your silence, your partner is left feeling like you are pulling a power play, and it feels awful.

While there's no universally agreed-upon amount of time to wait before offering an apology, check in with yourself and your partner to identify which side you tend to err on. You may need to be quicker to attend to their feelings, or you may need to slow down and give their feelings some room to breathe.

MARCH 18

Grief and loss are hard enough on your soul and psyche, but sometimes life puts us face-to-face with something even more extraordinary: ambiguous loss.

Ambiguous losses (a term coined by Dr. Pauline Boss) are losses that lack closure, that exist outside of ritual and linearity. The ambiguity and uncertainty in this type of loss complicate and delay healing, leaving us living in a liminal space—on hold, neither leaving nor arriving. Ambiguous losses come in two varieties:

- **Physically present but psychologically and emotionally absent:** *You're still here, but you aren't you. I need to therefore reorganize who you have been to me and who we are to each other.* For example:
  - A loved one with dementia
  - A child with special needs, especially the kind that involves a loss of prior skills
  - A divorced/separated partner
- **Physically absent but psychologically and emotionally present:** *You are gone, but I don't have closure. Therefore, you feel very much alive inside of me.* For example:
  - Migrating, especially sudden or forced
  - Losing someone in a situation where the body isn't recoverable
  - Ghosting or a unilateral breakup

Understanding ambiguous loss may validate the confusion and lingering knot of emotion you carry inside. Because your relationship with this person lives as a sort of "open tab" inside your mind and heart, you will need to meet this grief with tender loving care—honoring what the relationship meant to you, affirming your pain, and focusing on what is present and solid in your life today.

A healthy relationship boundary conveys, "Here's what I need in order to love you the way I want to love you."

A lot of talk about boundaries focuses on not tolerating certain kinds of behaviors in a relationship. The themes are self-protection, establishment of safety, and prevention of hurtful behavior. This framing is wholly understandable given how many of us have experienced relational harm. I am 100 percent in favor of enacting boundaries that ensure our autonomy, sovereignty, respect.

However, I want us to remember that boundaries *also* prime us for intimacy. Boundaries provide guidelines for tenderness and affection: "Here's the relational climate I need in order to open to you, to shine on you, to feel fully able to show you how much I adore you."

When you ask for a particular boundary, consider what it might be like to let your partner know that it's not *just* about protecting yourself from the harm you fear they may do to you. It is *also* about your desire to co-create a space where you can unfurl, drop down, exhale, and expand in love, service, care, and celebration.

Relational Self-Awareness Questions

- What is it like for you to consider that healthy boundaries are about *both* self-protection *and* intimacy?

- What vulnerability arises in you when you imagine saying, "Here's what I need in order to love you well and fully"?

- What is a relationship boundary that helps you feel more comfortable shining on your partner? Why?

The voice of your defensiveness shouts to you, "Respond now!" When this happens, just pause. Listen for the voice, even the whisper, of love.

Defensiveness is a symptom of a threatened brain; if left to its own devices, it will escalate a situation to protect itself. Pause. Take some deep breaths. Step away if you need to, saying something like:

- "I love us too much to keep talking right now."
- "I'm going to step away and collect myself."

When I feel defensive, I know that fear has taken the wheel. I ask myself, *What would love do?* Love trusts that it's better to be connected than right. When love takes the wheel, you don't need to feel defensive. You stop seeing the situation as win or lose. Rather than fighting against the other person, you're now fighting *for* connection. You can say:

- "This is a hard moment, but I want to understand what's going on for you."
- "You seem upset—can you help me understand?"
- "I want us to be on the same team."
- "It sounds like you're feeling X. Do I have that right?"

The best way to prevent resentment in the future is by showing up for your partner in the present.

Couples therapy usually begins because partners have lost their sense of connection with each other. In my office, we rewind the tape, looking back in the hopes of moving forward. Partners' stories often center on this theme: "You weren't there for me when I needed you."

Sometimes we don't ask clearly for the support we want and need in the moment. Instead, we hide, we bluster, we act like we are fine. Sometimes, even if we are clear with our needs, our partner's ability to offer support is blocked:

- Because they are also in pain

- Because our pain stirs up something old and overwhelming in them

- Because they are too distracted to hear us

- Because they are unskilled at providing empathy and relational care

In couples therapy, when there has been a missed opportunity for support, we work to shift from blame to shared mourning to rebuilding and prevention. Here are three suggestions for how you can show up for your relationship today:

1. **Keep your eyes open for *bids for connection*.** Research shows that happy couples respond to their partner's bids for connection (invitations, affirmations, musings, etc.).

2. **Ask your partner what helps them feel supported by you.** Then give a gentle nudge if they don't ask the same of you!

3. **Savor the good.** It is easy to focus on what's bugging you. Find the positive spin. Celebrate what's going well.

To have a thriving intimate partnership, you must learn to practice discernment. Sometimes it's about raising your concerns, and sometimes it's about letting stuff go.

Our pool of potential life partners is made up 100 percent of imperfect people. We choose from a menu of foibles, quirks, blind spots, and peccadillos. This is:

- **One part magnificent:** It means you don't have to be perfect either and you still get to be loved anyway. Halle-freaking-lujah!

- **One part infuriating:** It means you'll spend "'til death do you part" loving someone who leaves the fresh roll of toilet paper atop the empty roll of toilet paper.

Love requires us to let stuff go. What's worth our energy, and what isn't? This can be hard because the annoying stuff our partners do tends to be stuff we ourselves would never do. What helps us let stuff go is remembering that we're also no walk in the park! We present our partners with all kinds of opportunities to exhale deeply and remember how much they love us.

When it's time to let something go, make sure you really let it go. Exhale irritation and inhale grace/gentleness/gratitude. Imagine your heart opening up, big and wide. Call forth a list of things you love about your partner. When you do this intentionally, you guarantee that you actually *are* letting it go, instead of simply biting your tongue for now.

If you bite your tongue, it will come out sideways later today or next week, and your partner will feel caught off guard. If you're unable to let it go, it needs to be brought into the relational space so you can address it together.

The heart of repair is choosing to value connection over vindication. Because missed opportunities will happen. Because thoughtless acts will happen. Because sharp tones will happen. These unfortunate things will happen *not* because your partner isn't "the one," but because your partner is not perfect. Newsflash: You aren't perfect either!

Relational Self-Awareness Questions

- How did the grown-ups in your home repair relationships?
- Did they offer apologies?
- Did they proactively invite their partner to do something fun/ engaging/gentle to reestablish connection?

MARCH 23

Even if your Family of Origin provided consistency and care, you may still struggle as an adult.

It is a massive advantage to grow up in a family system that was able to:

- Meet your needs when you were little
- Adapt as you grew up
- Celebrate your independence as you launched

It is so helpful to grow up with grown-ups who modeled how to:

- Express differences of opinion

- Ask for what you need
- Tolerate frustration

However, a loving and stable Family of Origin does not inoculate us against struggle. In fact, one of the risks with this background is that we gaslight ourselves: "I had a good/normal/healthy family—WTF is wrong with me?"

Years ago, a graduate student of mine shared a story about an emotional breakdown she went through in college. She wondered if part of why she fell apart so completely (her words, not mine) was precisely because her family was her soft place to land.

Whether you lived in a supportive or disorganized **Original Love Classroom**—the household you grew up in—the past travels with you and shapes you. Keep this in mind as you're getting to know someone new or deepening a long-term relationship.

Relational Self-Awareness Questions
- What are your Family of Origin's main strengths?
- How have those strengths been assets to you during good times?
- How have those strengths carried you during difficult times?

You can feel badly that your choice creates pain in someone else while remaining clear and firm on your path.

Let's talk about this in terms of a breakup, though it applies to other hard choices as well. Deciding to end a relationship requires:

- Trust in one's own judgment
- Faith that the next chapter will be promising
- The ability to withstand the reactions of the other person

It is so hard to make a choice that you know will create pain in someone else. The understandable emotional response to knowing your choice will have a negative impact on another person is *guilt*. But you need to be careful not to confuse *guilt* and *regret*. Feeling guilt is a reflection of your capacity for empathy, not an indication that you have made a mistake. It's vital to learn to stay with your emotions, even the strong or painful ones. Emotions demand attention, not action. Hold steady. Observe. Breathe.

One of the most unkind things we can say: "This should not be so hard for you!"

We need to promise not to say this to each other. Not only are these words invalidating to a person who is already having a hard time, but they are also ineffective. In the history of the world, nobody has ever had less of a hard time because they were told they shouldn't be having a hard time. They only felt worse about themselves, thus blocking their access to their internal persistence and resilience. When we say this to someone else, all we are saying is, "I am uncomfortable bearing witness to your struggle. Be different so I feel better." Make the brave choice of sitting with someone and witnessing their challenge alongside them, supporting them as they make their way through it.

It's just as important to stop saying this to ourselves. If you are guilty of saying this to yourself, here's what to do:

- **Start to catch yourself when you're saying this.** Pay attention to the commentary inside your brain. You can't change anything until you become conscious of it.

- **Do not beat yourself up for beating yourself up.** You're already having a hard time. Don't add insult to injury.

- **Replace these words with something kinder.** For example, you might tell yourself, "This is hard."

- **Remind yourself of past experiences where you showed persistence and resilience.** Know that you possess internal strength.

- **Resist the urge to compare.** Don't line up anything about yourself or your situation against anyone else or any other situation. Just be with yourself and your current situation.

- **Reflect on whose voice this is.** When you were a kid, were you told this during moments of struggle? (This certainly helps you understand why you do this to yourself, but you'll still need to practice the previous bullets.)

MARCH 26

If you grew up with a harsh and critical parent, your partner's praise may feel like patronization.

Every single one of us has a part that longs to bask in the praise of someone whose opinion matters tremendously. Looking in someone's eyes and seeing acceptance and warmth reflected back is elemental to love. The need to feel valued by those we love is essential to our sense of well-being. If your Original Love Classroom included a harsh and critical parent, you learned to tuck that part of you away. As a result, you may have forgotten that part of you existed.

So what happens when you fall in love with someone who is not afraid to let you know that they think you're the bee's knees? It can feel *confusing* and *confronting*:

- **Confusing:** You may confuse affirmation with condescension or patronization, as if your partner is looking down on you rather than celebrating you. You may have deemed the need for praise to be a weakness. You might judge the part of you that wants praise and then inadvertently judge the giver of the praise as being manipulative or attempting to control or trick you. This is not your destiny! The first step toward healing is noticing what you do with incoming praise. With time and attention, you might be able to allow it and eventually, perhaps, welcome it.

- **Confronting:** Your partner's praise may illuminate something inside of you. Sometimes it is only when we receive something that we truly realize how long we've gone without it. In that space of contrast, we may experience grief for how long we were deprived. Here again, simply notice. Hold that part of you that is taking sips of affirmation with so much care.

A good thing (like support from a partner) isn't always an easy thing. Notice your reactions to praise and warmth and be willing to question them. What's keeping you from accepting your partner's compliment? What's the relational impact of not accepting your partner's compliment?

The process of building trust is both idiosyncratic and relational.

Getting to know someone new is a dynamic process of mutual disclosure. A process of peeling the proverbial onion. How we pace ourselves in that process is both idiosyncratic and relational:

- **The idiosyncratic side:** Some of us open like a garden gate, easily and readily. Others are more like a fortress, guarded and difficult to access. These individual differences are born of a blend of temperament, cultural factors, and adaptations to a traumatic experience or maladaptive relationship.

- **The relational side:** We decide whether, when, and how we will grant others access to our inner world by sharing something and tracking their response. This is less about us testing our partner and more about us orienting ourselves. We are getting our bearings in this strange new land called *us*. We share a little, and if we read empathy in our partner's eyes and we experience discernment about whom they tell, we are likely to share more with them. More quantity, yes, but also more interiority—that is, more of the facts and stories that live even deeper inside us. This is how trust builds in relationships.

Defensiveness is you protecting yourself at your partner's expense.

Once our walls go up, we are not available to the people who matter most.

We must develop the ability to notice when we've shifted from open to closed. But because it can be really hard to open right back up, we might need to call a time-out in order to regulate ourselves and shift back from closed to open. Rest assured though, this is not evasion—*regulation is not the same thing as conflict avoidance.* Stepping away to reset ourselves is an act of love. Try using this language to express your goal in stepping away:

- "I feel too upset to talk right now."
- "I need a little break."
- "I have to press pause and step away for a bit."

Once you've stepped away, your goal is to shift yourself from defensiveness to non-defensiveness.

- From certainty to curiosity
- From self-focused to relationship-focused
- From deflection to accountability

When you're the one who has initiated the break, be the one who initiates contact again. Try this language to open the door:

- "I'm ready to talk a bit more whenever you are."
- "I feel calmer now. Can we do something together?"
- "Thank you for giving me some space. How are you?"

When you make an effort to tend to your defensiveness for the sake of your relationship, you deserve to feel so proud of yourself. Know that you are investing in connection, safety, and growth.

Standing at a relational crossroads evokes profound questions about who you are and what you want from life. Beware of anyone who promises you easy answers.

Should I stay or should I go? A decision like this creates anguish in body, heart, and mind. It can feel like we're turning a kaleidoscope that brings into focus various facets of our dilemma:

- *What will it be like on my own?*

- *What if I regret my decision?*

- *What will other people think?*

A relational crossroads isn't brutal because you're indecisive or weak or broken. It's brutal because you are confronted with profound questions about your needs, your identity, your values, your morals, your past, and your Core Wounds. Meet yourself with gentleness and be discerning about the chorus of voices around you, such as friends who offer unsolicited advice or experts who promise you X number of steps to clarity.

Instead, surround yourself with people who can act like mirrors, reflecting you back to you. Seek out the people who help you find self guidance in those wise places that dwell within you. Your journey is unique, but you don't need to travel alone! Learning to listen to your own guidance will help you show up in a relationship as your most authentic and aligned self.

Validation sounds like: "That makes sense." "I can understand how you'd feel like that." "I get it."

The scene: Todd and I are taking a walk.

Todd: One of the best songs ever is "Despacito."

Alexandra: I agree 100 percent. I'll never change it when it comes on. But to be honest, I don't think Bieber adds much to that version.

Todd: You're right.

If you ever wondered what a decades-long marriage looks like, here's a solid snapshot. Can you feel the simmering sexual chemistry? This scene highlights not one but two instances of validation. Can you spot both?

Validation can be described as "deposits" in the relational bank account. Invalidation, on the other hand, is an emotional grind. A 2021 study on the impact of the pandemic on relationships found that couples with higher levels of invalidation were more likely to also have more thoughts of separation. Invalidation sounds like this:

- "That doesn't make sense."
- "You're wrong."
- "How could you say that?"

Validation isn't always easy, but it's infinitely easier when the topic is music—compared to emotions/sex/money/parenting, so keep an eye out for relational low-hanging fruit. Look for opportunities to be proactive and intentional with validation.

When you're in conflict about a topic that is tougher than music, look for (and comment on) the nuggets of truth/legitimacy/sensibility in your partner's perspective. You're not giving up anything when you do this. You're proactively doing your part to create an atmosphere of collaboration and care.

MARCH 31

We sometimes avoid difficult conversations because we are scared of how they will end. But the unfolding is beyond our control. What is within our control is how we start.

You know the feeling—something is weighing on your mind. There's a relational pebble in your shoe. You know you need to bring it up, but when you imagine the conversation, you feel sweaty and filled with dread. The problem is that the more you avoid, the more the pebble rubs. The delay makes the little thing into a bigger thing. If you're prone to silencing yourself, ask yourself: What is getting in the way?

One constraint that I hear a lot (especially from men) is that they can't start because they don't know where the conversation will go. They decide that the uncertainty isn't worth the risk. This constraint makes sense when we look at how men are socialized to always have control. That may work well in some settings, but it's antithetical to the collaborative setting of intimate partnership. Imagining that you can control an outcome implies that you can control your partner. Yikes!

In reality, all you can control is your side of the street: how you set up the conversation, and your intention to stay calm, caring, and curious. Here are a few tips for starting well:

- **Go Meta.** "When would be a good time to talk?"

- **Ask them to help you.** "I'm struggling with something and I wonder if you can help me talk it through."
- **Frame yourselves as a team.** "I want us to address this together."

You don't have to know where the conversation will go. Just start well. When we lead with more questions than answers and more curiosity than criticism, we create the conditions for conversations that deepen connection.

It's time to make yourself your home. A home that is both sturdy and gentle, both welcoming and safe. Becoming a home to yourself allows you to share that home with another.

We often talk about home as a place we grow up and leave. And for some of us, leaving home was essential, lifesaving, soul-saving. Creating a home of our own, with our own stuff, our own rules, our own rituals, provides immense healing to the Little One who felt devalued, unseen, misunderstood.

But home is also a place you cultivate inside yourself. An ongoing commitment to value, see, and understand yourself. This commitment to living as a home to yourself helps you create healthy relationships with others.

When you are uncomfortable in your own skin, you are at risk of perceiving that your partner (or coworker, friend, family member) feels similarly critical of you. Projection happens. We're all at risk of hearing other people's words in the most hurtful way possible, adding a negative spin to the neutral or benign. It's very hard to give someone else the benefit of the doubt if you haven't been giving it to yourself. Creating internal comfort helps you become more aware of the benevolent support around you.

Relational Self-Awareness Questions

- What images do you associate with home? If these are primarily negative, what images do you want to begin to associate with home?
- What does emotional safety look like to you? What color/shape/texture is it?
- If your "home of the self" had a motto, what would it be?

APRIL 2

Let go of the story that making a change in the service of love is the same thing as losing yourself.

Consider a scenario that happens all the time in couples therapy: Partner A makes a request of Partner B, and Partner B feels a rise of resistance. This resistance may look like one or more of the following:

- Criticizing Partner A for wanting this change
- Deeming the requested change silly or extreme
- Proclaiming that others don't need this change/wouldn't want this/would experience the exact same resistance

In this scenario, I would invite Partner B to explore their fear of making the requested change by asking, "Who are you afraid you will become if you make this change?" Partner B's answer may be something like:

- "I'm afraid of becoming a woman who works so hard to gain her partner's approval that she loses herself."
- "I'm afraid of becoming an emasculated man who can't stand on his own two feet."

Stories like this may be relics of painful Family of Origin dynamics in which subservience was required to keep the peace.

Even when someone's history makes their resistance understandable, the resistance needs to be addressed. Love requires us to expand, making space inside ourselves to accommodate the needs and desires of another. Love challenges us to figure out how to honor another without surrendering ourselves. When we do, we deserve to feel proud, not ashamed. Elevated, not diminished. Caring, not weak.

Your work is to figure out the story behind your resistance and discern how this story blocks your love.

When someone gives you a second chance, they are courageously engaging with the unknown. The more you can keep this in mind, the less terrifying their leap of faith will be for them.

Couples who dare to explore the possibility of coming back together after a breakup or a breach have their work cut out for them. The one who was left heartbroken must:

- **Hold onto both pain and possibility.** Do not deny the existence of either.

- **Resist the urge to label themselves a fool.** A shame-loaded story like that will only make a hard thing harder.

- **Practice clear boundaries with all the folks who want to share their opinions about the idea of a relational round 2.** You can simply say, "I hear that you are concerned" and move along. Resist the urge to explain/prove/defend. Conserve your energy.

The one who initiated the breakup (or caused the breach) must:

- **Express remorse without dissolving into a puddle of shame.** By its very nature, shame takes you out of connection.

- **Feel and express empathy for their partner.** Highlight again and again the courage it takes to even *attempt* to trust again. Say it loudly, proudly, and repeatedly. Their courage takes nothing away from you, and your willingness to shine on them is massively helpful in rebuilding trust.

Healing happens in the space between people.

When you and your partner become focused on trying to figure out whose fault it is, you're lost.

The word *fault* has no place in our relational vocabulary. It's a dead-end street. As couples therapists love to say, "You can be right or you can be happy." To which regular people love to say, "I'd like to be both, please and thank you very much."

So what are we to do? We need to learn to notice the urge to find fault and recognize it as a blinking indicator light. It's telling us that we are off-track, that we have begun to prioritize:

- Righteousness over humility
- Vindication over accountability
- Pride over vulnerability

This instinct doesn't mean that we're horrible people or that we're doomed as a couple. It means that we need to infuse our relational environment with things that support connection and health. All you need is one person to notice that you've gotten yourselves lost in the Forest of Finger-Pointing, and to say something like:

- "I think we're off track."
- "I don't like where this is going."
- "Let's see if we can pause and find a way to honor the hurt that *both* of us are feeling."

The moment one person steps out of the blame game, the game can't continue. How cool is that?

Your relationship with your partner, your relationship with your children, and your relationship with work exist as an ever-evolving, dynamic, and noisy conversation.

There's no such thing as "balancing work and family." This language points us toward a problem to be solved, a destination at which we arrive. Language shapes experience—when we talk about "balancing work and family," we send a message that reinforces perfectionism and fear of inadequacy. In this fantasy of balance, both partners relish their distribution of labor and responsibility—bills are paid, ambitions are pursued, and children's every need is met. When this fantasy rules the day, shame is the inevitable consequence. That nagging sense that we're doing it wrong makes a hard thing harder.

I have spent years at the messy intersection of wife, primary caregiver, and career-loving psychologist. On my best days, I move easily between these roles and responsibilities and feel grateful for this multidimensional life. On my worst days, I have an unrelenting sense that I am never quite in the right place.

A family is a system that needs to navigate multiple demands, all of which boil down to two essential elements:

1. **Economic:** Bringing financial resources into the home

2. **Caregiving:** Translating income into the goods and services that keep people alive, happy, and healthy

Housed within each of these elements are infinite opportunities for Relational Self-Awareness that encourage ongoing conversations about economics, caregiving, ambition, priorities, passion, and power.

- The work we do to bring money home also inspires our passions; engages us mentally, socially, and physically; and helps us feel like we are making a difference (at least sometimes).

- The work we do to care for our children also serves as a source of pride about caring for the next generation, a chance to decenter ourselves, and an opportunity to learn about patience and finding beauty in the ordinary (at least sometimes).

When you stop trying to achieve balance as an outcome and start embracing these elements as an unfolding process, you can be more realistic and self-compassionate.

Can you stay near me while I'm hurting? Can you hold my hand as tears shake my body and stain my face? Can you stay present even as you hear the cruel whispers of the old stories you've been told about crying? Please try. For my healing. For your healing.

Big feelings in other people evoke big feelings in us. Feelings are contagious. And many of us have spent lots of years developing stealthy exit strategies that help us move from discomfort to comfort. Bearing witness is a muscle we may never have learned how to flex.

- Maybe our Family of Origin didn't have language for feelings and didn't show feelings, so there were no opportunities to practice.

- Maybe our cultural identity afforded us a lot of privilege and comfort, and we didn't see/feel what we didn't want to see/feel.

- Maybe when we were a kid, someone who was big had big feelings that overwhelmed us.

- Maybe when we were a kid, nobody allowed us to sob and shake, so how on earth would we know how to do that for someone else?

- Maybe we grew up feeling so responsible for everything and everyone that another person's pain is wholly inseparable from our responsibility.

We tend to exit our discomfort by trying to change the other person. We may say things like the following, inside our heads or out loud:

- "It's not that big of a deal."
- "Other people have it worse."
- "Calm down."
- "They didn't mean it."

Your strong reactions in the face of conflict or big emotions don't come from nowhere. Identifying your Origin Story is the first step in your journey toward agency and growth as you strive to become a more compassionate and supportive partner.

> We will continue this topic in tomorrow's entry.

APRIL 7

Some of us need to enroll in a "witness protection program." We need a program that can help us learn how to protect the essential skill of bearing witness to the pain of another person.

#TherapistHumor

Holding space for someone else's big feelings takes practice. To hold space, you have to be both grounded and connected.

- **Grounded:** You don't get lost in your own panic, judgment, shame, or guilt. You stay present.
- **Connected:** You attune yourself to the other person's experience without casting judgment or getting overwhelmed.

Your witness protection program begins the moment you get wise to yourself: *A-ha, there I go again, trying to change someone's feelings because I'm uncomfortable.* From that savvy place, you can drop the rationalizations, the problem-solving, the defensiveness. You can feel your chest open, your breathing steady. You can stay here, in this moment, trusting that witnessing heals them *and* you.

When partners need to make a decision, it's easy to slip into an "either I get what I want or you get what you want" mindset.

A relationship is a thing unto itself. A third entity. Like Aristotle said, "The whole is greater than the sum of its parts." This perspective is hard to hold onto because a relationship is also made up of one *me* and one *you*, and sometimes what each one wants is *not* the same thing. Sometimes even the halfway option between your want and your partner's want isn't entirely obvious. For example, you want a dog; your partner doesn't want a dog; you cannot adopt half of a dog. Being at odds with the person you most want on your team is profoundly uncomfortable. So what might happen next?

- One person might try to resolve the discomfort by giving in.

- One person might try to resolve the discomfort by cajoling, begging, guilt-tripping, or pouting.

But how about a third path? What if you let go of the decision itself and go a bit deeper? Identify the deeper fears you each have:

- *If I don't get what I want, I am afraid* . . .
- *If you don't get what you want, I am afraid* . . .

Getting vulnerable with yourself and your partner about the feelings beneath the decision topic can activate empathy and create an entirely different way of imagining the decision—as an opportunity to clarify your individual and collective values:

- What value of yours does this tap into?
- What value of your partner's does this tap into?
- As you play with possible next steps, what would each path highlight about what you value as a couple?

New options may emerge as you clarify what matters to you and why. There's no way to get around the reality that love demands mutual accommodation. Shift out of the win/lose, either/or mindset by focusing on a choice that supports the *relationship*.

Sexual pleasure is about being versus doing, enjoyment versus accomplishment.

By its very nature, pleasure is hungry, unruly, selfish. Seeking pleasure begins with a sense that you are entitled to it. That you are worthy, by nature of your mere existence, of feeling good.

It turns out that feeling good can feel fraught. Ironic, perhaps, but true. Taking time to explore your relationship with pleasure is a vital part of expanding your **Sexual Self-Awareness**—an ongoing curious and compassionate relationship that you cultivate with your sexual self. I invite you to start *outside* the bedroom.

Relational Self-Awareness Questions
What are the stories you've internalized about permission to:

- Receive?

- Delight?

- Focus on yourself?

- Follow what feels good instead of a "should"?

Your assessment of someone's attractiveness is irrational, subjective, and complicated.

When you assess someone's attractiveness, your evaluation is informed by factors that are both out of your control and out of your conscious awareness. Here are just two examples:

1. **Cultural conditioning:** Social science research shows that beauty can only be understood in a particular time and place. Different parts of the world prize different body shapes, and a single part of the world has prized different body shapes during different historical times. All your life, you have been internalizing social messages about attractiveness, consciously and unconsciously.

2. **Your crew:** Your perception of your partner is inevitably informed, at least in part, by feedback from your friends and family. This is wholly understandable—you want your partner to be celebrated by your loved ones and to integrate seamlessly into your larger social network. At the same time, when you are building a relationship with a partner, you have enough on your plate just trying to figure out how *you* feel about the relationship.

> If your crew is overtly critical of your partner's looks, you will want to assess the quality of those connections. Their judgments reveal much more about them than you or your partner.

Remember:

- Attractiveness is about more than a booty or smile. It's about a soul.

- Our physicality is forever changing. We gain and lose weight. Hair changes. Bodies age.

- Attractiveness and sexual compatibility are not the same thing. Desirability is infinitely less about six-pack abs and infinitely more about presence, empathy, and solid communication skills.

APRIL 11

Some of us fall in love while others step into love. The steppers are often the ones whose hearts have known immeasurable pain and loss.

For some of us, love is ushered in with a fantastic fall, a swirling and obvious undeniability. For others, love is a sacred evolution, an easing in, a step and a breath followed by a step and a breath. The latter may be particularly true for those of us who are survivors of trauma:

- Those who were betrayed in a prior intimate relationship
- Those who endured maltreatment in childhood
- Those who lost someone near and dear

For these people, falling in love might feel really out of control and scary. We need to go slowly, keeping our feet on the ground and ensuring safety over and over again. If that's the case for you, you may not experience the "I'm in love with you" feeling. I want to give permission for that to be okay. You may need to let yourself feel sad that one lingering impact of your past pain is that you open up gingerly and mindfully.

But there's a world of difference between feeling sad and feeling ashamed. We are obsessed with creating better/worse hierarchies out of how we do this thing called "being a human." Enough already! None of us are broken. There is no right or best way. There is only your way. Trust your process.

APRIL 12

The imagining of a boundary begins inside of you and is made real in the dynamic space between you and your partner.

We come into relationships with legitimate fears:

- *I don't want to be a doormat.*
- *I don't want to do harm.*
- *I don't want to lose myself.*
- *I don't want to be emotionally unavailable.*

Therefore, we must be intentional with our boundaries. Far from a list of rules, boundaries are alive, dynamic, and relational. The boundaries we need at one point in our life are different from what we need at another point. The boundaries we need when we first meet our partner are different from what we need as we deepen into a trusting relationship.

Your best and bravest boundary work is about doing two things:

1. **Improving your awareness of your internal world:** This is the only way to know when someone is intruding on your boundaries. For me, it feels like a twisting in my gut and a growing sense of resentment.

2. **Getting comfortable asking for feedback from the people in your world:** That's how you keep from stepping all over someone else's boundaries. Strive to be safe enough for them to be honest and direct with you.

Boundary work is the work of a lifetime. When you can effectively communicate your boundaries to those you love and honor theirs at the same time, you are on our way to deeper intimacy.

APRIL 13

Let's stop saying, "That job/relationship/ experience was a waste of time."

Begin to view the words *waste of time* as a declaration of your frustration and pain rather than a statement of fact. When you view something as a waste of time, you express something powerful that lies beneath this idea. For example:

- *I am angry that I wasn't treated better.*

- *I am ashamed that I stayed.*

113

- *I am afraid of what I missed out on while I was in it.*

- *I am anxious about what's next.*

Naming any or all of those feelings is more self-compassionate than self-critically stamping the experience with a "waste of time" label.

Another cruelty of the wasted time mindset is that it keeps you stuck imagining the life you "would have had" if you hadn't been doing exactly what you were doing. Since you can't return to the path not taken, your work is to grieve that imagined chapter of your life so you can fully inhabit your life right now. Honor the pain of what (in hindsight) you wish hadn't happened so you can begin to move forward.

Relational Self-Awareness Questions

- What situation have you described as a waste of time?

- How would you describe the pain that underlies those words?

- What lessons can you take away from the experience?

- What might be different for you if you could trust that you are learning and growing on your current path?

- Might you be able to imagine holding both the grief of (imagined) lost opportunities and the hope of what's next?

APRIL 14

Intimacy is a progressive and revelatory exploration of what's possible between two hearts, two bodies, two minds, two lives.

Intimacy itself has facets or dimensions:

- **Emotional intimacy:** Granting access into each other's stories, memories, hopes, and present-moment experiences
- **Sexual intimacy:** Creating a shared arena for expression and communication via touch, movement, breath, sensation, and pleasure

We need to remember that facets of intimacy don't exist as silos. Emotional intimacy readies us for sexual intimacy. Sexual intimacy opens us to more and deeper emotional intimacy.

This is why the "third date rule" (sleeping together on the third date) should be thrown out with wearing "jorts" and eating oysters (sorry not sorry). We need to stop acting like readiness for sexual intimacy can be plotted on some external timeline. Readiness for sexual intimacy can only be determined within and between the hearts, minds, and bodies of those in the relationship. That's intimacy. Up close. Curious. Patient. Willing to sit with question marks.

APRIL 15

Shame paralyzes. Responsibility mobilizes.

Our interpersonal dynamics and the larger societal systemic dynamics mirror each other:

- What is healthy for our one-to-one relationships (with partners, kids, friends, family members) is healthy for our society at large.
- What is destructive for our one-to-one relationships is destructive at the societal level.

Family therapist Terry Real teaches that there are three relational stances:

- **The one-up stance:** Grandiosity

- **The one-down stance:** Shame

- **The face-to-face stance:** Connection

Those of us who are White do harm to BIPOC folks when we get stuck in either the one-up stance or the one-down stance. The one-up stance is obviously harmful:

- White supremacy is about toxic beliefs in superiority.

- Other patterns like denying the problem ("All lives matter") and getting defensive ("Not all White people . . .") also reflect a one-up stance.

- These responses say "I don't need to engage with you," and they prevent healing.

The one-down stance is similarly harmful:

- Feeling guilty about being White makes us ask BIPOC folks, directly or indirectly, to take care of us or make us feel better.

- Feeling ashamed when someone points out our blind spots or when our hurtful words/actions prevent us from figuring out how to create change.

- If we are lost in shame, we may retreat and become unavailable to work with others to figure out a way forward.

The face-to-face stance is the heart of being what Dr. Ibram X. Kendi calls *anti-racist*. We create change by seeing how we are part of, and responsible to, a larger collective.

APRIL 16

When you marry someone, you become a member of their family and they become a

member of yours. We must meet the synergies with celebration and the clashes with curiosity.

Every relationship is the merger of two life stories. Two family stories. Two cultural stories. We need to approach these layers thoughtfully because:

- Our partner arrives in our world with traditions, rituals, preferences, and tendencies that are unlike ours.
- Our knee-jerk tendency is to assume our way is the normal/right/ good way, which makes our partner's way the odd/wrong/bad way.
- Very often what seems to be a personality difference is really a family or a cultural difference.

With reflection, attention, and care, these spaces of difference become opportunities for you to grow in compassion and for your relationships to grow in intimacy. With this in mind, in moments of friction, disappointment, or confusion with your partner's family, try this mantra:

If my partner, their family, and their people approach life differently from me, my family, and my people, it offers me the chance to experience life from my partner's perspective. If I can suspend my judgment and tend to my anxiety, I will grow.

APRIL 17

It's far easier to see a relationship challenge as a reflection of your partner's deficit than to see a relationship challenge as a dynamic.

The shift from blame and finger-pointing to dynamics and dances is challenging for many of us. Why? Because part of us is invested in the idea that a relationship challenge shines a light on a deficit in our partner.

We can exhaust ourselves making that case. I don't think we try to be obstinate; we just have never learned to study our reactivity!

When we're upset, it's likely a lot of people could stand beside us and validate the hell out of our complaints about our partner. But when our *modus operandi* is proving that we are victims of our partner's thoughtlessness or deficiency, we cut ourselves off from an opportunity for insight and liberation:

- Liberation from society's expectations of us

- Liberation from our old stories that we are not enough as we are

Let's look at an example: A woman becomes furious at her partner when he questions a parenting choice that she has made. Is he missing an opportunity to offer support to his bone-weary partner? 100 percent. Does her reactivity highlight where she remains trapped and therefore triggered by her partner's alternative perspective? 100 percent.

What is she trapped by?

- **Society:** She has been sold a bill of goods that says her worth as a woman depends on how her kids are doing. This raises the stakes on every parenting choice she makes.

- **Old story:** She was not mothered well and is terrified that she cannot mother well either. His question feels like a confirmation of that bone-deep fear.

This relationship challenge highlights where she is not liberated. Not because she is a bad mother and partner but because the ties that bind are heavy. If she stays exclusively focused on the fact that he is "undermining" her, she will miss an opportunity to heal.

Attraction happens. Attraction is notoriously unruly and transgressive. You aren't the victim of your attractions. You make choices about what you do in the face of that attraction.

Dr. Shirley Glass, one of the first therapists to write about infidelity, offers this helpful gut check: If you wouldn't want your partner to see a video or read a transcript of an interaction you're having with someone else, it's likely that you're "playing with fire"—that is, saying or doing things that would feel hurtful to and erode trust with your intimate partner.

Trust is an essential ingredient for an intimate relationship. We need to be able to trust our partner and we need to feel that we ourselves are trustworthy. Practicing healthy boundaries helps us feel sturdy, grounded, and proud of who we are in our relationship. You cannot control when you feel the pull of attraction toward someone other than your partner, but if you do sense these feelings, you can meet that energy with Relational Self-Awareness.

Relational Self-Awareness Questions

- What unmet need inside of you are you attempting to fill with this outside attraction?

- What unmet yearning/longing are you experiencing in your relationship?

- Is something in your relationship evoking an unhealed pain from your past that makes you want to hide or distract yourself?

If you grew up with a critical parent, you may feel confused by your partner's strong reaction to what feels very much to you like a neutral comment.

Kids have zero psychological boundaries. What is said to them sinks right in. A critical grown-up powerfully shapes a kid's entire sense of self. If you grew up with a critical parent, you were basically in a years-long training program where you learned to thicken your skin:

- You learned how to take an emotional hit and keep on chugging.

- You learned how to stay quiet in the face of judgment (especially if pushing back would have led to louder critique).

- You learned a skewed version of relational dialogue.

Let's focus on that last point. A critical grown-up *normalizes* things like unsolicited harsh feedback, character assassination, teasing, and pointing out any and all missteps. For people who grew up in this type of Original Love Classroom, this just feels like how people "do" relationships. So when your partner reacts strongly to something you say (their eyes well up with tears, they pull back, they express shock, etc.), you may feel legitimately confused. To you, teasing someone when they make a mistake just feels normal. Benign. The way it's done.

Your brave and humble Growing Edge is to begin connecting the dots between your past and your present: "Because of my Family of Origin dynamics, my threshold for verbal harshness is really freaking high. Being able to tolerate that when I was little was a Coping Strategy that I don't need any more. I have to remember that my partner didn't grow up like that, which means they don't have thick skin like me."

Your challenge is to soften your approach without feeling terribly about yourself: "The default setting of my words is harsh. I can have compassion for how I came to be this way even as I work on softening. It's what my partner needs . . . and frankly, it's better for me!"

Change can happen without shame. You aren't broken. You're evolving.

If you are struggling to make a decision, ask yourself, *What would I choose for myself if I had an unshakable belief in my ability to choose?*

Standing at a fork in the road can activate profound self-doubt:

- If your Family of Origin was very top-down and authoritarian, you may not be very practiced in the art of choosing your own adventure.

- If you occupy one or more marginalized identities, the world may have presented you with more roadblocks than open doors. Getting/having to choose feels scary, and you may be guided more by a desire to avoid a potential threat than a desire to claim a potential reward.

Rather than saying "I'm so indecisive," see what happens when you say, "Making choices for my life is a Growing Edge. I am committed to loving myself as I learn how to decide for me."

Consider this question: *What would I choose for myself if I had an unshakable belief in my ability to choose?* Meditate on it, journal about it, or talk about it with a trusted adviser/friend. This question provides you with a different perspective on the decision. It may help you occupy a space beyond the limiting story about your "silliness," "indecisiveness," "history of bad decisions," or whatever harsh story you are at risk of telling yourself about yourself.

The fact that grief is woven into the fabric of choice means we are real, not wrong.

When we are young, the future feels like a wide-open expanse of possibility. With every choice we make (school, major, job, partner, etc.), the expanse narrows, creating a series of mini-griefs. For example:

- Choosing to marry requires that you grieve the loss of your single life.
- Choosing to parent requires that you grieve the loss of flexibility.

Whatever path we choose inevitably highlights another path we did not choose. Sometimes we think the only way to cope is avoiding the grief by avoiding the choice. Stay open. Plant no flags. Take nothing off the table.

But our refusal to choose can backfire. We send ourselves a message that we *can't* choose:

- *I have commitment issues.*
- *I am too damaged.*
- *I am not meant for "X"* (whatever X is).

A different way to cope with the inevitable grief of choice is by inviting your attention back to the bounty within the choice you've made. Challenge yourself to do two things at once. Grieve the loss of one chapter so you can delight in the new chapter. As the saying goes: "Don't worry that the grass is greener on the other side. Water your side!"

Is she nagging? Or is she being crushed under the weight of a centuries-old inequitable distribution of domestic and emotional labor created and perpetuated by the patriarchy?

Old habits die hard. Gender role socialization is ingrained. We've done a better job empowering women as workforce leaders than we have empowering men in the domestic realm, as evidenced by the fact that men between ages 18 and 34 in heterosexual relationships are no more likely than older couples to equally divide household labor.

Household labor is an umbrella term that covers so much beyond cleaning toilets and doing laundry. It also means school forms and plans with in-laws and noticing when supplies are low and doctors' appointments and putting cards in the mail and decorating the house for holidays. So much of emotional and domestic labor is invisible. While mixed-sex couples are at obvious risk of replicating male/female models of domestic responsibilities, queer couples have been socialized in heteronormativity too and can struggle with inequitable distribution of labor based on income, gender expression, or personality.

If you are a partner who does less of the domestic work, banish the word *nag* from your vocabulary. It's a word that can only be spoken from a victim stance: "After all I do for her, she has the nerve to ask me again and again to put my bowl in the sink. She needs to stop nagging." The word drips with entitlement and loss of context.

If you have the urge to utter that word, take it as an indicator that your partner is exhausted and resentful. Widen your perspective. Start scanning your home for what needs to be done. If you don't want to be asked/ reminded, get in the driver's seat.

When we can stay present to our feelings, we can use our past experiences to guide our next steps and new choices.

We are primed for reflecting on the past at certain times, such as when we are:

- Facing a developmental milestone like turning a certain age, graduating, launching a kid out of the nest, or retiring

- Considering a big change like a breakup, divorce, job change, or move

- In a crisis—our own or that of someone we care about

During these times, we are likely to ask ourselves, "How did I get here?" This question brings intense scrutiny of the choices we've made (and not made) every step of the way, as well as the choices we were unable to make or that were made for us. Our work in times of transition is to pair reflection on the past with grace, not judgment.

It is impossible to guarantee 100 percent safety in an intimate relationship. At the same time,

we cannot be expected to take relational risks in the absence of relational trust.

Because our partner is a separate being, we are forever at risk of losing them. Separateness is *both* the prerequisite for intimacy *and* the root source of the inevitable, unsolvable insecurity we experience in an intimate relationship. Intimacy demands that we invest ourselves emotionally, sexually, spiritually, logistically; however, that investment puts us face-to-face with the threat of loss—to another person, to death, to anything.

Since this problem cannot be fixed, it must be contained. Held gently. Discussed tenderly together. Love holds up a mirror, giving us the chance to observe:

- *How do I begin to behave when I feel scared to lose what matters to me?*
- *How do I reckon with the limits of my control?*

Our partner cannot make our trepidation go away; the most they can do is empathize with our fears and express their own. At the same time, we cannot be expected to take emotional (or sexual) risks in the absence of trust. Trust is enacted through:

- Reliability
- Consistency
- Care
- Empathy
- Alignment of words and actions

Trust isn't a talisman that wards off pain. Rather, trust is what helps us feel sure that the reward is greater than the risk.

Although love cannot be anything other than complex, we can learn to be curious, savvy, and reflective in the face of love's complexities.

One of the symptoms of relational distress is one partner telling a very simplistic story about their problem:

- "You don't respect me."
- "You shouldn't watch porn."
- "You are too beholden to your mom."
- "You don't help out enough around here."

These straggly little stories elicit defensiveness, counter-complaining, and polarization from the other partner:

- "You don't respect *me*!"
- "You shouldn't judge my porn use."
- "At least I talk to my mom!"
- "I do plenty around here."

Romantic love is complicated because it's hard to balance two people's needs, differences, and preferences. Romantic love is also complicated because old pain that started long before you ever laid eyes on each other gets activated in an intimate relationship.

You cannot make love easy, but you can learn to become more thoughtful and measured, less reactive and defensive. The heart of Relational Self-Awareness is commitment to ongoing curiosity and compassion in relationship with yourself. This lets you begin to disentangle the past from the present and witness your partner as they attempt to do the same.

Biting your tongue solves the moment of conflict while sowing the seeds of longer-term resentment.

Dr. John Gottman's research has shown that happy couples have a *low negativity threshold*. This means that partners in a successful relationship are able to raise and resolve concerns in real time. Nobody needs to bite their tongue. Nobody needs to walk on eggshells. Couples with a low negativity threshold have cultivated a relational ecosystem in which it is safe to give and receive feedback.

Having a robust yet gentle feedback loop between partners lets both of you learn how to support each other. Neither one stockpiles a whole mess of unmet needs. If you find yourself biting your tongue, consider it a flashing indicator light that something is amiss in your relationship. Remember that it is incumbent upon you to find words and use a tone that invite your partner nearer.

Sexual monogamy does not have to be boring. But it does have to be cultivated.

When couples commit to a journey of Sexual Self-Awareness, sex becomes a playground—a space of escape, silliness, joy, and healing where couples never make the same love twice. As couples deepen into commitment, sexual desire does not die, but it tends to change. Couples who choose sexual monogamy must also choose to cultivate their erotic connection rather than take it as a given.

Our connection to our sexual selves and our intimate partner is precious, but it is also fickle. Sexual desire is susceptible to the vicissitudes of life: stress, illness, exhaustion, tension. When we are stressed out, sex can slide down the list of priorities. Stay open to the possibility that allowing yourself to feel good might be the perfect medicine for your overwhelm.

You need and deserve a definition of "feel-good" that suits you, not the sexual script you've learned through your culture. Every erotic encounter, whether alone or with a partner, ought to begin with the question I learned from my dear friend Shadeen Francis: "What do you want to feel?" This question sets you and your partner up to build an experience together.

What a skill it is to say goodbye to an experience or a relationship without devaluing its place in your life.

A butterfly outgrows her chrysalis. This doesn't mean the chrysalis was fake, meaningless, or not worth it. It means the chrysalis served its purpose. In the same way, you will outgrow a job, home, friendship, relationship. Can you say goodbye without belittling the place that experience holds in your heart? In your life? In your transformation?

It is easy to trash something when it ends, calling it silly, lame, embarrassing, or a waste of your time. Let's look at why you might devalue your experience:

- **You are in pain.** You have been mistreated, misunderstood, or betrayed.

- **You imagine it will be easier to go if you feel mad.** It is easier to leave behind something that was bad for you than walk away from something that was good for you.

- **You fear your goodbye won't otherwise stick.** You don't quite trust yourself to look ahead rather than in the rearview mirror.

Now let's look at the potential consequences that can result when you use devaluation as a Coping Strategy:

- **You hurt the person or space that you're leaving.** You could avoid this if you instead let yourself sit with the complex knot of feelings you actually have about this ending.

- **You create shame inside yourself for needing that step for your evolution.** My kids often ridicule their former habits or pronunciations—I feel so protective on behalf of their little selves. "Don't judge that Little You," I remind them. "If you hadn't done that then, you wouldn't be here now!"

- **You compromise your ability to integrate the loss.** Your ability to create meaning is limited when you are hellbent on devaluing.

We think belittling what something meant to us will help us feel better, but it can end up hurting us further, making us hesitant to embrace anything new out of fear that we will later regret it. Choosing trust instead helps us let go with self-compassion and move into a new chapter with an open and curious heart.

What's essential here is to make space *both* for the feelings you have about the experience itself (anger, sadness, disappointment, etc.) *and* for the lessons you've learned through the experience. You deserve peaceful departures and gentle goodbyes.

Instead of spinning your wheels trying to figure out whether your loved one can't or won't make the change you've asked for, see how your perspective shifts when you simply say they aren't.

Person A makes a request of Person B:

- "Let me know if you're going to be late (because you know I worry)."

- "Reassure me that you think I'm a good parent (because I feel insecure right now)."

- "Keep your grades above a C+ (because we're sacrificing a lot to send you to this school)."

If Person B doesn't do what they've been asked, Person A's feelings about it depend on many factors: the history of the problem, Person A's personality/Core Wounds, Person B's personality/Core Wounds, the story that Person A tells about Person B's behavior. Based on their feelings, Person A is going to *make meaning* from the situation that will shape their next steps:

- **If Person A decides that Person B won't do what they've asked, their story steers toward blame.** Person B is willful, lazy, mean, entitled, and Person A is (therefore) a sucker, a doormat, a victim. This path may create anger and hurt in Person A, leading to a set of next steps that might include consequences, demands, and/or an ultimatum.

- **If Person A decides that Person B can't do it, their story steers toward excuses.** Person B is compromised, limited, overwhelmed, needing help, and Person A (therefore) needs to support, rescue, let go. This path may create sadness and disappointment in Person A, leading to a set of next steps that might include reducing expectations, increasing support or intervention, and/or working on acceptance.

Often, we flip-flop between these two paths. Won't versus can't. Demand versus release. Expect versus surrender. Hold the line versus let go of expectation. Relationships are complex and there are few (if any) easy answers. But I want to invite you to explore what happens when you find a place *beyond* the "they can't" versus "they won't" binary:

- *They* aren't *letting me know they are late.*
- *They* aren't *praising my parenting.*
- *They* aren't *getting above a C+.*

See what happens when you drop the quest for meaning and simply meet reality on reality's terms. This third path may help you feel less emotionally entangled and more able to problem-solve with clear eyes.

APRIL 30

When you gain an insight about your past, you may want to process it with the people who were there at the time

(family member, ex-partner, etc.). But your insights can belong only to you.

I was working with a client to heal from a breakup, revisiting old incidents with new awareness. Putting pieces together. Identifying patterns. Peeling back layers. She found herself wanting to reach out to her ex. As we explored this urge, she realized that she felt selfish keeping her new insights to herself.

This feeling is very common for broken-up partners. The urge to share insights may reflect a desire to:

- Alleviate the suffering (or imagined suffering) of another person

- Gain closure or control by creating a shared narrative of what happened and how

- Show your ex that you're fine—fine enough to have solved the puzzle of what went wrong

You either will or won't share your insights with the people in your life. They will either welcome or block what you share. What matters most is that you meet the urge to share with curiosity, teasing out the elements that create your motivation. Then the choice is just the choice!

MAY 1

Pleasure, by its very nature, is hungry, unruly, and selfish. Seeking pleasure begins with a sense that you are entitled to it—that you are worthy, by virtue of your existence, of feeling good.

The ability to access erotic pleasure is predicated upon deservingness:

I deserve to feel good, it's okay to let go, I can have this. Dr. Lori Brotto's research has shown that teaching mindfulness skills to women helped them quiet the noise inside their heads and access pleasure. Specifically, women who practiced mindfulness during sex experienced more desire, more arousal, and more orgasms. Pleasure begins with feeling permission to be present and grows with a partner who is similarly attentive and emotionally attuned.

Relational Self-Awareness Questions

- What is the noise inside your head that takes you out of the moment?
- To what degree do you believe that feeling good is bad or risky?
- What do you want to believe and feel instead?

MAY 2

You get to build adult relationships that don't play by old rules of engagement.

Many of us grew up in a Family of Origin that was under tremendous stress. This stress may have been imposed by macro factors (immigration, racism, poverty, incarceration, sexism, natural disasters, etc.), micro factors (addiction, personality disorders and other mental health challenges, abuse, disengagement, etc.), or intricate combinations of both.

A system under stress grows brittle and rigid, unable to adapt or flex with life's ebbs and flows. In that brittle state, individuals get cast in particular roles that interact to create an illusion of stability.

When we live in a world like this, we then grow up into:

- The caretaker who cannot focus on self

- The angel who never asks for anything

- The troublemaker who offloads competence to stay connected

If you've only had the chance to show up in a relationship in one particular way, that's the one particular way you'll keep showing up. However, just because something is familiar doesn't mean it's fated. You have always been multifaceted—the other parts of you were just buried under necessity and loyalty. You now have the chance to re-find and reclaim the roles you'd like to play.

MAY 3

For those who learned to play nice, shrink back, or focus on everyone else, pleasure is a much-needed act of rebellion. For those whose bodies have been traumatized, pleasure says, "You hurt me, but you didn't break me."

Sexuality has been shrouded in fear and silence and shame for so long. One consequence is that many of us struggle to feel deeply, truly, fully entitled to pleasure. Finding our way back to pleasure can start with exploring the stories we carry about it. Many of us feel so disconnected from what makes our bodies feel good that it's hard to even know where to begin.

Many of us struggle with sexual pleasure because our first or predominant sexual experiences have been experiences of pain. If this rings true for you, please know that you can heal. Your vibrant sexuality is there, even if it is buried under trauma.

As you resource yourself with therapy, books, podcasts, and community support, I want you to set your sights higher than just making the pain stop. Easing pain is necessary but not sufficient. I want you to feel fully entitled to envision the reclamation of sexual pleasure and erotic joy within your body. Step by step. Bit by bit. You deserve nothing less, and you always have. You deserve a vision of your sexuality that is bold, unapologetic, dynamic, evolving, permission-giving, loving, joyful, subversive, holy, and brave.

Relational Self-Awareness Questions

- How do you view pleasure? Is it selfish? Dangerous? Immoral?
- What keeps you from feeling deserving of/authorized to seek pleasure?
- What might be different if you began to take your pleasure seriously?
- What steps can you take (or do you take) to ensure that your partner will prioritize your pleasure?

MAY 4

If you are recovering from a chaotic childhood, an ambiguously defined intimate relationship will create more wounding than healing.

Some people thrive in an ambiguously defined relationship. They reap the benefits of connection, play, and sex without the work of accountability and intimacy. Perhaps a "situationship" works well for these people because their life is in transition and they need to stay agile and flexible. Perhaps a situationship reflects the current depth of their self-awareness—staying in the shallows suits them because they fear the deeper waters of their soul.

But here's what I know for sure: If you are busting your ass learning to swim so you can dive safely into your own depths, tolerating a poorly defined intimate relationship will wound you in familiar places. Why? Because you'll have to act again and again as if you *don't see* what you see, *don't feel* what you feel, *don't know* what you know. Just like when you were a kid.

If you grew up in a chaotic Family of Origin, you survived by acting fine when you weren't. You relied on one person: *you.* In a weird way, you have everything you need to tolerate low-accountability love. But your healing rests on striving for more than just tolerance. Don't you finally deserve a relationship that makes space for all of you? One where you don't have to leave out the messy parts so that someone else feels okay? For those who seek deep connection and the healing that comes from a trusting partnership, a situationship will likely fall short.

MAY 5

Your tendency toward impatience may have an Origin Story about a need for control that emerged during a time when your life felt out of control.

My impatience is big, old, and deep. (Perhaps yours is too.) When I was a kid, a lot of my family life felt pretty overwhelming to me, so I controlled

what I could control. My room. My homework. My feelings. Early
Coping Strategies can become enduring personality traits.

> Personality traits are *also* genetics or mysteries of consciousness,
> or they develop for other reasons. I am not suggesting we
> need to map all of who we are onto our early years.

Our impatience can make it hard to be on someone else's schedule or
to adjust our pace to accommodate others. So what *do* we do with our
impatience?

- Sometimes we need to stretch ourselves to relinquish control.
- Sometimes we need to say to the other person, "I actually will
  need to do this on my time frame, so catch up with me later."
- We always need to offer reassurance to the kid who lives inside of
  us, reminding them that what was required then is not necessary
  now.

When we take the risk of flexing to accommodate someone else, the
kid inside us learns to let go a little and trust.

MAY 6

If you struggle to treat yourself with kindness, you will deflect others' efforts to treat you with kindness.

We do not need to practice self-compassion 24/7, but we need to be savvy
enough to recognize when our inner critic is kicking up dust. When our

inner critic is in charge:

- **We are at risk of deflecting the positivity that others try to offer us.** Deflecting positivity from other people is not a very nice thing to do. If someone offers us a compliment, and we pooh-pooh it because we don't feel deserving, we deny them the yummy pleasure that comes from watching us absorb and enjoy their praise. Our inner critic hurts us *and* them!

- **We are at risk of distorting the neutral or helpful things that other people say because our ears are primed for negativity.** You'd be surprised to know how many fights begin because we assume that someone has rejected or criticized us when, in fact, it's our inner critic who is so intent on finding confirmation of our inadequacy that it makes something of nothing.

Our work toward wholeness and gentleness spares us the pain of self-criticism. It also spares the people around us from the fallout of our self-criticism.

MAY 7

When you and your partner are muddling through a relationship challenge, ask yourselves and each other this question: "What can we do to protect the rest of what's great about our relationship from the impact of this problem?"

When a couple is dealing with a relationship challenge, it can feel as if that challenge fills every cubic inch of the relational space, as if the problem has become the sum total of who the couple is. That's why I love to invite couples to sit with the question above. The mere posing of the question reminds people that they are more than the problem they share. It also shifts the couple's focus from their problem to their strengths. Because guess what? A couple can be *both* burdened by a problem *and* lovely/loving/strong/diligent/kind/sexual/playful.

We *have* problems, but we *are not* problems. When a couple needs to find their way, it is everything outside the problem—their strengths, resources, and gifts—that will see them through:

- Their strengths will help them persist in the face of challenge.

- Their resources will help them find support and care.

- Their gifts will help them see possibilities.

MAY 8

Take time to celebrate the small victories: your own and those of the people you love.

Small victories—a day without conflict, a task completed without (or with less) prompting—definitely matter. But sometimes the small victory:

- Seems too small to make a difference

- Feels too obvious to be celebrated

- Is so long-awaited that it has outlasted your excitement

Let's explore some blocks that can keep you from celebrating small victories and some ways to address them.

- **Block 1:** You grew up with grown-ups who were hard to impress. You didn't get credit for the ordinary and the expected, so your radar is calibrated to only notice the big stuff.

- ○ *Try:* Blessing those grown-ups for their mindset (I'm sure it has had lots of payoffs, like making you a hard worker), then freeing yourself to notice the little stuff.

- **Block 2:** You worry that if you celebrate small victories, it will have a paradoxical effect: You (or the person you love) will stop trying because you/they got the reward of affirmation.

  - ○ *Try:* Remembering that what you focus on, you get more of. Celebration begets motivation.

- **Block 3:** You waited so long for this small victory that you're too annoyed to affirm it.

  - ○ *Try:* Honoring your annoyance. It's real! What is also real is that this person did their part. They weren't doing a thing, but then they did a thing—yay! Your request mattered to them. Let that sink in.

Life is hard. Adjust your lens so you can savor every possible drop of sweetness and notice every shift or change or improvement that happens inside or around you. You need all the sweetness to combat the heavy, the scary, and the overwhelming. Give yourself and each other the gift of celebrating small victories.

As we work toward creating a more just world, we need to ensure that empowerment extends to the bedroom. Intimate empowerment is about pleasure—the right to feel good.

Feeling good is predicated upon:

- Feeling entitled to feeling good

- Knowing what feeling good feels like for you

- Partnering with someone who feels good about you feeling good

Women, those who love them, and those who make love to them must (and deserve to) value women's pleasure. As a couples therapist and relationship educator, I know that challenges related to sex are both very common and very hard to talk about for couples. Our culture is screwed up about sex and, in particular, deeply uncomfortable with women's pleasure.

Although the clitoris has been the centerpiece of sexual pleasure for those with a vulva for centuries, collective ignorance has reigned. In fact, the full anatomy of the clitoris wasn't mapped until the spring of 2000, and only about 50 percent of college-aged women can accurately identify 80 percent of the external female genitalia. (Only about 25 percent of college-aged men can.)

Creativity and play can keep monogamy from becoming monotonous, but vulva-bodied people (and their partners) can't unlock their sexual imaginations until and unless they have information, entitlement, and support in the endeavor.

MAY 10

Family dysfunction manifests as a constriction of possibilities.

When people feel overwhelmed, they may cope with their pain by narrowing down their world. They create shortcuts and simplifications to make life feel more manageable. One way this happens in families is when grown-ups cast kids into roles. Kids get the message that "I need you to be *this way* because it's all I can handle," and they learn to embody those roles without question. As Dr. Gabor Maté says, kids trade authenticity for belonging because their very survival depends on it.

Two things are true at once: rigidity of roles is an effort to cope with pain, *and* narrowness around what is tolerated or permissible does real damage to kids' development. In contrast, a hallmark of a healthy family system is that our insides get to match our outsides:

- We can move between being happy, silly, ambitious, tired, artsy, sporty, social, and quiet.

- We get to play different (age-appropriate) roles at different times.

- Our evolution is celebrated. Changes are met with curiosity rather than combat.

In a healthy family system, we get to be multifaceted and magnificent.

Relational Self-Awareness Questions

- Has your Family of Origin become more rigid or more flexible over time?

- Can parts of you be witnessed and celebrated today in ways they couldn't when you were young? If not, how do you ensure that those parts are nevertheless witnessed and celebrated?

- Are you able to get to know the members of your family in new ways today? What is that like for you?

We self-sabotage when we doubt our worth.

Many years ago, Oprah Winfrey and the inspirational speaker Iyanla

Vanzant came together for a reparative conversation on an episode of *The Oprah Winfrey Show*. Back when they were close, Oprah and her team had been working with Iyanla and her team to create an opportunity for Iyanla. But along the way, something happened, Iyanla retreated, and their friendship had a falling out.

During their live-on-TV conversation, Oprah verbalized a mix of:

- Hurt ("I thought we shared a vision")
- Confusion ("I don't understand what happened here")
- Irritation ("Why did you act like that?")

The part that has always stuck with me is Iyanla's response: "I hadn't worked hard enough for it. I hadn't struggled enough. I couldn't receive it. I couldn't recognize it. I didn't even know what it was." Iyanla blew up the opportunity because she could not rest comfortably in her worthiness.

Self-sabotage is what happens when we make an easy thing hard. It may show up in behaviors like procrastination, avoidance, gossip, dishonesty, and overcommitting. It is a blinking indicator light pointing us to our struggle with worthiness:

- Worthiness to have comfort
- Worthiness to have success
- Worthiness to have ease
- Worthiness to have connection

We heal a lack of worthiness through the daily practice of Relational Self-Awareness. We ask ourselves, *What would I choose for myself right here right now if I had an unshakable sense of my worth?* And then we choose that.

It's okay to ask for affirmation.

Should we be able to affirm our own worthiness? Absolutely. Should we be able to turn to trusted others to affirm our worthiness? Absolutely!

Some people think it's weird to need validation. But you know what's really weird? Watching how someone acts when they need validation but they don't feel able to ask for it. The need instead comes out in all kinds of indirect and unhelpful ways! Although we cannot outsource our worthiness, we can certainly turn toward each other for robust reinforcement. If we choose not to express how much we value affirmation, we leave ourselves at the mercy other people's interpretations of our needs. In other words, we expect other people to read our minds!

If we need affirmation, we need to let our partner know. For example, let's say Partner A is the primary breadwinner while Partner B is the primary homemaker. Partner B knows (as all at-home partners know) that what she does all day is largely invisible. If Partner A doesn't validate her efforts, Partner B knows she's at risk of getting passive-aggressive. ("I suppose you think I sit around all day eating bonbons?") So what can Partner B do when Partner A gets home? She could ask, "May I give you a tour so you can see all of my hard work today?" And what does Partner A say? "Of course! Lead the way!" Then Partner A affirms the daylights out of Partner B.

Validation doesn't need to happen every day, and it cannot replace the cultivation of self-worth. But if there's a day when Partner B knows her bucket is a bit low, it's far better for her to ask for what she needs instead of lying in wait and pouncing if Partner A doesn't offer it.

Rather than feeling *ashamed* of our need for affirmation, what if we feel *proud* of our ability to ask for what we need? Validation feels good to receive and feels good to give.

Relational Self-Awareness Questions

- What messages were you given growing up about seeking affirmation from others?
- How do you feel when you ask for affirmation?
- How do you feel when you receive affirmation?
- How do you feel when someone asks you to validate them?

In being asked, we merely lean into the desires of another. In asking, we cultivate courage and declare our dreams.

I am a thousand times more comfortable with being asked than I am with asking. It makes sense—there's vulnerability in the process of asking.

Many of us prefer waiting to be asked because the act of asking brings the risk of being rejected or laughed at. The risk of trying and failing. The risk of getting it wrong. But I think there's something deeper that precedes those risks. Allowing ourselves to get in touch with what we want can make us feel quite vulnerable.

I think this is in part gendered. As women, we can spend a lifetime orienting ourselves to the desires of others: our supervisors, teachers, love interests, kids. This way of being is familiar. It keeps us busy, valued, and connected.

Regardless of your gender, I invite you to consider your relationship with *asking*. Imagine yourself asking for:

- A date

- A raise

- Help

- An opportunity

What fears get activated for you? Where do you get blocked? In identifying the dream/desire/goal, or in articulating it? Asking involves a requisite amount of healthy entitlement. To what degree do you feel a sense of healthy entitlement? When you were little, who celebrated your bold declarations and your audacious ideas?

Being asked is lovely. It makes you feel desired, seen, needed. But you need also to experiment with asking. This is how you feel into your agency, your power, and your voice. Identifying the block is the first step toward transforming it.

MAY 14

As you heal, you will begin noticing that when you share your story with someone else, you are seeking connection with them, not approval from them. Self-compassion fuels connection.

If you carry a lot of judgment, fear, and/or shame about your story, your disclosure to someone else will actually be an attempt to win their *approval*:

- Their validation of your experience will feel essential because they are giving you something you don't yet know how to give yourself.

- Their invalidation of your experience will feel like confirmation that your suffering did not and does not matter.

If you have worked to move yourself toward a deeper understanding of/compassion for your story, your disclosure to someone else will be an opportunity for *connection*. It becomes a chance for them to know you more deeply:

- Their validation of your experience will deepen the connection between the two of you because you will feel safe to share with them again in the future.
- Their invalidation of your experience will cue you to be careful about whether and how you share with them again.

However, your overall well-being does not depend on anyone else's response to your story—you can always validate yourself.

Someone who tells you that you are "overreacting" is telling on themselves. Focusing on you allows them to avoid reckoning with their own behavior.

Acting any old way in a relationship has consequences.
Even if you feel hurt, when you scream/name-call/seek revenge/humiliate the other person, you are participating in a process that erodes trust and connection. Being a Relationally Self-Aware person means feeling your hurt *and* addressing your pain in an empowered rather than reactive way.

Let's say that you let your partner know that they did something that hurt you and they respond by telling you that you're overreacting.

Your partner is deflecting, shifting the spotlight off them and onto you. What they are really saying to you is that what you're asking for—their accountability and acknowledgment of harm—currently exceeds their relational capacity. Your partner is telling on themselves, but they are doing it in an underhanded way. It would be more courageous for them to say something like, "Yikes, you're holding up a mirror in front of my face, asking me to look at myself, and I'm not available for that right now because":

- *I've lived a life of privilege, and I'm not accustomed to accommodating others.*

- *I am afraid that if I look at my behavior, I'll drown in a pool of shame.*

- *I am unskilled at the art of repair.*

- All of the above.

When your partner tells you that you're overreacting, that's your cue to press pause:

- Don't try to convince them that your feelings are legit because they've just told you that they're not available to bear witness.

- Don't get louder—they will just tell you that you're proving their point.

- Don't keep trying to engage them.

Instead, step away for the moment. Otherwise, you'll burn yourself out trying to do emotional labor for you both. Tell your partner that you're hurt and confused and want to process with them, but that they've shown you that they're not available right now. Ask your partner to please approach you when they feel ready to talk in a way that honors both of your perspectives and needs. This is what a healthy boundary looks like during a moment like this.

What are the sneaky stories you've been telling yourself about how you can show up in the world and how you cannot?

The world projects possibilities and restrictions onto people based on identity variables (age, race, gender, etc.). We need to explore the sneaky ways we've internalized those stories. Internalized identity rules sound like, "Because I am X, I cannot also be/do Y." For example:

- *Because I am a mother, I cannot take a pole dancing class.*

- *Because I am forty years old, I cannot become a student.*

- *Because I am well-known in my community, I cannot go to therapy.*

- *Because I do CrossFit, I cannot do Zumba.*

- *Because I am a man, I cannot ask my partner to hold me.*

There are two results that come from obeying an internalized identity rule:

1. **A feeling of stuckness or devitalization:** Someone who is considering a career change but who believes they are "too old" to go back to school is likely to feel an increasing sense of boredom at work as they tamp down their curiosity to pivot toward a new opportunity.

2. **Judgment of those who transcend these rules:** Mama A, who craves a pole class but feels like she can't sign up, is far more likely to judge the mama who is getting her twerk on than Mama B, who simply isn't interested in giving pole dancing a try.

Criticism is the language of those who self-deny! By noticing what you have deemed permissible and forbidden, you can begin to imagine new possibilities for your life. Whether or not you take the pole dancing class, you will learn a lot from exploring the story that says you cannot.

Relational Self-Awareness Questions

- What is the internalized identity rule you're bumping into?
- What are you afraid of if you break this rule?
- Whose voice does this internalized identity rule sound like?
- What is the consequence of obeying this internalized identity rule?
- What might the consequence be of pushing back against it?

MAY 17

Don't get it twisted: In an intimate relationship, sometimes advice is control masquerading as generosity.

When we fall in love with someone, *interdependence* is par for the course. You lean on your partner. They lean on you. Your choices impact them. Their choices impact you. When you build a life together, you and your partner become a "we." That's good and delicious. And you can weather life's storms a little more easily when you multiply life by the power of two (as the Indigo Girls said). However, advice-giving can be tricky business.

Take this scenario: Partner A is launching a new project. Partner B sees all kinds of things they think Partner A could be doing differently or more quickly or better. If Partner B cares about the health of the relationship, it is incumbent on Partner B to practice great discernment in figuring out when and how to share those observations with Partner A. What happens all too often is that Partner B offers advice freely and boldly, couching it by saying, "I love you and I want what's best for you." This may very well be part of the story, but I also want Partner B to check in with themselves about all that is stirring inside of them, which may include any or all of the following:

- Envy that Partner A has this new venture
- Fear that if Partner A succeeds, they will leave
- Resentment that they are investing resources in a venture that may not succeed
- Jealousy that this project is getting more attention than they are

Sometimes when we scratch the surface of "I just want what's best for you," what lies beneath is actually "I want to be in charge of you." None of these hidden emotional layers are bad or wrong. In fact, these deeper layers remind us that loving someone gives us the opportunity again and again to attend to our own stuff. We get ourselves into trouble when we act as if all we are trying to do is give advice. The work of loving and being loved requires us to lean into the complexity rather than resist it.

MAY 18

A complaint blocks intimacy because there's no risk and no vulnerability. A request invites intimacy by bravely offering your partner a window into your world.

The distinction between a complaint and a request is subtle and profound.

It's so tempting to complain. Complaining is cheap and easy—the McDonald's of relationship behaviors. Complaining feels, at least for the moment, like it keeps you safe. You don't have to look within yourself. Instead, you can focus on what's "out there"—usually, your judgments about the other person's behavior. But complaining compromises intimacy. It usually sets up the other person to get defensive and to withdraw.

What happens when you take that urge to complain and use it as a cue?

Say you're feeling the urge to complain to your partner ("You're so distracted," "Your mother is crazy," "This house is so messy," etc.). Noticing these thoughts is a gift, letting you know it's time to transform your complaint into a request. Deep breath. Hand on heart. Say quietly to yourself, "What do you need, Dear One?" Ahh—the request emerges. Tender. Vulnerable. But oh, so inviting.

A request holds the potential to pull your loved one close. A request invites witnessing:

- "I miss you so much."

- "I'm struggling in my relationship with your mother. Can we talk about it?"

- "I need some help cleaning up our home."

It may not be easy to open up like this, but it sure is worth it.

<hr/>

MAY 19

Rather than demanding, "Why won't you be self-reflective?" ask instead, "What's keeping you from looking inside of yourself right now?

What's keeping you from taking a deep breath and wondering how your words, your choices, your tone may be part of our problem here?"

There's a world of difference between an invitation and a demand. One is infused with curiosity. The other is filled with judgment.

If you feel like you've been knocking on your partner's door for weeks/months/years, this is a big ask. But I know for sure that how you ask matters. I want you to be surrounded by the support you need, so you can invite instead of demand.

Let's say you are brave enough to invite. And let's say your partner's response gives you a window into their inner world. *What you do next matters.* Here are a few suggestions:

- Celebrate this as a win.

- Express gratitude for their disclosure rather than exasperation that it took so long.

- Refuse to use what they shared with you in a future conflict.

MAY 20

At the heart of a happy intimate relationship is a deep and abiding friendship.

The most successful intimate relationships are based on a deep friendship. For some couples, this is literally the case because the couple was friends before they layered in romance/sex. For other couples, even though their relationship began with romantic interest, they also view each other as friends.

Let's look at the role of friendship in love. Friendship is about:

- **Mutual admiration:** Happy couples really like each other as people.

- **Shared history:** Research shows that it takes about 200 hours of time together to develop a deep friendship. Time spent talking, exploring, and engaging in activities together becomes the stuff of collective memory.

- **Support:** Happy couples are cheerleaders, wanting the best for each other. New opportunities generally feel exciting, not threatening. (And if a partner does feel threatened, they can own that feeling, share it with the other, and work on it as a team.)

- **Investment:** Happy couples know that love is a renewable resource. They take responsibility for investing time and energy to stay connected and curious about each other (rather than asking, "What have you done for me lately?").

What a gift it is to treasure and be treasured.

MAY 21

Keeping score in an intimate relationship is a symptom of a deeper problem.

Relational scorekeeping sounds like this:

- "I initiated sex the last five times."

- "We went to visit your family the last three Thanksgivings."

- "It has been thirteen days since you last unloaded the dishwasher."

Two things are true at once: Scorekeeping is common, *and* scorekeeping is just not sexy. So what are lovers to do? Treat the scorekeeping as a symptom of something amiss in the relational ecosystem. If you can avoid slipping into mutual finger-pointing, you can explore *why* unsexy numbers are creeping into the space between you.

I have all kinds of hypotheses about what drives scorekeeping:

- **Maybe the couple is locked into a transactional gender script.** This script may read that women provide men with sex in exchange for protection and financial security. This may give each partner a metric to measure the degree to which they each feel taken care of in the relationship, but this metric is based on functionality, not intimacy. Both partners need to value themselves and each other for their unique and enduring traits, not the relational "service" they provide.

- **Maybe one partner has a related Core Wound.** Perhaps this Core Wound comes from being taken advantage of, and it has brought into the relationship a tiny accountant who runs numbers to self-protect. The couple needs to figure out how to put this tiny accountant into retirement by reassuring it they are safe.

- **Maybe—in fact, undoubtedly—the couple needs to boost presence, attention, and connection.** The fix is that the couple needs to invest in their love!

Find a space beyond blame and shame and dig a little deeper there. Beneath the numbers is an important story about attention, connection, respect, and trust.

If you don't like when someone follows up with you about an unfinished task, offer them an update. If you don't like getting reminders, write yourself a note. If you don't like taking direction, see how you might take initiative. If you are sensitive to feeling controlled, directed, or micromanaged, get into the driver's seat.

Let's talk about the overfunctioning/underfunctioning dynamic.

The partner in the overfunctioning role:

- Does most/all the heavy lifting (emotionally, practically, financially, sexually, domestically, etc.)

- Gives a label to the partner in the underfunctioning role (lazy, entitled, etc.)

- Feels overwhelmed, lonely, and misunderstood

The partner in the underfunctioning role:

- Waits to be told what to do, shirks duties, does not keep their word, retreats

- Gives a label to the partner in the overfunctioning role (rigid, controlling, etc.)

- Feels overwhelmed, lonely, and misunderstood

When a therapist is working with a couple like this, the first order of business is helping the couple see this as a pattern. A couple needs to move from pointing fingers to looking together at their unique "choreography" as a couple:

- The more one partner overfunctions, the more the other partner underfunctions.

- The more one partner underfunctions, the more the other partner overfunctions.

These roles are entwined. If either partner changes up their moves, the dance cannot continue in the same way. This is complicated, but I'm inviting you into a new perspective:

- The only person you can change is yourself.

- Changing yourself changes the system.

- Do not underestimate your power.

> The overfunctioning/underfunctioning
> dynamic is not relevant to situations of disability.

MAY 23

When you remember that attending and agreeing are not the same, it becomes far easier to listen without defensiveness.

Relational truths are local and personal. Our experiences of self and each other are forever perceived through the lens of our cultural locations, personalities, gender role socialization, Family of Origin experiences, and sensitivities from past relationships. The happiest and healthiest couples are the ones who keep that in mind.

When your partner raises a concern with you about you, the process goes much better if you remember that *attending* to this concern is not the same thing as *agreeing* with this concern. Rather than closing yourself off by defending or rationalizing, you can remain open to your partner. You can offer the bold invitation of saying to them, "I want to make sure I understand what you're saying." Without sarcasm. With care.

Reflecting your partner's concern back to them is powerful medicine. It is you *attending* to your partner. The more heard they feel, the more likely they'll be able to tolerate the fact that you have a different perception of what happened.

So many dust-ups that happen in an intimate partnership are not fixable. Therefore, we need to be able to offer empathy across differences, again and again. If you can say to your partner, "From where you are standing, your reactions make sense," then they're much more likely to be able to say the same to you.

Regulation needs to precede communication.

Emotionally regulated: You can identify and articulate your thoughts and feelings while working to understand the thoughts and feelings of the person you're talking to.

Emotionally dysregulated: You are too flooded/triggered/activated to understand and express your thoughts and feelings in a way that the other person can receive.

When you realize you have moved, or are moving, from regulated to dysregulated, your best and bravest work is to pause. Your goal, over time, is to widen your zone of regulation so you can stay engaged in difficult conversations for longer periods of time, able to speak and listen with care and presence. Being human means that some days your bandwidth is narrower than other days, so you need to press pause with grace and respect.

The body doesn't lie. It speaks to us in energetic shifts, whispers, and tugs.

The body is a powerful source of knowing. It is also a source that has been systematically silenced and maligned. There has been and continues to be collective fear of the power wielded in women's ways of knowing. As Audre Lord said, "For women, this has meant a suppression of the erotic as a considered source of power and information within our lives." We have learned that anything connected to the erotic is dangerous, dirty, sinful, and that our sexuality exists only in the service of others.

What might change if women begin to view their connection to erotic energy as a resource? What if it was a source we could turn to for healing, joy, creativity, and connection? This notion subverts everything we have learned about gender, power, and sex. This isn't about "boosting your sex drive" or "being a better lover." Instead:

- It's about remembering what you might have forgotten.
- It's about trusting the wisdom of your body.
- It's about refusing to split yourself up into nice parts and naughty parts.

It is time for a collective shift from sex as duty to sex as celebration. From sex as performance to sex as expression. From sex as shameful to sex as healing.

Relationship doubt may reflect your difficulty in trusting your ability to choose.

Sometimes relationship doubt indicates that the relationship you are in is unhealthy, and your best and bravest next step is couples therapy or a graceful ending. At other times, relationship doubt is a symptom of an *individual* problem rather than *relational* one.

Modern love is a choice. Choosing:

- Indicates and reflects freedom

- Puts you in the driver's seat

- Necessitates that you live with the consequences of your choices

When you choose to be in a relationship, you declare something profound to yourself, to your partner, to the whole damn world. If/when you experience relationship doubt, resist the urge to simply:

- Pick your partner apart

- Survey your friends and family for their hot takes on your relationship

Instead, explore your relationship with yourself.

Relational Self-Awareness Questions

- To what degree do you trust yourself to choose wisely?

- Is this doubt familiar? When is another time you have felt it?

- Who told you that you're too silly/impulsive/emotional to chart your own course?

- What experiences in your life have shown you that you can, in fact, choose well?

Sometimes your overt irritation about the little stuff is pointing you toward your yet-to-be-witnessed hurt about the bigger stuff.

If you notice yourself persistently and peculiarly irritated with stuff that seems small and petty, get curious. Perhaps your nervous system is fried. When we're stretched too thin, noises are too noisy, messes are too messy, touch is too touchy, and people are too people-y. Your irritation might just be showing you that you need a cup of tea, a cozy blanket, and some time in a room by yourself.

But keep open another hypothesis—you might be feeling hyper-sensitive about the little stuff because your concern about the big stuff is being left unattended:

- You raised your concern, but your partner is deflecting, being defensive, or diminishing it.

- You are consciously or unconsciously avoiding bringing your concern up.

Unaddressed concerns rarely dissipate. Instead, they just tend to come out sideways:

- In a snarky comment about the spoons

- In a big reaction to an unmade bed

- In a critical response to a slow-poke partner

If you realize that your cranky mood is fueled by something in the relationship, you must take the following steps:

1. Validate your concern for yourself so you can enter the conversation on solid ground.

2. Ask your partner for time and space to explore the concern together.

3. Enter that conversation with a willingness to name your tender feelings, rather than criticize your partner for the thing they did.

4. Enter that conversation with a desire to begin putting your hurt in the past and a curiosity to begin moving ahead.

5. Ask for what you need.

MAY 28

We need to let our loved ones know when we're having an "off day"—not so they can give us a free pass but so they can offer grace and accommodate accordingly.

Your interconnectedness is undeniable. When something is going on inside of you, it will affect the people around you. That's why it is an act of generosity to give your loved ones a heads-up:

- "My PMS is kicking my booty today."

- "Heads-up: I'm feeling edgy because of my big presentation tomorrow."

- "If I don't seem like myself, it's because I slept poorly."

But this is not a "get out of jail free card." We don't get to make a declaration and then act any kind of way. It's still our job to regulate ourselves as best we can, or at least to take ourselves out of the fray so we minimize our impact on others.

Talking with the people around you about your internal state is an alert, not an excuse. A bid for connection, not a misplacing of responsibility. This is about acknowledging that what's going on inside you shapes the space between you and others. When you offer this alert, you give the people around you a chance to be a bit gentler.

> Gentleness is *not* the same thing as walking on eggshells!
> (See March 5 entry for more on this distinction.)

Relational Self-Awareness Questions

- What keeps you from letting people around you know when you're having a rough time?
- What do you fear will happen?
- Who do you feel you "become" if you acknowledge that you're a bit off?

MAY 29

When you raise a concern and the other person can't or won't engage with you, you must hold onto two truths at once: Their defensiveness creates relational harm and their defensiveness reflects internal pain.

When someone who matters to you won't engage with you on an

important topic, two things are true:

1. The cycle of reaching out and being blocked hurts like hell—you feel lonely, devalued, like a fool for "putting up with this crap."

2. Unless you're partnered with a sociopath, hurting you is rarely the motivation that drives their defensiveness.

Therapists often highlight the difference between *intent* and *impact*. People defend themselves against stuff that overwhelms their ability to cope. Stuff that feels emotionally charged. Stuff that holds a direct line to a Core Wound. Where do you go from here?

- Make sure you're taking care of your "side of the street" by acknowledging your imperfections and taking responsibility for the ways that your behavior is less than ideal.

- Remember that defensiveness is data. See what happens when you shift to curiosity: "Can you help me understand why this conversation is hard for you?"

Relational Self-Awareness is a learned skill, and your partner may be in Relational Self-Awareness 101. Depending on someone's cultural background, gender role socialization, personality, Family of Origin, and other aspects, they may well be more unskilled than obstinate. What helps you muster a bit more patience and curiosity? While repeatedly excusing your partner's defensiveness will become too tiring to sustain, your patient persistence—accompanied by a steady belief that they can transcend this unhelpful response—may be the motivation they need to grow.

An intimate relationship is: More an ellipsis than a period. More an evolution

than a declaration. More a verb than a noun. More a liquid than a solid.

To be in a relationship is to be in an ongoing process of evolution. This is both exciting and terrifying.

- If we are evolving, what if we begin to head in different directions?
- How do we hold both the being and the becoming?
- How do we hold both the commitment and the change?

I haven't found any easy answers to these questions, but I have been thinking a lot about something my husband Todd once said. He shared that, as my partner, he anchors himself in two words: patience and service. His devotion to patience helps him weather the little storms and keep his eye on the big picture. His devotion to service helps him remember that he cares for a "we" that is bigger than himself.

Relational Self-Awareness Questions

- What feels exciting about the fact that you get to grow and change in your intimate partnership?
- What feels scary about the fact that change is inevitable?
- What do you want to be able to remember when you feel a change happening in your relationship?

MAY 31

To love someone requires us to wrestle with acceptance.

Holding the tension between accepting someone and asking them to change is exceptionally hard. Far from mindless surrender, acceptance means leaning into being an inevitably imperfect human who loves another imperfect human.

When you love someone, you must be willing to engage in a process of *shedding* and *expanding*. Shedding fairy tales that say true love is perfect and problem-free; expanding to hold a more nuanced experience of loving and being loved. You must find a way to hold steady as your expectations and your reality crash headlong into each other. Your partner cannot be your:

- Knight in shining armor

- Mother you never had

- Savior

- Hero

Of course they can't be, your rational self says. But if you dig deeper, I suspect there's a part of you that struggles to hold onto this truth. A part of you that craved a fairy tale. Not because you are broken or naïve but because craving a fix for the endless complexity of being a human is so very understandable. It is painful to shed the illusion that love should be straightforward and easy.

Further, it can be so very hard to find the line between "settling" for someone less than perfect and accepting that nobody is perfect. I can't tell you where that line is because love is messy and paradoxical. (And I encourage you to be suspicious of any "expert" who says they can tell you where that line is.) But here's what I do know:

- Loving someone over time means riding forever cycles of connection-disconnection-repair, and you *both* are responsible for all three steps of the cycle.

- Nobody, no matter how wonderful, can be everything to you. The fact that you love your partner and your partner disappoints you proves that point. Needing friends, colleagues, family members, and a pet in addition to your intimate partner in order to feel fulfilled does not mean you're settling. It just means that you require a village to meet your needs.

- Accepting your partner and asking for change are not mutually exclusive.

JUNE 1

When we get activated, we risk muddying the past and the present.

Painful moments activate painful memories. We can begin to act now the way we had to act then, operating from an outdated set of beliefs and accessing only a limited set of skills. We become self-protective and self-referential. We struggle to hold empathy for the person we are struggling with.

I don't think our old pain ever really goes away. I think we just get better and better at noticing when the past is getting confused with the present, and then making a different choice. We learn to catch ourselves when we regress from empowered to powerless. The creeping in of negative self talk may be the clue:

- "I'm too scared to handle this."
- "I'm worthless/stupid/unlovable."
- "Nobody understands me."

Or the clue may be found in our behaviors:

- Fight (making threats, raising our voice, etc.)
- Flight (walking away, leaving a text unanswered, etc.)

- Freeze (saying nothing, feeling numb and confused, etc.)
- Fawn (accommodating, pleasing, mollifying, etc.)

Your work in that moment is to meet the present moment on the present moment's terms. When old pain gets activated, pause and put your hand on your heart. Take some deep breaths and say out loud to yourself, "This is my trauma, not my truth." This mantra helps you begin to sort the here-and-now from the there-and-then. This mantra helps you remember that there is so much more to you than your painful memories. Responding to the present pain with care and awareness offers healing to Little You.

Meet your regret as a student meets a teacher and allow it to point you in the direction of your growth.

"If I knew then what I know now . . ." With these words, you position yourself at a fork in the road.

- **Path 1:** Self-criticism, anger, blame, shame, depression, panic
- **Path 2:** Repair, apology, boundary, reflection, accountability, self-compassion

Looking back is inevitable. Perhaps regret is too. But what is not inevitable is the story you attach to what you see in the rearview mirror. That story determines whether you will end up feeling stuck or accepting, whether you'll use the past to berate yourself or to challenge yourself.

Path 1 is tempting because it provides a seemingly simple answer—figuring out whose mistake led to this unfortunate turn of events:

- You may feel pulled toward *shame*, beating yourself up for what you did or did not do, could or could not do.

- You may feel pulled toward *blame*, pointing the finger at others who failed, betrayed, or disappointed you.

Even if you start off down this path, you can still catch yourself and course correct.

On Path 2:

- You strive to remember that there is no such thing as a perfect parent, perfect career, perfect response, or perfect partner.

- You remind yourself (or your sacred allies remind you) that your past holds the power to teach you.

- You work on revising your story to be gentler and more forgiving in the hope that someday it can become an offering to others—not to save them, but to support them.

JUNE 3

There's no way to bypass the vulnerability of dating.

I can't stand all the relationship advice that treats dating like it's a game:

- "Play hard to get."

- "Get them to come to you."

- "Don't seem desperate."

I am not advocating the other extreme: diving in with both feet, ravenous and without boundaries. Rather, I am inviting you to explore the scripts and beliefs that shape your thoughts, feelings, and behaviors around dating.

Two common patterns in dating breed cynicism and stifle the chemistry of romance:

1. **Narrow gender scripts:** Women who date men sometimes feel they need to tamp down their enthusiasm because our culture judges women who take the lead or come on "too strong." Men who date women sometimes feel as if they are walking a tightrope, afraid of being judged as either creepy or wimpy. Queer folks feel boxed in by homophobic scripts of all sorts.

2. **Bread-crumbing:** In the high-volume context of online dating, people keep multiple lines of communication open, paralyzed by options and afraid of "choosing wrong." Energy gets diluted and no match can get traction. It's terrible to feel like nothing more than someone else's option.

The bigger picture: Dating is hard no matter what, and our rigid notions of gender scripts and the ambiguity of modern commitment don't help. If you're out there in the dating world, give yourself some grace!

Relational Self-Awareness Questions

- When you feel yourself starting to like someone, what do you do?

- Do you allow yourself to enjoy the feelings of attraction or tamp them down because they generate vulnerability?

- Do you allow the other person to enjoy your admiration of them? Or do you fear that if they know you like them, they'll take advantage of your openness?

One of the fastest ways to destroy emotional safety in a relationship is to weaponize something your partner has shared during a subsequent moment of conflict.

To love someone is to "get the goods" on them. As trust builds, they unlock ever-deeper inner sanctums of their soul. As they show you around, you become:

- A witness to their stories
- An ally in their battles
- A carrier of their secrets

These are sacred honors and must be treated as such. Letting each other into tender memories is the essence of intimacy. The promise we must make to be granted access into the inner chamber is that we won't use that information as a cudgel when we are mad, sad, or scared.

Here's where it gets tricky: to love someone is also to experience moments of frustration toward them, disappointment in them, even doubt about your relationship with them. You must resist the urge to leverage their vulnerability just because you're mad. This means committing not to saying, in the heat of the moment, things like:

- "Maybe your last partner was right when they said you're so X!"
- "How could you do that after what your mom did to your dad?"
- "Why aren't you doing X after you told me last week you're so ashamed of yourself?"

Weaponizing tender knowledge about your partner erodes emotional safety and trust. It also spikes defensiveness in your partner, escalating the conflict between you. It pretty much guarantees that whatever originally upset you will go unaddressed.

When you need to share an observation with your partner about their behavior and you suspect that their behavior is driven, at least in part, by a Core Wound that they revealed to you in a vulnerable moment, you must remember to proceed with caution. Tossing it out in the heat of battle is a low blow. If you know that your comment has landed below the belt, apologize. Make it right, in the name of love. Emotional safety—being able to trust that our tender spots won't be used against us—is essential for a healthy intimate relationship.

JUNE 5

Growing up in a home with predictability and consistency creates advantages in adulthood.

We talk often about how contexts like race, ethnicity, and socioeconomic status create advantages. Another advantage comes from the secure attachment created by emotional and relational stability within the Family of Origin.

If you grew up in a home with grown-ups who struggled (with mental health challenges, addiction, etc.), this affected all aspects of your development. You may have needed (or still need) time to recover and to create stability for yourself as an adult. Your education, career, and intimate partnership trajectory may have been impacted in ways that leave you feeling behind or delayed, relative to your peers.

It's a profound kind of grief to acknowledge the lack of the Family of Origin we wish we had. But it can also create shame about the dysfunction of our family and what their struggles prevented them from providing (support, cheerleading, advocacy, etc.). No matter what your perspective is toward the people who raised you, you deserve to be proud of the work you're doing to heal and grow as you create security within yourself.

What might be different if, instead of penetration, we called it envelopment?

Words connote and imply, reinforce and limit. Words carry an energy of their own. Language holds the power to constrict or expand our erotic imaginations. The words we use to describe the many aspects of sexuality create specific energy around those experiences. That's why I invite heterosexual couples to sit with the word *penetration* and examine how it contrasts with the word *envelopment*.

Penetration confers agency upon *him*. He does; she is done to. He gives; she receives.

While language is not the sole cause of the orgasm gap between men and women, language can reinforce our perceived limitations. It's vital for women to feel sexual agency to:

- Identify and follow sensation in their bodies

- Lead the action, if and when they want, and verbalize what they want and need every step of the way

- Enjoy the fullness of their pleasure without fear of being deemed too much (too loud, too quiet, too wet, too dry, etc.)

What might be different if we called it *envelopment* instead? This word recognizes *her* agency. She envelops; he is taken in. She contains; he is

173

surrounded. *Envelopment* elevates the co-creative process that is the heart of intimacy. Might he feel less pressure to perform and more permission to be present? Might she feel less pressure to be pleasing and more permission to be pleased?

> The purpose of this entry is to invite you to reflect on the ways language limits possibility. The example is heteronormative and likely to resonate less with queer readers. However, queer couples are also boxed in by patriarchy, and I invite you to explore how terminology, especially around sexuality, may limit what you feel able to ask for, experience, or enjoy in your intimate relationship.

JUNE 7

Intimacy-blocking language: "You make me . . . (feel crazy, so mad, so insecure)." Intimacy-promoting language: "When you do X in situation Y, I feel Z."

The words we choose both reflect and shape the reality of our relationships. One of the most common intimacy-blocking language choices we make is saying, "You make me feel crazy/so sad/so mad." As a therapist, I have trained my ears to catch this language. Although none of us love to be redirected, I guide my clients toward a vital shift: using an *XYZ statement*.

You may ask, "Why does it matter how I say it? I'm upset and my partner needs to know. The words are merely the means to the end." Here's why:

- **Reason 1:** Saying, "You make me . . ." gives away *all* of your power. You send yourself the message that you are wholly at the mercy of your partner's whims. Yes, partners are interdependent, but remember that there is always space between your partner's words/actions and your response. You get to *choose* when and how you engage, what gets into your soul and what is not welcome.

- **Reason 2:** Saying, "You make me. . ." sets your partner up to push back by saying some version of "That's not what happened." Then you're going to argue about what happened, and arguing about reality is the least fun, least sexy, least productive use of anyone's time. Own your experience and share that.

What's the alternative? An XYZ statement like this: *When you did X, in situation Y, I felt Z.* "When you didn't empty the dishwasher again at the end of the night, I felt taken for granted, hurt, and frustrated." Can you see how this conversation opens up possibilities for empathy and connection, rather than staying stuck in blame and shame?

JUNE 8

The work of a marriage is to do everything we can to make the promise of forever feel like a privilege, not a prison.

What makes marriage today so beautiful and complicated is that we strive to hold two truths at the same time:

1. "I'm here because I *want* to be here."

2. "I'm here because I committed myself to being here."

You'll have days when you are certain about your place in your partnership. You'll also have days when your relationship feels really, really hard. Here are four things I know for sure about marriage:

1. It's okay to go to bed mad. Sometimes sleep is the answer, and sometimes a new day brings perspective as well as the capacity for apology.

2. Sex changes over time, but not necessarily for the worse. Like every other aspect of a marriage, erotic connection requires compassion, awareness, and dialogue.

3. It's hard to let yourself be loved when you feel unlovable. Do it anyway!

4. The things you love about your spouse and the things that drive you crazy tend to be two sides of the same coin. What a delicious cosmic joke!

Relational Self-Awareness Questions

• How do you define marriage?

• How is marriage different from dating or living together?

• What intrigues you about marriage?

• What scares you about marriage?

• Who are your marital role models? Why?

JUNE 9

Telling your partner that you're bored is a threat, not an invitation.

Feeling flat or disengaged in an intimate relationship can feel upsetting and confusing, but we need to resist the urge to make our boredom our partner's problem to solve. Intimate relationships experience chapters of enthusiasm and chapters of tedium. Sometimes one partner seems more invested and engaged while the other seems passive and apathetic. These ebbs and flows can feel disorienting and scary:

- "Is this the end of us?"

- "Do I need to dig in? Or cut my losses?"

- "Where is the line between my responsibility and your responsibility?"

Feeling flat, in and of itself, is not a problem. What is a problem is behaving as if it is incumbent upon our partner to keep us engaged/excited/surprised. Noticing this mindset slipping in gives us the power to shift it. Invite reflection on the belief that undergirds the feeling of boredom:

- **Does it feel scary to ask for what you want?** Waiting to be entertained is a handy way of avoiding vulnerability. Try to embrace the scariness of initiating novelty as part of the thrill you're looking for.

- **Is there a gender script at play?** "Men should woo women." "Women should hold men's sexual attention." These scripts are sneaky. Be on the lookout for them and push back against them.

- **Is there a rigid and narrow cultural script at play?** "We should always be excited to spend time together." "If our relationship doesn't look like date night on *The Bachelor*, what's the point?" Drop the static images of desire and romance and focus on being present to what feels real and authentic to your relationship.

Check in with yourself about the belief that drives the boredom. Rather than seeing your boredom as a sign that your relationship is doomed or broken, treat it as an invitation to experiment with something different. While there may not be an easy answer or a quick fix, the feeling of flatness is a worthy piece of data, one that needs to be unpacked within each partner and between partners. Be brave enough to do something about it.

Silent spaces are ripe for shame.

When I ask people what they learned in sex education, I hear things like this:

- "I learned about STIs and that's about it."
- "I learned to feel ashamed of my sexuality because queer sex was completely omitted."
- "I learned that so-called premarital sex would harm me—body, heart, and soul."

Many of us need to undo the harm we experienced in sex education. As of this writing, only seven states in the U.S. require that LGBTQ identities and relationships be included in school sex ed curriculum, and only 17 states require sex ed to be medically accurate! At most, students receive information about the biology, physiology, and public health of sex. Necessary, but far from sufficient.

Relational Self-Awareness Questions

- Reflect on whether your sex education provided you with information on any of the following topics (and let yourself feel whatever sadness and anger arises if/when you reflect on the fact that nobody offered you guidance on these vital matters):
  - The idea that your sexual orientation simply is—it's not good or bad, right or wrong, sinful or holy

- The relational dynamics of sex—how to know when you are ready to become sexual with a partner and how sex shapes the dynamics of a relationship
- How to communicate and collaborate with a partner before, during, and after sex
- How to address sexual problems that commonly arise for individuals and couples

• Write a letter to your adolescent self that addresses your early experiences with your sexuality. Begin with "Dear Younger Me" and consider these prompts:
  - What I wish you had learned in sex education was . . .
  - Please be gentle with yourself around . . .
  - I want you to understand that sex is . . .
  - When it comes to your sexuality, I am proud of you for . . .

How do you feel as you reflect on your sex education? Grief for the information and support you needed but did not receive? Anger at the shame-loaded approach the adults in your life took? Grateful that you were surrounded and affirmed during your transition from childhood to adulthood? Whatever you feel, meet it with compassion and a commitment to giving yourself the sexual resources you need today.

Changing your mind is a sign of growth, not weakness.

Rather than doubling down on your stance in an argument, consider trying these phrases instead:

- "I hadn't viewed it like that before."

- "Thank you for showing me another perspective."

- "I want to sit with what you've said because it's new and it feels important."

These are gentle verbal off-ramps that point us to a new or expanded perspective.

One of the constraints to growth is that some of us have learned that changing our minds is equated with being weak. How tragic it is to hold onto a limited or limiting perspective simply because you fear being humiliated for changing! So much of how you mend and strengthen an intimate relationship is about reckoning with who you have been and who you want to be. Far from humiliation, leaning into the discomfort of growth ought to be a source of pride.

Imagine how you'd feel if someone said to you any of the sentences I shared on that list. I know that if I heard them, I'd feel validated, witnessed, empowered. I'd feel safe enough to bring my next difficult topic to that person. This is how you move from debate to dialogue, from conflict to connection. This is how you heal and grow.

JUNE 12

Every sexual problem is a couple problem.

I was doing a daylong training with therapists and talking about erectile dysfunction (ED). Specifically, I was musing about how the ads for ED medicine both reflect and reinforce shame: "Call this number and get your ED pills sent to your door without ever having to talk with a doctor." An older man raised his hand and shared that he had ED due to a medical condition. He said he and his wife grieved for a couple of years, but he never felt shame. I admired his ability to discern the difference between sadness and shame. Furthermore, I suspect that by staying with sadness instead of slipping into shame, he and his partner could experience grief as a coming-together that, I hope, brought forth all kinds of lovely re-imaginings for them to be intimate with each other. Re-imaginings that allowed them both to remember that the whole body is a source (and a receiver) of pleasure.

When a sexual problem arises between you and your partner, two paths are available:

- **Path 1:** Get stuck in blame and/or shame.
- **Path 2:** Approach the problem as a team.

On Path 1, distance grows. On Path 2, the relationship becomes a source of comfort and creativity as you face the challenge together. I wish Path 2 for you, if and when you need it.

JUNE 13

Make sure that you don't spend so much time analyzing your relationship that you forget to be in it.

Learning to practice Relational Self-Awareness can create a sense of urgency. We may feel like we need to be self-reflective and/or having deep and meaningful conversations all the time. This happens because:

- It is liberating to learn how to peel back layers and connect the past to the present.

- It is a relief to have time and space to process painful experiences inside yourself and with others whom you trust.

- It is thrilling to feel increasingly competent and confident in your relationships.

However, just because you could be swimming in the deep end 24/7, it doesn't mean you have to be! Cultivating an intimate relationship that values Relational Self-Awareness makes it safe to be easy-breezy with your partner. You can make up silly nicknames and watch trashy shows because you know that when one of you feels hurt, confused, or anxious, you both will put your goggles on and start to swim. Together.

JUNE 14

Healthy conflict is standing up for yourself without putting your partner down.

When we practice care and caution, conflict becomes a gateway to deeper intimacy. Let's get practical—here are three phrases to banish from your vocabulary:

1. "You make me so [mad, crazy, etc.]."

2. "You always . . ." / "You never . . ."

3. "You're just like your [mother, father, etc.]."

Now let's break these phrases down:

- **The problem with #1:** No one actually makes you feel any kind of way. When you say this, you give away your power. The feeling of powerlessness is the seat of all kinds of "below the belt" behavior. Instead, look at the facts. Your partner did a thing. You have a feeling about the thing. Start from that place. Talk about the feeling. (For more on this, refer to the June 7 entry.)

- **The problem with #2:** It's likely inaccurate that your partner is getting a perfect A or a total F. Extreme language reflects the intensity of your feelings but will likely just lead them to highlight the exceptions. Instead of focusing on a track record, name the hurt you feel right now.

- **The problem with #3:** You likely know this tendency of their mother/father from a prior vulnerable conversation. Pointing it out in this context will feel hurtful and reduce the chances of future vulnerable shares. Again, simply name your hurt.

JUNE 15

Conversations about sex are never done.

My son asked me to explain what #MeToo means. I told the story from the beginning, from the movement launched years ago by Tarana Burke to the boost given by Alyssa Milano's tweet in 2017. I told him that this tweet inspired millions of people to step forward and name their trauma, many for the first time. We talked about:

- How shame is often a byproduct of trauma, and that when a person feels they need to stay silent about painful things that have happened to them, they have a hard time healing

- How much harder it is to change a culture when lots of people within that culture have been silenced by painful things that have happened to them

- How shame can become the start to recovery when someone tells their story

- How having many people tell their stories makes our schools, workplaces, and communities safer for everyone

- His responsibilities as a man regarding consent

A woman who had been sitting at the table next to us walked over. "I didn't mean to eavesdrop," she said. "I am a survivor, and it means a lot to hear you two talking like this." I was so touched that she approached us to share this!

If you think you've talked to the young people in your world about sex, consent, and pleasure, talk again. What the next generation hears, understands, and integrates at age 14 is different from age 16 and age 18. We continue to change, and our culture continues to change. Therefore, we must continue to talk.

Relational Self-Awareness Questions

- How did you feel when you first heard about the #MeToo movement? Why?

- How has the #MeToo movement affected you personally? Do you talk differently about sexual harassment and sexual trauma? Do you feel more able to offer support to those who are survivors of sexual violence?

- How do you want to talk with the young people in your life about the #MeToo movement? What do you want them to know and remember?

Your partner arrived to you with life chapters lived before you and without you.

You missed your partner's early years. There were victories you weren't there for, griefs you can't fully understand, loyalties to people that are deeper than you can fathom, and choices made without your input, knowledge, or guidance.

As you learn your partner's story, you will feel stuff: jealousy that you missed out on celebrations, sadness that you weren't the one who provided comfort, confusion about why they did what they did when they did it, anger at connections to people that don't make sense to you.

Some of your emotional reactions will reflect your capacity for *empathy*: "That must have been such a thrilling time for you," "I'm so sad you went through that alone," "I wish I had met your brother."

Some of your emotional reactions may reflect your *fear*: "Why did you do that?" "I don't understand why you tolerate this treatment from that person," "What did that relationship mean to you?"

The reactions themselves are not the problem. It's what you do when the reaction arises. When fear takes over, you may become controlling: "I don't want you talking with them anymore." "You need to promise me _____." The more controlling you become, the less opportunity you'll have to hear what your partner has learned from their pre-you history.

Investigate your reactions for how they relate to your Core Wounds and tender spots. The more you commit to owning your reactions, fears, and judgments about your partner's past, the more your partner will be willing to talk with you about the lingering impacts of their past. Let your mantra be one (or all) of the following:

- *There is space for me.*

- *There is time for me.*
- *I lead with love, not fear.*

Growing up in a Family of Origin that was not able to provide emotional support means you learned how to survive overwhelming situations on your own.

Kids who had to endure stress and pain all by themselves become adults who are labeled by others as "emotionally unavailable." This is not an excuse but a context. It's so hard to feel like someone is shutting you out. When someone is emotionally unavailable, there is an Origin Story that likely began long before this person met you. Their Origin Story may well draw your compassion, but it does *not*:

- Invalidate your pain
- Require you to give them another chance
- Mean that you can fix them

Someone who is emotionally unavailable can, of course, become emotionally available by learning to:

- Adopt a growth mindset
- Move from a solo to a relational orientation to life
- Sit with emotional nuance

Still, remember that your investment in someone else's growth cannot supersede their resistance or unwillingness. You cannot do someone else's healing work for them.

Is it healing to allow yourself to receive the comfort of another? Yes. Is it confronting as hell? Also yes.

When someone is accustomed to being alone with their pain, it can feel quite unnatural for them to allow another person near when they are hurting. Instead of the "comforter" rushing in with suggestions and interventions for the "comfortee," I often encourage asking, "How can I support you right now?"

But what if the comfortee has *zero* idea how to answer that question? (I hear this follow-up a lot.) This may happen because:

- **They have been socialized in the masculine.** They learned that needing help/comfort/care is a sign of weakness and to be avoided at all costs.

- **They have been socialized in the feminine.** They learned not to take up space. Being the comfortee is all about taking up space!

- **They occupy one or more marginalized identities.** The world has shown them their feelings don't matter by centering the experiences of those with privileged identities at the expense of their own.

- **Nobody in their Family of Origin was there to provide comfort for them.** They learned how to turn an inherently relational process into a one-person show.

- **The motto in their Family of Origin was "Suck it up, Buttercup!"** Sitting in their feelings rather than invalidating or denying them is a bizarre new world.

These are just a few possible reasons why the comfortee may not be able to provide direction. What, then, can the comforter do?

- **Accept that receiving comfort is going to be a Growing Edge for their partner.** Look for signs of progress, not perfection.

- **Offer multiple choice options for the support they can offer.** The comforter doesn't need to create an exhaustive list, but the effort and action conveys a lovely willingness and might help the comfortee feel "permission" to admit what they need.

- **Let them know you are there when they need you.** Say something like, "I hear that you don't know right now what would feel good. I'm not going anywhere. Please connect when you're ready."

I hope this helps you take a relational approach to comfort.

JUNE 19

The chances are slim that you and your partner will be ready for the next step in your relationship at exactly the same time. The space between your pace and theirs is ripe for misunderstanding and hurt.

Let's say Partner A is ready for the next step in a commitment sequence (defining the relationship, meeting the family, moving in, marriage, etc.) and Partner B is not ready for this step. This **Pace Discrepancy** (as I call it) shifts us from an individual to a relational framework.

Without a relational framework, a Pace Discrepancy can take on a life of its own. Partners will unwittingly and unintentionally end up confirming their worst-case scenarios. The more the Slower-Paced Partner avoids conversations about commitment and the future, the more the Faster-Paced Partner pursues those conversations. The more the Faster-Paced Partner pursues those conversations, the more the Slower-Paced Partner avoids them. This dance of pursue-and-distance keeps each of them from understanding whatever tender/vulnerable/valuable complexity may be hiding behind the behavior. Without understanding that tender complexity, each partner is left to assume, to project, to interpret according to their worst fears:

- The Slower-Paced Partner perceives the Faster-Paced Partner as controlling and needy.

- The Faster-Paced Partner perceives the Slower-Paced Partner as unreliable and commitment-phobic.

When a couple can look together at their Pace Discrepancy, new possibilities will arise. The new possibilities might be for the couple to make a change (speeding up or stretching out their timeline) or for the couple to rest more comfortably in a solution that pleases both of them a little but neither of them completely.

> We will continue this topic in tomorrow's entry.

JUNE 20

Usually, a desire to talk with your partner about the future of your relationship reflects a desire to dream together, not a desire to

create demands. It is a quest for clarity and affirmation, not control and promises.

Although a Pace Discrepancy is common for couples, feeling more ready to talk about the future than your partner is a tender place to be. Here is where the rubber hits the road: Does your partner want to explore with you how you ended up with this Pace Discrepancy, and how you can both protect the relationship from its impact? Your relational work is to move from a perspective that is "my way versus your way" to a perspective that is "us looking together at the Pace Discrepancy."

A helpful place to start is unearthing hidden assumptions and expectations about the pace at which a relationship "should" develop. Consider these notions for yourself, then discuss them together with your partner. (You can use the Relational Self-Awareness questions below as a jumping-off point.) My hunch is that you will find that your partner has internalized a different social clock than you have. My hope is that unearthing this difference will create curiosity inside both of you rather than judgment.

Relational Self-Awareness Questions

- What kind of timelines do you have in your head? (*I should be married by this age, I should not have a baby until I/we have hit a particular milestone*, etc.)

- Which of your cultural identities (country of origin, gender, ethnicity, religion, race, etc.) most powerfully informs your timelines? Why? How?

- In what ways has your Family of Origin shaped your timelines?

- In what ways have your friends shaped your timelines?

- In what ways have the media and society shaped your timelines?

Feedback helps us grow.

You know you're improving your Relational Self-Awareness when someone offers you a piece of feedback on the impact of your words or actions and your gratitude is bigger than your resistance. This means:

- You're shedding brittleness in favor of heartiness.
- You're letting go of perfection in favor of realness.
- You're offloading righteousness in favor of connection.

When you have that experience, make sure to celebrate yourself! When someone is giving you feedback from a place of care (not cruelty), put yourself in their shoes. See if you can feel empathy for the risk the other person is taking. Decentering your embarrassment/defensiveness/guilt can help you see the feedback for the gift that it is. An opportunity to grow yourself and your relationship. The more we can lean into our discomfort, the richer our relationships will be.

Getting what you need can awaken hidden vulnerabilitics.

Let's say you make a request: for help around the house, for touch, for a little gift that says, "I was thinking of you while we were apart." And your partner gives you what you need. Pay attention to what happens next for you. Being given what you need seems like it should be all puppies and rainbows, but many of us really struggle to receive what we've requested.

Practice Relational Self-Awareness by exploring what happens when it's time for you to receive.

Do any of these resonate? When your partner gives you what you've asked for . . .

- You pooh-pooh it—they only did it because you asked for it.
- You worry about what they will want from you now or in the future.
- You feel guilty because they have extended themselves.

Receiving requires you to lean in. The more skin you have in the game, the more it might hurt if you lose the person. Perhaps you prefer to caretake because letting someone care for you is foreign and feels risky. This is often the case for those of us who had to take care of grown-ups when we were kids. As you struggle with this, remember to offer some compassion to your partner. It's likely sad for them when you block their efforts to provide. Bit by bit, learn how to let someone attend to you. Make a practice of letting them love you.

JUNE 23

Our past travels with us in one of three ways: The Path of Repetition, The Path of Opposition, or The Path of Integration.

Our past is the pair of glasses through which we experience our adult intimate relationships, with blind spots and distortions created by our early experiences. We connect the dots between then and now by talking about the three pathways by which the past travels with us. Which one sounds most familiar to you?

The Path of Repetition: You are repeating now what you witnessed or experienced then. For example:

- The grown-ups in your Family of Origin yelled a lot, and you are similarly prone to outbursts.

- There were lots of secrets in your Family of Origin, and you struggle to let people in.

- Your Family of Origin rarely expressed affection, and you are generally uncomfortable with hugs and kisses.

When you find yourself creating a life that bears a strong resemblance to what you saw growing up, even if you swore you'd never "become your parents," you need to offer yourself fierce self-compassion and, from that place of gentleness, challenge yourself to tweak your behavior.

The Path of Opposition: You are doing the opposite of what you witnessed and experienced in your Family of Origin. For example:

- The grown-ups in your Family of Origin yelled a lot, but you tend to shut down or placate during difficult conversations.

- There were lots of secrets in your Family of Origin, but you wear your heart on your sleeve.

- Your family rarely expressed affection, but touch is your love language.

Your desire to flip the script makes sense. You said hell no to the pain you saw and experienced and committed yourself to the opposite in your future relationships. However, a 180-degree shift is rarely the answer. Sure, you don't look like your parents, but you may be stuck in an equally limiting box (*My parent yelled, so I never do . . . but I also don't advocate for my needs*)

The Path of Integration: This is the path of Relational Self-Awareness, a path that honors:

- The gifts and limitations that existed within your Family of Origin
- The ways you were seen and the ways you were ignored
- The parts of you that were celebrated and the parts that were neglected

The Path of Integration liberates you from the old patterns so you can create new possibilities today.

Liking someone makes you human. Letting them know makes you brave.

Dating is courageous; it's easier to be courageous when you can let yourself like someone. When you feel entitled to pursue these feelings, it means you trust yourself to handle the messiness.

Pro tip: If you remind yourself how good it feels to be liked, perhaps it will be easier to let someone know you like them. There's a kindness—a generosity of sorts—in letting someone know you think they are pretty amazing. Drop the story that liking someone puts you in the weaker position.

To take root and grow, a new intimate relationship needs mutual investment of energy. When each person must wait for the other person to give a clear indication that they are interested, a potential connection dies on the vine. Your work is to trust yourself to lean in.

If you cannot cut yourself slack, then when your partner asks for empathy, you will call it coddling.

Coddling is a word we use to justify withholding empathy. It's part of a ridiculous notion that tenderness breeds weakness. In fact, validation and empathy are far more effective motivators for change than shame and humiliation. It's really hard to offer another person a greater degree of gentleness than we offer ourselves. I can tell you that in my own marriage, there's a strong positive correlation between my self-criticism and my Todd-criticism.

The practices I use to move myself back to a place of deeper self-compassion are also a gift I give my husband! Mindfulness practices slow us down so we can notice the chatter inside our minds. Noticing is the first step to shifting/challenging/redirecting. If you are accustomed to . . .

- Driving yourself hard
- Acting with relentless persistence
- Suppressing vulnerable emotions
- Learning things the hard way

. . . you are at risk of making a false equivalence between *empathy* and *coddling*.

When you have the urge to use the word *coddling*, explore why you are feeling critical of the fact that someone is receiving accommodation or care. Check in with yourself: Perhaps your judgment stems from the fact that you could use a bit of TLC yourself!

Every couple must define for their relationship where privacy ends and secrecy begins.

Privacy is about your relationship with yourself. It's an essential space of autonomy and freedom. Solitude is a precursor to intimacy, so be free to embrace your private life. When you share with your partner something from your private world and they receive it as an offering, not a confession, you invigorate the space between you. Your private world doesn't threaten your connection because it's lovely and necessary to keep some *me* in *we*.

Secrecy, on the other hand, is a relational red flag. A secret indicates that you don't feel able to bring your truth into the space between you and your partner. Maybe because you struggle to trust people, including your partner. Or maybe because your partner struggles to help people (including you) feel safe in their presence. Secrets are a symptom of a problem that lives inside of you and/or between you and your partner. To diagnose the problem, we have to look at the full tapestry into which this secret is woven.

Regardless of how they come about, it's undeniable that secrets compromise intimacy. You are not fully present to the relationship if part of your energy is occupied with keeping your secret from your partner.

Privacy nourishes connection to yourself and lays the groundwork for intimacy with your partner. *Secrecy* blocks the ability to hold yourself in warm regard and erodes trust with your partner. Couples must define for their unique relationship where the line is between that which is private and that which is secret. As you consider this definition, remember:

- These conversations are hard, but they build intimacy.

- It's painful when one person's private information is perceived as another person's secret. Being proactive rather than reactive about relational boundaries builds trust and prevents misunderstandings.

- Rather than negotiating what's "good" and what's "bad," focus your conversation on this question: *What are the central values of this relationship and how do we know when we are embodying them?*

Bring in support when you're navigating a challenging life chapter. Let go of support during life chapters of ease and flow.

I work with clients for a while, then release them to the wild (so to speak) with the knowledge that they can reach out if and when they need a tune-up. So often, they do!

Don't think about therapy as something you do once in your life, for a few months, to learn more about yourself or to fix a problem. Even in the best of therapy relationships, whatever you figure out will need to be revisited. After all, when the context of your life changes, your core issues are inevitably reawakened. Not because there's anything wrong with you, but because life never stops cracking you open. If you let in the idea that you may very well be in and out of therapy forever, therapy becomes a reflection not of your brokenness but of your willingness to grow, your desire to live with awareness and care.

Let your partner know how you want to receive acknowledgment for your efforts.

You've heard of love languages, right? Let's talk about your *recognition languages*: preferences or idiosyncrasies in how you like to be praised. For example:

- Partner A asks Partner B to make a change that Partner A thinks will improve the relationship.
- Partner B makes that change because they are humble and brave.

I urge Partner A to acknowledge the heck out of Partner B because:

- Making a change can feel hard/vulnerable/scary.
- Leaning into what someone else wants/needs is so loving and wonderful.
- Validation/praise/recognition will increase the likelihood that Partner B will keep up this new improved way of doing that thing. Research shows that Partner A's acknowledgment is reinforcing.

In my experience, the acknowledgment piece can be easier said than done. Partner B may be finicky about how they like their recognition to be offered. I've met many a person (often a *male* person) who falsely equates praise with patronization, which puts their partner in quite a pickle!

Therefore, I want Partner A to say, "I see you making this change that I requested. I want to shine on you in a way that feels good to you. Do you like jazz hands? A text? Flowery language? A hug? A high five?"

Alternatively, Partner B could get ahead of the matter by saying, "I love you, and I'm going to make this change. But I might feel a bit skittish about how you compliment me. A simple wink and a nod will be plenty!"

We are all quirky people in relationship with other quirky people. How lovely it is to learn the landscape of each other's quirks.

If you're ready to go before your partner and you just stand there quietly, you are a freaking hero!

In couples therapy, I've unpacked so many fights that go something like this:

Partner A: "We agreed that we were going to go grocery shopping. I was ready. Partner B wasn't ready. Partner B expects me to wait around!"

Partner B: "When I came down, you weren't even ready. You were sending an email!"

Partner A: "I was sending an email because I was filling time waiting for you!"

Sound familiar?

At one level, timeliness is for sure an individual difference tied to factors like personality traits (some people just never feel rushed), cultural identity (folks in different parts of the world have different relationships with time), and health status (mental health challenges and disabilities can lead some to be more insistent on timeliness or less able to attend to timeliness).

On another level, timeliness is a relational dynamic, one that I would argue can go quite deep:

- **The one who is waiting may feel disempowered, taken for granted, unseen, foolish:** They may feel vulnerable that they are accommodating someone else.

- **The one who is being waited for may feel guilty and inadequate:** Alternatively, they may (perhaps unconsciously) derive a sense of security when their partner is waiting for them.

If you are the one who tends to wait for your partner, I invite you to feel proud when you practice patience. Someone needs to "hold center." When it's done with neutrality and ease, it's a beautiful way to show love.

Relational Self-Awareness Questions

- What story do you tend to attach to the act of waiting?
- What story do you tend to attach when your partner is waiting for you?

> We will continue this topic in tomorrow's entry.

JUNE 30

When you've kept someone waiting, acknowledge it.

Your partner knows they have been waiting for you. You know your partner has been waiting for you. I can't stress enough how important it is for you to acknowledge this.

I know it's tempting to do one of the following instead:

- **Minimize it:** "It was only four minutes!" or "There's no time we actually *have to* arrive."

- **Rationalize it:** "I have more steps to get ready than you" or "You got to catch up on Twitter."

- **Ignore it:** "Okay, let's hit the road!"

- **Excuse it:** "My mom called" or "I had to clean up that spill."

These responses may be completely true. But they miss the mark. Why? Because a thing happened. It's a misdemeanor, not a felony . . . but it's a thing with potential to hang in the space between you as you head out together. Rather than risk this thing shaping your next interaction, neutralize it with acknowledgment. Recognition sets up a reset that lets the two of you have a lovely dinner or a playful outing.

Acknowledgment doesn't equal self-flagellation. It isn't "I'm awful," "How can you stand me?" or "I ruined our day." In fact, all of those keep the focus squarely on you because now your partner may feel responsible to pull you out of the shame hole you're digging. Acknowledgment sounds like:

- "Thank you for being patient."

- "I am sorry that I lost track of time. I am really happy to be here with you now."

- "I kept you waiting! How can I help you move on so we can have fun?"

To supercharge your acknowledgment, pair it with some eye gaze, a squeeze, or a booty shake. If this is a chronic issue, you might try to prevent it by adding some "scaffolding" for yourself. For example:

- Set a timer on your phone to stop what you're doing and start getting ready.

- Keep your phone out of reach when you're getting ready so you don't start scrolling when you should be showering.

- Ask for help! If your out-the-door list is longer than your partner's, how can they help expedite?

Problematic cultural messages about sex and gender create the conditions for fake orgasms.

If you are faking, you are far from alone. Research indicates that a lot of women fake a lot of orgasms, especially women who have sex with men. If this sounds like you, the first thing you must do is be gentle with yourself. Resist the urge to turn a "we problem" into a "me problem." Especially if you have been socialized in the feminine, system-level issues have set you up to fake your orgasms:

- Inadequate sex education
- Inaccurate depictions of sex in mainstream porn
- Intolerable gendered messages that teach women to be self-effacing rather than authorized and men to be dominant rather than attuned

We are set up for lackluster sexual experiences that may lead women to fake in order to protect their partner's ego and to honor a sexual script that says that sex can only end if there are orgasms. Sexual Self-Awareness is about finding our way home to our truth. And sometimes our truth is that we haven't been truthful about our orgasms.

We will continue this topic in tomorrow's entry.

202

Faking an orgasm creates two disconnects: a disconnect between you and your body and a disconnect between you and your partner.

It makes sense that straight women are most susceptible to faking orgasm:

- Women in general learn to be people-pleasers who avoid rocking the boat.

- A woman whose man brings performance-based self-esteem into the bedroom knows that her orgasm stabilizes his self-worth.

- Penetrative sex tends to be less orgasm-producing than other options on the erotic menu.

Faking an orgasm is a self-abandonment. It's your communication to yourself that your pleasure doesn't matter. It is also a miscommunication to your partner, sending the message that a sexual activity is working for you when it isn't. Over time, faking an orgasm repeatedly with the same partner will compromise intimacy and emotional connection, and it will keep you from working together to figure out behaviors that would be more orgasm-producing for you.

Hold self-compassion for the ways our culture has set you up not to value your own pleasure. Hold empathy for the fact that your partner might feel hurt and confused by your disclosure. It may feel like a confession of a betrayal, but it is not. You both need to remember that every sexual problem is a couple problem, and that disclosure reflects your desire to refine your erotic "dances" into something more collaborative, generous, and truthful.

> My friend, Dr. Laurie Mintz, says disclosing that you have been faking
> may not be necessary or wise. Instead, you can simply ask your partner
> to focus on whatever you need more of (clitoral stimulation,
> affectionate touch, words of affirmation, pretend play, patience, etc.).

JULY 3

Couples cycle between closeness and distance, connection and disconnection, ease and tension. Our work is to relish the rises and accept the falls.

An intimate partnership is a series of rises and falls. It's ironic, but true, that closeness can evoke distance. Isaac Newton would say that for every action there is an equal and opposite reaction, right? It's easy to say we crave closeness, but when we get it, it may be followed by tension/closing back up, which can feel frustrating and disheartening. To understand this better, let's look at both the internal and the relational pieces.

Internal: When you can become aware of the urge to close up after having been open, you are practicing Relational Self-Awareness. Pause. Explore what begins to stir within you when you are together. This space may feel incredibly vulnerable. Letting your partner see you is courageous. *Noticing* the urge to close back up gives you the option to make a different choice, like talking with your partner about how frightening it can be to feel so connected.

Relational: As connection begins to ebb, naming your feeling of deflation instead of assigning blame can invite a shared humility about the inevitability of love's cyclical nature. Rather than trying to figure out whose fault it is, get curious.

When we feel good, we can't even remember why we ever felt bad, and it's easy to think that this is our new permanent residence: *Phew! We made it! We have finally arrived at a place of peace!* When the tide begins to turn and our tones become sharp, the urge might be to:

- **Feel shame:** "Why can't I just allow things to be okay?"

- **Assign blame:** "Why do you have to start trouble?"

How different to just name the disappointment: *What a bummer that we're starting to feel tense with each other!* Naming the disappointment invites you to sigh together about the "fall from grace." From that place of shared deflation, you may see a pathway to repair: a kitchen make-out, a game, a walk, a little space. Accepting the ebbs helps you work with them.

JULY 4

When you feel the urge to offer someone unsolicited advice, dive into self-reflection instead.

Unsolicited advice is a boundary violation because we're exiting our own lane and entering someone else's without asking first. When we have the urge to offer unsolicited advice, we are invited into a learning opportunity about our *motivation*. We often get stuck at the tip of the iceberg: "I am trying to be helpful!" If we stay at that level, the other person's reaction to our unsolicited advice feels to us like they are being "too sensitive" or "making a mountain out of a molehill." Again, we were just trying to be helpful! But if we peel back a layer, that's where the good stuff is. The stuff that says more about *us* than the person we are trying to advise.

Relational Self-Awareness Questions

- Do you want to offer unsolicited advice because you're feeling some kind of way about this person? What kind of way? Are you trying to connect? Are you feeling threatened/jealous and trying to establish a bit of authority?

- Does their behavior remind you of any of your own? Do you want to change this part of them because it reminds you of a part of yourself that you haven't accepted?

- How do you want them to respond to your unsolicited advice? What does that tell you about what you're needing/wanting in your life? How might you give that to yourself/ask for it more directly?

Moving from self-sabotage to self-empowerment is much less like flipping a light switch and much more like adjusting a dimmer switch.

In finding our voice, we may swing from one extreme to the other. We go from *I have no voice, I accommodate, I submit, I placate . . .* to *I voice my thoughts, feelings, reactions, beliefs, and perspectives when I want and how I want, to hell with the impact on anyone else.*

Sometimes we overcorrect. We go from silence to shouting. We are so insistent on being seen that we lose sight of the other. I have endless compassion for how challenging it is to move from self-abandonment into self-reclamation. I want to gently name that empowerment does not have to be loud, demanding, and unyielding. Empowerment can be quiet, clear, and kind. We may feel our way into a middle space by experiencing both extremes and moving to the center. It's helpful to have a vision for that middle space of intimacy. We're talking about changing patterns and dances. Your new moves don't need to be dramatic to dramatically change your relationship.

Obligation and love are not mutually exclusive, but if we've been led by obligation for much of our lives, we may need to step out from under what we think we should be doing so we can feel into what we want to be doing.

Our goal is *not* to create a relationship with zero obligations but to cultivate an atmosphere with enough freedom that obligations end up feeling like care. For example: "If left to my own devices, I would not choose to take your mother out to dinner, *and* I will do it with an open heart because I know that I *also* have the freedom to choose activities that feel 100 percent mine."

Relational Self-Awareness Prompts

- When I make a choice to prioritize me, I tend to feel . . .
- When I make a choice to prioritize my partner, I tend to feel . . .
- When my partner makes a choice to prioritize themselves, I tend to feel . . .
- When my partner makes a choice to prioritize me, I tend to feel . . .

A happy and healthy intimate relationship is grounded in rituals that convey the notion of *I'm glad I'm here, and I'm glad you're here.*

Research by the Gottman Institute has shown that happy couples invest time and energy into rituals. In relationship terms, a ritual is just an ordinary activity that has been infused with a measure of intentionality and planning. Couples create rituals around a huge range of activities:

- Cooking
- Walking
- Morning coffee
- Happy hour
- Before bed make-out sessions
- Snuggling
- Tech-free time
- Game night
- Gardening
- Working out

Different parts of ourselves come forward when we hold time and space for a different way of doing the same old thing. While disengaging is the first step toward all kinds of relationship trouble, turning toward each other is protective and preventive. Great intimate relationships happen because people invent and invest.

What intimacy-promoting rituals do you and your partner enjoy? Why?

Healthy boundaries sit at the intersection of empowerment and care.

A healthy boundary is a Both/And:

- I can *both* hear myself *and* listen to you.

- I feel *both* protected *and* connected.

- My behavior is *both* truthful *and* loving.

If you have historically been a bit of a doormat but are now practicing healthy boundaries, the people on the receiving end of your expressed needs may experience you as "rude" or "hostile." Their misunderstanding arises because this behavior of yours is new to them. Far from being rude, your commitment to healthy boundaries reflects how much you value the relationship.

When you practice healthy boundaries, you are not afraid of what others are going to do or say because you can trust yourself to respond with love, clarity, and firmness:

- **A healthy boundary is not confrontational.** It is spoken in the service of the relationship.

- **A healthy boundary is not an escalation.** It is a clarification and a redirect.

- **A healthy boundary is not critical or blaming.** It is an articulation of what's needed to continue an activity, a conversation, a relationship.

You know you embody healthy boundaries when your behavior is intended to help you show up for, engage with, and appreciate the people in your life.

When your partner makes an effort to change their part of a painful pattern, let them know that you notice. Your observation is a powerful validation.

Research devoted to understanding how couples get stuck in dysfunctional patterns and how they develop newer, healthier patterns has shown that when one partner takes the risk to try out a new and softened behavior, their partner tends to respond in kind, shifting the couple from a vicious cycle to a virtuous one. For example, Partner A tends to get critical ("You told me you were going to walk the dog, and you haven't yet!"), then Partner B tends to get defensive ("Stop pestering me!"). Partner B has agreed to work on being less defensive, so the next time Partner A gets critical, Partner B tries a new move. Instead of getting defensive, Partner B says, "Ah! I definitely told you I would walk the dog. I'm going to hit send on this email and head out the door!"

Partner B made a change, yes? However, it turns out that the adjustment that makes the difference is Partner A's *response* to Partner B's changed behavior. What happens next is that Partner A's shoulders drop and their face softens. Partner A even says, "Can I come with?"

Partner B changed their move (and deserves credit for that), but it's also Partner A's willingness to lean into the change that helps the new dance really take root. Love is all about celebrating your lovely dance moves and healing the ones that leave you with sore feet.

As we begin to lean into and cultivate deeper intimacy with a partner, we offer healing in the present to the anxious kid we once were.

If you witnessed volatile relationships in your Original Love Classroom, love and chaos likely got connected in your brain. You learned to adapt to tension:

- On the one hand, thank goodness you learned to adapt. It's what helped you grow up into the resilient soul you are today.

- On the other hand, every adaptation that you've developed (because you needed to develop it) carries with it a consequence. If you adapted to unpredictability, steadiness feels dangerous.

Having chaotic and unpredictable early relationships may lead you to unconsciously code an intimate partner as "boring" when they offer you their steady presence. Your neurophysiology whispers to you, *Where are the fireworks? Something must be awry.*

Your healing work is to identify the connection you've made between love and stress. Thank that Coping Strategy for keeping you safe when you were little, and let it know that you don't need it anymore. As you begin to associate love with commitment, honesty, and predictability, you rewire your brain and body and offer healing and care to Little You.

When someone is upset, expressions of empathy and expressions of concern land very differently.

Partner A is feeling upset about a difficult dynamic involving their extended family. Partner A wants to talk about the upsetting situation with Partner B. Partner A is tearful, moving between sad and mad, talking about who said what to whom, and all the ways it activates old feelings in them.

When someone we love is upset, we are hardwired to get upset too. (Thank you, mirror neurons!) As Partner B listens to Partner A, they likely feel very differently inside their body than how they feel when, for example, making dinner.

In my experience, Partner B's best move is to just stay with empathy. Empathy in action might look like:

- Putting their phone away, minimizing distractions, gazing at Partner A's face

- Making gestures (getting Partner A a glass of water, a tissue, a blanket, etc.) that offer comfort to Partner A as they process

- Being quiet (empathy doesn't need to be talky) or perhaps saying things like, "ugh," "this is hard," "your upset feelings make sense"

Empathy is very different from concern. Expressions of concern like, "I'm worried about you" or "Maybe you need to talk to someone" can feel invalidating. If Partner B has honest concerns about the state of Partner A, I'd encourage them to invite a separate conversation at another time. Expressions of concern are sometimes warranted, but often empathy is the beginning, middle, and end of the story. Upset feelings come and go. They exit particularly gracefully when witnessed and tended with the empathy of someone we love.

When someone lets you know that your words or actions have been hurtful, your harmless intent does not negate your hurtful impact.

Not meaning to cause harm does not negate harm. Even if you wouldn't be hurt if the roles were reversed, you don't get to decide whether the other person's reaction is legitimate. When someone tells you that you've been hurtful, pause. Take a deep breath and slow yourself down so you can meet this moment with the kind of care and grace it requires.

Tending to the hurt means you:

- **Focus on what happened.** Position yourself like a reporter, putting together the sequence of events. Drop the emotion and the meaning; simply focus on the facts.

- **Seek to understand their world.** "Can you say more about how you felt?"

- **Reflect it back to them.** "What I'm hearing you say is _____. Have I got that right? What else do you need me to understand?"

- **Discern what the repair will look like.** To what degree is it relational—that is, a process for you to work out together? To what degree is it personal—something you need to examine on your own?

Your true north is seeking to understand rather than to be understood. You may feel incomplete, wanting them to understand where you were coming from. If you meet the moment with empathy, your chances are greater that they'll be available at a later time to learn more about your perspective.

All of this is even more important to get right when you occupy a position of achieved or ascribed power in the relationship:

- Boss/employee
- Older/younger
- Male/female
- White/BIPOC
- Parent/child

As a society, we have internalized a problematic story that the powerful don't need to apologize, validate, or see the powerless. Feel proud of yourself when you bust up that old story with your willingness to be accountable!

JULY 13

In an intimate relationship, you are forever loving across differences.

We will never fall in love with our clone. In an intimate relationship, we are forever navigating differences of all kinds (cultural, temperamental, personality, etc.). When confronted with a difference, it's easy to judge our way as better/more normal and our partner's way as deficient/odd.

Let's imagine that Partner A is content in their career while Partner B is highly ambitious. In their worst moments:

- Partner A judges Partner B as neurotic, ruthless, materialistic.
- Partner B judges Partner A as lazy, complacent, disengaged.

Each partner's internal experience is painful too:

- Partner A feels inadequate in Partner B's eyes. *Nothing I do is ever enough.*
- Partner B feels lonely and invalidated. *I am not celebrated and appreciated.*

By laying out the judgments and the internal experiences, partners invite each other into a deeper understanding of the difference between them. No right. No wrong. Just two people struggling to feel seen, heard, understood. Imagine if the conversation across this difference was predicated upon a sense that each partner holds an element of truth, a stance worthy of exploration:

- There is beauty in coasting—enjoying what *is* rather than constantly looking to analyze, improve, strive.
- There is beauty in growth—imagining what might be possible, uncovered, explored.

Differences must be met with curiosity and patience for intimacy to thrive.

JULY 14

To love someone for the long haul is to be granted a front row seat to their evolution. This is both a privilege and responsibility.

One of the great joys of an intimate partnership is having a live-in cheerleader. But the person who gets to clap for the good stuff also sees our screw-ups, which can feel less than amazing.

The thing about evolution is that it's far from a straight line. There are highs and lows. Victories and failures. Seasons of brilliance and seasons of barely-hanging-on. Victories are sweeter when we get to share them with people who love us. Even failures are more tolerable when the people who love us keep on loving us regardless!

Letting ourselves be loved in the lows offers sacred healing. My wish is for you to cultivate a relationship that welcomes the celebrations, the crises, and all the ordinary moments in between.

Can you plant your worth more deeply than your most recent win? Can you let your partner sit in your front row? Soak it in. Let it fill you up and sustain you. Oh, and when you're sitting in the front row, be the one who claps loudest for your partner. Be unabashed in your fandom. Shine on them.

JULY 15

Deep listening is the heart of intimacy.

There's a profound difference between giving advice and holding space. We know (or we are learning!) that when someone we love is struggling with a decision, it is far better to witness than advise. If we know this in theory, why is it so hard to do in practice? Here are a few possible reasons:

- **Your person might be pulling for you to give them an answer.** The interior experience of going round and round about a decision is anguishing, and it's wholly understandable to wish for someone to just provide direction. As an empathetic person, you likely feel like giving them an "answer" is the kindest thing you can do.

- **Perhaps your Family of Origin regularly ignored your views and opinions.** When someone turns to you for advice, this is like medicine for your soul! The Little You who felt unseen is jumping for joy that someone is all ears and wanting your input.

- **It's an ego boost when someone seeks your advice.** It can make you feel wise and important.

You must give attention to what comes up when someone you love is standing at a fork in the road. When you are able to resist your urges to advise, direct, and fix, then your loved one is able to connect to whatever feels good and right and true for them. Getting to be part of their process is a privilege and an honor that builds trust and safety.

The central task of a new relationship is to discern whether the conditions are ripe for intimacy to take root and grow.

Question: Is intimacy an individual capacity or a relational dynamic?

Answer: Yes. (It was a trick question!)

Individual capacity: To create intimacy within a relationship, both people need the capacity and willingness to tune into their internal experience and communicate what they find. Self-reflection and intimacy go hand-in-hand. You can only reveal to your partner that which you have discovered inside you.

Relational dynamic: Intimacy emerges within a relationship when people commit to demonstrating care, reliability, consistency, sincerity, trustworthiness. Intimacy is the prize that two people win for proceeding with gentleness and grace. The work of Relational Self-Awareness creates the sturdiest foundation for intimacy.

What a gift kids receive when grown-ups pause and ask *themselves* why they are reacting the way they are.

Although this is a book about partnering, let's take a moment to talk about parenting. Our reactions to our kids tell us so much about our wishes/fears/wounds/beliefs. For that reason, I want to highlight how we as parents can (and must) bring the skills of Relational Self-Awareness into our relationship with our children.

Recently, my teen daughter was talking about a stressor in her life. I was offering empathy and reflection in the conversation. There was a turning point when I moved into fix-it mode and proposed a solution that felt invalidating to her. She exited the conversation shortly thereafter. She opened up to me, I got "fixy," and she closed up.

I rewound the tape in my mind to that turning point and asked myself what was going on inside of me that led me to propose a solution. I quickly identified my desire to "take away" her stress. When she struggles, I feel anxious, and my knee-jerk response is to figure out how to remove the source of struggle. In hindsight, I wish that I would have asked her if she wanted to process or problem-solve. Instead of trying to manage her problem, I could have brainstormed possible paths forward and helped her feel into the path that felt best for her.

Parents don't have to get it right every time. But we do need to be willing to notice when our words/actions keep connection open with our kids and when our words/actions close doors. Our kids' feedback helps us course correct. We can hold authority *and* accountability. Track conversational sequences with your kids. Notice when your reactivity (anxiety, anger, sadness, etc.) spikes. Remember that shift points you toward your Growing Edge.

One of the more unhealthy relationship behaviors we fall into is breaking up (or threatening to break up) reactively during a fight. Reactive breakups both reflect and activate Core Wounds.

The words "I am done with this relationship" may be fueled by wildly different motives, so let's first distinguish between *intentional breakups* (IBs) and *reactive breakups* (RBs).

IBs are:

- Planned
- Done by someone who may be upset but is not triggered
- More likely to stick
- Necessary to end a relationship

RBs are:

- Impulsive
- Done by someone who is triggered/flooded
- Less likely to stick
- An indicator of relational insecurity

If you are someone who is prone to initiating an RB, begin to unearth the Origin Story that fuels this behavior. Beneath the surface of your tendency may lie feelings of being powerless or deeply misunderstood.

You may lack skills around self-soothing. Conflict may feel wildly triggering for you, likely for very good reasons. Perhaps in your Original Love Classroom conflict was frightening, and you were alone with huge feelings. Be gentle with yourself while you investigate the origin of your tendencies. Learn to honor the power of your words so that if and when you declare that you are "done" with the relationship, you know that you have been thoughtful, clear-headed, and intentional about your decision.

Growth is a spiral staircase.

You can practice Relational Self-Awareness for a long time, but you will never be done learning because your context will change:

- You'll fall in love.
- You'll suffer a loss.
- You'll have a baby.
- You'll get a promotion.
- You'll move.
- You'll adopt a pet.
- You'll make a new friend.
- You'll hit menopause.

When our context changes—whether the change is chosen or unanticipated, delightful or dreaded—we are invited into a deeper relationship with ourselves. When our context changes, ghosts of the past rear their heads, giving us another opportunity to rework the story from back then in the soft light of now.

The difference, with our Relational Self-Awareness, is our ever-expanding understanding as we continue to circle back through our old stuff like a spiral staircase. We'll never stop stumbling, but we won't make the same reactive/unaware/self-destructive choices now that we used to make then. We begin to see each stumble not as a failure, but rather as an opportunity to pause and reflect.

One of the most intimacy-promoting sentences is "I'd like a redo, please."

Maybe you say everything right the first time. If you're like me, though, you sometimes take your foot and put it straight into your mouth. You may be guilty of speaking before you think because of one or more of the following:

- Along with your many gifts and talents, you are saddled with a short-ish fuse.
- You were "hangry."
- You walked into a room and all the people asked you for something at the same time.

When your tongue is sharper than you'd like it to be (or sharper than the people around you would like it to be), you have two choices:

1. Double down with a blame-y phrase like, "I wouldn't have said what I said if you hadn't done what you did."

2. Ask for a redo.

To ask for a redo, you need to first notice that you don't like how you handled a moment. This takes self-awareness, humility, self-compassion.

You must be able to separate your less-than-awesome behavior from your perfectly imperfect self. You must remember that your worth is not contingent upon being beyond reproach. You must trust that revisiting an interaction will help people trust you, not think less of you.

How do you ask for a redo? Just put it out there: "Eek! I don't like how I handled that. I'd like a redo." Then respond to the moment in a different way—with more empathy, attention, patience, and/or humor.

Asking for a redo doesn't absolve you. But a redo is a tool you can add to your communication toolbox for moments when you're crabby.

Relational Self-Awareness Questions

- What might keep you from asking for a redo?

- What might keep someone else from granting you a redo?

- How might you make the redo into a relationship agreement?

Being listened to, carefully and deeply, is one of the greatest gifts we can receive from someone we love.

As the old saying goes, we have two ears and one mouth for a reason: Listening is more important than talking. But listening is more than just sitting quietly. It is quite an active process. In fact, it's a process that requires we:

- Quiet our minds of other distractions (what's next on our to-do list, what's happening on our phones, etc.)

- Decenter our own experience (focus intentionally on what the other person is sharing rather than comparing it to our experience)
- Open our heart so we can feel the emotion that undergirds the words

You can set your potential listener up for success by first Going Meta, which in this case, means that you are checking in with them and asking directly for what you need. This might sound like:

- "Is now a good time for you to listen to me talk something through?"
- "Do you have the bandwidth for a situation I want to share with you?"
- "How would you feel about being a sounding board for me?"
- "Would you be able to listen/reflect instead of advise/counsel?"

Then, affirm the amazing benefits of being deeply listened to by expressing your gratitude at the end.

JULY 22

Every conflict has both lyrics and music. We can navigate upsetting moments more skillfully by learning to attend to both.

We cannot avoid moments of misunderstanding, frustration, and disappointment. The best we can do is learn to approach those moments with care, skill, curiosity, and grace. Every conflict has both *lyrics* (a theme) and *music* (a form).

Lyrics: Conflict can be sparked by any topic, but couples tend to struggle most with sex, money, in-laws, parenting, and domestic labor. Issues with no easy answers. Often unsolvable, in fact. Because these topics require collaboration or coordination, power struggles can easily ensue. Smart minds differ on how to handle these topics but agree they are connected to deeper issues: *Do you see me? Do I matter? Are we okay?*

Music: Couples therapists talk about three main choreographies of conflict for couples:

1. **Pursue/pursue:** I get louder, then you get louder, then I bring in three more topics, then you bring up something from six months ago.

2. **Pursue/distance:** The more I try to engage you, the more you shut down, and the more you shut down, the more I try to engage you.

3. **Distance/distance:** When something upsetting happens, I get quiet and withdrawn. When I pull back, you pull back in response.

The skill is to hold dual awareness: We're talking about Topic X *and* we are talking about Topic X in this particular way.

If you can notice the process, then you can comment on it. This opens up a new avenue for collaboration. See what happens when you make a comment about the process, like, "Look, we're doing that thing again, where the more I want to talk about this right here right now, the more you shut down." (This is another example of what we call *Going Meta*— talking about how you are talking.) This skill moves both partners from a "me versus you" stance into a "we" stance that turns conflict into a fresh opportunity for intimacy.

Our well-being is determined, in part, by the degree to which we can move with, instead of against, the passage of time.

Our son was a couple weeks old when we had our first family outing. We packed up all the things and headed to my mother-in-law's condo in the city to watch a football game with the Solomon crew. My mother-in-law asked me to go with her to the grocery store to grab some snacks. After about four minutes in the store, I felt a wave of panic. It was the first time I was away from my baby, and I could not deal with it. I was desperate for her to hurry up and pay already, so I could get back upstairs to hold him. In that moment, I was hit with a profound and painful a-ha: Parenting is basically a steady progression of letting go.

This lesson is one that I have had to learn again and again. Whether or not you are a parent, I suspect you have been learning this lesson too. For some of us, our first response to transition of any kind is resistance. But you must be resolute about loosening your grip to reduce your suffering . . . and the suffering of those around you. After all, fighting against reality can make us rather tough to be around, am I right?

Relational Self-Awareness Questions

- What (or who) helps you when it's time to let go?
- How do you hold both the sweetness and the bitterness of letting go?
- What do you want to remember next time you're facing a transition?

To create a thriving intimate partnership, you must soften.

Many of us are invested in being hard:

- Hard muscles

- Competitive edges

- Sharp thinking

- Agile responses

Hardness has got us where we needed to go, safely and in one piece. Hardness has been the secret to our success. Our hardness has been protective and motivating.

However, love requires softness. We must open, bend, flex, adapt, adjust, and accommodate. We must make space for someone else. How cruel it is that our culture holds softness in contempt, equating it with weakness, when in fact, some of the best stuff in life is soft. Puppies. Babies. Fleece blankets. Sweaters. Brie cheese. Let us be unafraid to embrace some softness:

- Softness is what allows us to let our partner know how very much they mean to us.

- Softness is what allows us to say in a difficult moment, "I am letting go of my need to be right so I can understand you."

- Softness is what allows us to spoil our partner and feel expanded and proud—not embarrassed—about spoiling them.

Relational Self-Awareness Questions

- What helps you remember that softness isn't weakness?
- What helps you feel proud of how much you love someone, rather than ashamed of it?
- What might it be like to thank your hardness for its protection and drive while asking it to share the stage with softness?

JULY 25

Protect your most important relationships by discerning when you're actually frustrated by a moment rather than by a person.

Sometimes there's an inverse relationship between relational safety and emotional inhibition:

- The more emotionally safe we feel, the less vigilant we are about ensuring we are polite/appropriate.
- The less emotionally safe we feel, the more vigilant we are about ensuring we are polite/appropriate.

The classic example is the kid who keeps it together all day at school and then comes home and acts foolish for their parents.

In some ways, it's so lovely that in our most precious relationships, we feel so darned at home that we put our feet up on the coffee table and yawn without covering our mouths, so to speak. But it's a sad paradox that the people who have the most invested in us sometimes get our most raggedy-ass edges. Remember, there's a world of difference between feeling frustrated by a moment and feeling frustrated by a person.

So often we take out our frustration with a moment on a person. Usually it's a person we love to the deep depths of the ocean. If this resonates, don't beat yourself up; instead, see if you can allow yourself to feel helpless/sad/frustrated without identifying a target. Lots of stuff in this life just *is*. Spare your people by dropping the story and embracing reality in all its messy realness.

For long-distance couples, goodbyes and hellos carry additional weight.

The practice of Relational Self-Awareness is all about connecting your *stir* to your *stuff*—understanding how your unique profile of sensitivities, wounds, and triggers affects the way you give and receive love. The more you can understand and share the map of your interior, the more you can enlist your partner's compassion and support.

Couples in a long-distance relationship live in cycles of separation and reunion. One activity that builds Relational Self-Awareness is reflecting on your individual histories of being separated from people who matter to you deeply. Knowing each partner's landscape of tender spots positions you both to be thoughtful about how you handle these transitions.

Relational Self-Awareness Questions

- Does one of you tend to be slower to warm up when you are together after being apart?

- Is one of you at risk of picking a fight before you are away from each other?

- Do you need different pathways back into connection? What are each of your pathways?

Empathy is presence + attunement.

When our partner comes to us with a problem, we are at risk of advising, directing, and solving rather than holding space. Gender role socialization can help us more deeply understand the Origin Story behind our rush to fix.

Years ago, Dr. John Gray wrote a wildly popular book called *Men Are from Mars, Women Are from Venus*. It was predicated upon the idea that men tend to offer problem-solving in situations that demand empathy. This book sold about a zillion copies because it resonated so well. Gender role socialization teaches men to lead/solve/fix, leaving many men to falsely equate empathy with weakness. I spend a good bit of time in my therapy office helping men reclaim their innate empathic abilities.

But women are not off the hook here. In fact, because women are socialized to derive a lot of self-worth from our relational identities (dutiful daughter, perfect mother, good wife, etc.), we can get a bit haughty and think we hold the corner on the market of relationship dos and don'ts. This can lead us to be directive and bossy about what people should and shouldn't do in their relationships.

No matter your gender, remember that empathy builds trust. Here are a few tips for practicing empathy:

- Problem-solving can sometimes reflect urgency to get a conversation over with. Find a time to talk with your partner when you don't feel rushed.

- Bring your full attention to the conversation (phone down, eyes up, no distractions).

- Listen fully. This means not planning what you'll say next.

- Reflect back what you're hearing.
- Imagine how it might feel to be your partner, experiencing this problem in the way that they are experiencing it.

All too often we leave our admiration unspoken and assumed.

Sometimes there is a disconnect between the feelings in our hearts and the words coming out of our mouths. If you sometimes leave your admiration unspoken, explore what might get in your way:

- **Perhaps you think this person knows how you feel and therefore verbal expression of your feelings would be superfluous.** If this lands for you, check in with yourself: What feels risky/silly about stating the obvious? How can it ever be wrong or silly to put more love into the world?

- **Perhaps you feel vulnerable when you imagine verbalizing how you feel about someone.** Check in with yourself: Do you worry that they will take your admiration and use it against you later?

  - If this person really would hold your verbalized admiration over your head, something is amiss in this relationship. Admiration ought to fuel connection, not domination.

  - Maybe this person wouldn't hold your verbalized admiration over your head, but you have a tender spot because of a prior painful experience in this area. If so, remind yourself, "That was then, this is now."

- **Perhaps you hold back because you fear you'll be stammer-y, blush-y, and weird.** To that, I say, go for it anyway! Being awkward makes the admiration more sincere.

Admiration, like love, is a highly renewable resource. You can share it without the risk of running out.

<hr>

JULY 29

You can relate to yourself with both accountability and gentleness. In fact, you must.

Some days I get really cranky. On those days, I can be terrible company. So I put myself to bed early. The next day, when I feel like myself again, I acknowledge my crankiness to my husband and kids and offer them an apology. We all move on.

To make amends with my family, I need to get right with myself. Doing so requires me to hold a Both/And: *both* accountability *and* gentleness:

- **Accountability:** I am responsible for the gnarly energy that I sometimes bring.

- **Gentleness:** I understandably get overwhelmed at times.

I can avoid accountability by making my bad mood about them, blaming their demands, stresses, and messes. I can avoid gentleness by making my bad mood about me, my inadequacy, and my inability to balance work and family. Each of those dead-end roads can get tempting. (I've driven down them many times.) Being expansive enough inside to hold both truths helps me reset, internally and relationally.

You are not responsible for being a ray of golden sunshine at all times. But you are responsible for being aware that a storm cloud hanging over your head has an impact on the people you love. The fact that others are affected by you does not make you a bad person. It makes you a connected person.

How do you and your partner respond to the challenges of being alive? Do you: Close or open? Shrink or expand? Harden or grow?

As a therapist, I certainly help clients develop skills:

- How to fight fairly
- How to ask for what they need in a way that invites collaboration, not resistance
- How to listen
- How to apologize and forgive

But the skills are just a means to an end. They help couples create the safety they need to open up. To be vulnerable. To expose their tender underbellies, where all the good stuff resides.

Even if two people get along swimmingly, life is full of stressors. What matters is how we respond to the stressors. In the face of a stressor, our work is to move from stuckness to flow. We get there by naming what's happening for us: *Ah, here I go again. I'm doing that thing I do when the stuff hits the fan.*

Conflict happens. Noticing it is key. When we notice conflict, its entire landscape changes. Rather than knowing only one way to cope, we begin to see multiple paths forward. As we slowly loosen the grip of our resistance, we open ourselves to the lesson that is housed inside every stressor. That little wedge of light between the crappy thing that happened and our response to it creates the potential for connection. Now it's you and me, side by side, together in the trenches. And the thing about the trenches is they're a hell of a lot cozier when you're in there with a buddy!

You deserve to feel good.

Sexual desire can be a fickle beast, impacted by any number of internal and relational factors: stress, medication, body image, conflict, dishes in the sink, time of day, sleep. But especially for women, one of the factors that can compromise desire is feeling bad about feeling good. So many of the messages that we give girls and women set them up for this confusing internal conflict:

- "Put others first."
- "Don't take up space."
- "Control your appetite."
- "Don't inconvenience people."
- "Don't be greedy/needy/demanding."

Sexual healing begins by recognizing and dismantling these wildly unhelpful messages. You deserve to feel good. You deserve to be partnered with someone who loves to make you feel good. Things that feel good are intrinsically motivating. It's far easier to want sex when you feel (reasonably) confident that you're going to feel good throughout the experience.

Relational Self-Awareness Prompts

- I feel good about feeling good when . . .
- I want to remember that . . .
- I know I deserve . . .
- What I want my partner to know about my pleasure is . . .
- What I need/want from my partner is . . .

AUGUST 1

When you have the urge to judge your partner for their emotional response, see if you can slow down and get curious about the reaction you're having to their emotions.

Partner A and Partner B go to a party. On the way home, Partner A vents to Partner B about a confusing interaction Partner A had with the host of the party. Partner B feels a rush of irritation and says, "I thought it was really fun. Why don't you just focus on what went well?" Partner A feels invalidated and judged. Partner B feels deflated and disconnected.

To be part of a couple is to participate again and again in micro-sequences of emotion/meaning/cognition/behavior. (I swear, I can take a 30-second snippet of a couple's conversation and create an hour's worth of analysis out of it—that's how many layers and nuances of intention, interpretation, and impact are happening all the time!)

In a moment like the one described above, I want Partner B to resist the urge to foreclose on a simplistic narrative like, "Partner A is so glass-half-empty!" I want Partner B to instead get curious about two elements:

1. *Why was this conversation with the host of the party so upsetting for my partner?* This is the heart of Empathic Attunement.

2. *Why am I so reactive to my partner's upset feelings?* This is the heart of Relational Self-Awareness.

By bringing curiosity to both these elements, a frustrating moment becomes an opportunity for intimacy. In the presence of curiosity:

- Perhaps Partner A can come to the realization that the conversation with the host activated old feelings of not-enough-ness that reach back decades. Partner A's reactivity is fueled more by old insecurity than current problems.

- Perhaps Partner B can begin to recognize that their reactivity to Partner A's upset feelings stems from Partner B's tendency to attribute a loved one's unhappiness to some failure on Partner B's part. Partner B's empathy is blocked by emotional over-responsibility.

The responses we have to our partner's emotions have a lot to teach us about ourselves.

AUGUST 2

People who rush to forgive are often people who learned early in life that their feelings come second to someone else's comfort.

If your partner hurts you, you need time and space to feel your hurt, and they need to bear witness to the harm they caused. Even if their shame threatens to swallow them whole, part of their recovery is their reckoning. If your partner rushes that reckoning, they're at greater risk of reoffending.

It might be really hard for you to allow your hurt to fill the space between the two of you. You may be so accustomed to accommodating others that being the center of our attention might feel foreign and vulnerable. You may have learned as a kid that interactions go more smoothly when you repress your feelings. Now is the time to break that habit.

Eventually, recovery will need to be about *both of you*: why you were at risk, how you lost each other, how your Core Wounds created problematic patterns. But first, your work needs to be about *you and only you*: your anger, sadness, envy, confusion. You deserve your partner's steady presence so you have time and space to feel your feelings.

AUGUST 3

When it comes to humor, context is the difference between hilarious and hurtful.

When people ask what made me fall in love with Todd, I say these two things:

1. I felt 100 percent myself around him.

2. I adored his sense of humor.

Nearly 25 years of marriage later, I'd still list both of those. Here's what's also true: There are times when his humor lands on me hurtfully rather than humorously. It's never his intention to tease in a way that feels bad, but sometimes that's the impact nonetheless. In those moments, Todd dials it back and I own my tenderness. We move along.

Humor can often be tricky in a relational context. The same joke might land well at one time and poorly at another time. If I'm being hard on myself already, my skin is as thin as rice paper, making it easy to hear a dig when none is meant. If we are feeling prickly or distant with each other, humor may be a bid for connection, but it might fall flat.

In this way, humor is a bit like touch. The same touch can feel titillating in one context and annoying in another. The space between two people is forever being navigated and negotiated. What's tricky about humor is it exists at both a *manifest* level (a silly joke) and a *latent* level (an expression of an underlying theme).

If your partner makes a joke and it feels hurtful to you, let them know that it felt hurtful to you. It will be good for your relationship for your partner to spend some time exploring the latent, under-the-surface theme that might have motivated their "joke." It is possible to bring latent content to the surface for exploration without it meaning that anyone was bad/wrong/stupid.

AUGUST 4

Scheduling sex can help couples protect time and space for erotic connection while neutralizing subtle but painful dynamics around initiation.

For some of us, stress is an aphrodisiac. A welcome respite from the heaviness of real life. For others, stress is a buzzkill. When time feels tight and/or our well-being and security are on the line, orgasms and play feel frivolous. How sex affects your mojo is idiosyncratic. No right. No wrong. Just truth. What gets tricky is when two people who share a sex life are affected differently by stress, and therefore, have different levels of interest/availability/motivation. Enter the idea of scheduling sex. Here are some potential benefits:

- **Creating eagerness:** If you know you're making love on Thursday at 9:00 p.m., you can spend the day building anticipation within yourself, flirting with your partner, and speaking kindly to keep the erotic space between you feeling good.

- **Eliminating constructed roles:** If one of you typically initiates or makes the bid, scheduling can neutralize a tender dynamic. The pursuer feels less responsible for carrying the torch for two. The pursued feels freed from the job of gatekeeper.

- **Prioritizing your connection:** When couples schedule sex, they are saying to themselves (and each other) that their sexual connection matters: *We prioritize us.*

- **Creating a routine:** When sex is scheduled, it becomes like a practice (not unlike a yoga practice): *We meet in this space together at this time to practice our love in this way.*

If you decide to experiment with scheduling sex, make sure you bring a spirit of curiosity. Notice the impact it has on each of you and on the dynamic between you.

AUGUST 5

When you've been betrayed, anger must be a stop on your journey but not your final destination.

We may not consciously experience anger in response to a boundary violation:

- We may move into *shame*, figuring that our boundary was violated because of something we did.

- We may go *numb* because feeling anything is simply too much.

- We may get *scared* of feeling any anger lest we are consumed by it.

If you are doing post-betrayal work with the person who betrayed you, they must hold space for your anger. The relationship between your partner and your anger must be one of reverence. Your anger doesn't get to say or do whatever the heck it wants, but it does deserve to be witnessed.

Relational Self-Awareness Questions

- What might be different if you were to trust that your anger is part of your journey but not your whole journey?

- What if you hold open the possibility that your anger is a teacher that may guide you to the next chapter of your story?

- What might be different if you could trust that your anger is a feeling, not an identity?

AUGUST 6

What makes conflict so painful is that we are: Desperate to be heard but too upset to listen. Desperate to be understood but too upset to be understanding. Desperate to be validated but too upset to offer validation.

It's not conflict itself that sinks a couple's relationship. It's how the couple handles conflict.

Life is frustrating, and opportunities for misunderstandings and hurt feelings abound. Plus, your intimate relationship *will* activate your Core Wounds (and your partner's Core Wounds)—so rather than fighting your partner, you are often fighting a ghost. What helps is practicing Relational Self-Awareness regarding your "conflict story": How did your Family of Origin deal with conflict?

- Did people escalate by yelling, blaming, or slamming doors? That's terrifying for a kid, making it wholly understandable to avoid conflict like the plague.

- Did people sweep stuff right under the rug, walking around in icy silence or trading sarcastic quips? That's confusing for a kid, making it wholly understandable if you have no clue what healthy conflict looks like.

Even if you had the privilege of watching grown-ups manage frustration with grace and care, it's still hard! When we get activated, the mature part of our brain (the prefrontal cortex) goes offline and the fight/flight/freeze/fawn part of our brain (the amygdala) takes over. Fighting fairly is about doing what it takes to move ourselves from a *me versus you* space back into a space where listening, understanding, and validating are possible. In other words, a space of empathy.

If that's not possible, our best and bravest move is to take a time-out: "I'm scared of saying something I'm going to later regret. I need to step away for the sake of us." If you call the time-out, you're in charge of rescheduling the conversation so it doesn't become a tool of avoidance.

When handled with empathy, conflict can be a gateway to greater intimacy.

Healing intergenerational wounds can feel confusing at times, especially for those of us who are parents ourselves.

Male client: My son talks to me in a way I never would have talked to my father.

Me: Congrats!

Male client: ???

Me: Your son is not scared of you the way you were scared of your dad. He feels safe enough in your presence to push and test and use his voice, and this is a gift.

Our healing means that we are creating a home environment that is very different from the one we grew up in. This means that our kids behave in ways we never could have behaved when we were kids:

- The grown-ups in our home would have punished us too severely.
- The grown-ups would have fallen apart.
- The grown-ups weren't paying close enough attention.
- We wouldn't have dreamed of taking up space because we knew how stressed the grown-ups were.

Whatever your Origin Story, what feels clear to you is that there are behaviors in your own kids' repertoire that you know darn well were not in your own repertoire.

Be clear—I am not positioning myself as pro naughty behavior. I am pro kids feeling safe enough to express themselves and to try out different ways of relating to the world around them in order to figure out what feels good/connected/rewarding and what feels yucky/disconnecting/not-worth-the-hassle. Like little scientists making sense of the world around them. In order to experiment, you need to feel safe.

My client's son felt safe enough to experiment with different ways of relating to his dad because his dad had committed to doing his own healing work.

So in a moment when your fear and self-doubt grip the wheel, you might say that your kids are "entitled" and "disrespectful." But when you find yourself heading down that dead-end road, I want you to remind yourself that their behavior may very well reflect the safety that you are creating in your home because of your commitment to your healing. When your kid acts up, the first thing to do is give yourself a big ol' hug. Extend compassion to yourself first. Reframe their "misbehavior" as a sign that they feel safe in your presence. Perhaps safer than you've ever felt. And that's so effing cool. Then figure out how to meet the challenging moment. When you tend to yourself first, you will parent your kid from a place of love, not fear.

AUGUST 8

A no might not be a rejection. It might in fact reflect the depth of someone's investment in the relationship.

Healthy relationships are infused with *both* heartfelt yeses *and* loving nos. The word no might be a way of saying, "I love us too much to acquiesce in the name of appeasement." If you ask something of your partner, and they say yes with their mouth while the rest of their body silently screams no, resentment is going to build. As resentment builds, their wide-open heart—the one you cherish so much—will begin to close in self-protection. Resentment erodes authentic connection.

To love you fully, your partner must be able to say no to you without guilt and without fear of retaliation.

- Your partner's work is to say no with love and clarity.
- Your work is to handle whatever their no stirs up inside you.

In the face of your partner's loving, healthy-boundary no, you might feel the rise of a thousand old stories:

- *I screwed up.*
- *I'm too needy.*
- *People always leave me in the end.*

You might feel the sting of tender feelings like sadness, shame, fear. Your brave work is to pay attention to your stories and feelings. The more you can sit with your stuff, the less likely you are to act on your stuff (punishing, withdrawing, begging, etc.).

Your commitment to practicing Relational Self-Awareness will help you understand healthy boundaries as an expression of love. Your partner can be your ally, reminding you of their love for you, their belief in you, and their pride in your relationship. But ultimately, you must resist the urge to turn their no into a statement about your own worth.

AUGUST 9

Allowing yourself to receive the love you've been craving is harder than you think.

Opening to love, leaning in to love, receiving love, trusting love. These choices are vulnerable as hell. If you keep your partner at arm's length, you can live an illusion of safety and control. If you let them in, you are giving them some serious power:

- What if they betray you?
- What if you disappoint them?
- What if they die?
- What if the relationship falls apart?

But it's more than that. Letting your partner love you is an affront to your story of worthlessness/wretchedness/undesirability. A self-critical story is no fun, but if you've been carrying it around for a long time, its familiarity can be comforting. A story about being chosen/valued/seen/nurtured is a new story. One that needs to be walked around in for a while. Broken in like a new pair of shoes.

We come by our self-critical stories honestly. They are born of trauma, disappointment, hurt. But you must know that you are bigger than the self-critical story you tell yourself.

Relational Self-Awareness Questions

- What are the ways you block love?
- What are you afraid of?
- What is the fear-loaded belief that makes it hard to allow yourself to receive love?
- Imagine yourself receiving love. What are you doing? What are you thinking? What are you feeling?

Between the toxic cultural messages you internalized and the intense vulnerability

inherent in sex, you need to heal your relationship with your sexual self.

Most of us need sexual healing. As we grow up, we are deluged with sex-negative messages that create deep associations between sex and danger/death/fear/sin/shame. For people whose sexual identities, gender expressions, skin colors, and bodies are systemically marginalized in our culture, a message of *You are wrong as you are* is suffocating. Those internalized messages meet up with the unavoidable truth that sex evokes profound vulnerability—a nakedness both physical and psychological. What a perfect storm of struggle!

To struggle with honoring and integrating our sexual self is understandable. But if we can't name that struggle, it goes underground, cordoned off from the rest of who we are. That which has been marginalized is ripe for shame and acting out. Our sexual healing begins the moment we recognize that we were denied access, by forces well beyond our control, to gentle conversation about and wholehearted exploration of our sexual self.

AUGUST 11

A common symptom of relationship distress is that partners stop giving each other the benefit of the doubt.

If you've ever taken an introductory psychology class, you learned about the *fundamental attribution error*. This is "the tendency for people to underemphasize situational explanations for an individual's observed behavior while overemphasizing dispositional and personality-based explanations for their behavior." (Thank you, Wikipedia.) In other words, we tend to tell more generous stories about ourselves than about the people around us:

- If you are talking on your phone while paying for your coffee, the story I am likely to make up about the situation is that you are rude and entitled.

- If I am talking on my phone while paying for my coffee, the story I am likely to make up about the situation is that I'm strapped for time and need to multitask.

In intimate relationships, research shows that people who are in unhappy relationships tend to make meaning out of their partner's negative behavior (forgetting something, saying something critical, etc.) by focusing on *undesirable traits* rather than on *situational factors* (including their own behavior!). In these cases, the story we make up about our partner's behavior has little to do with *context* and everything to do with *character*.

Imagine that Partner A is heading to the grocery store. Partner B says, "Please pick up Parmesan cheese." Partner A comes home with absolutely zero Parmesan cheese. In a happy relationship, the story Partner B makes up about the situation is that Partner A forgot, and the omission is a frustrating bummer. In an unhappy relationship, the story Partner B makes up about the situation is that Partner A is thoughtless and insensitive, and the omission proves that Partner A cares about nothing more than themselves. What's so painful is that the second story:

- Feels subjectively true to Partner B

- Reinforces Partner B's feelings of hopelessness

- Pushes Partner A even further away

We are meaning-making creatures, and we need to be mindful of the stories we make up about ourselves and each other.

It's okay to ask for what you want and need. Kindly and directly.

Asking for what you need in a manner that is *kind* and *direct* can be really hard to do. This is because asking is vulnerable. You may have a history of your needs going unmet, perhaps in your Family of Origin. You may occupy one or more marginalized identities, and you have learned from the world that you are here to serve, not ask. You may have had partners who conflated being asked with being controlled.

Even if you are comfortable with asking, you may have a Growing Edge that leads you to accessorize your requests with some intimacy-blocking moves, such as bringing in reinforcements:

- "My therapist says . . ."
- "Everyone knows . . ."
- "Any normal person would . . ."
- "You should want to . . ."

You must resist the urge to bring in reinforcements. Enlisting the validation of others will likely put your partner on the defensive. Your request deserves to stand on its own.

Try out one of these mantras to help you feel brave and grounded before you ask:

- *My need stands on its own.*
- *My need is worthy because it is mine.*
- *I don't need to have the views of other people to affirm what I feel/need/know.*

Then, practice making your ask with confidence and calm.

What a gift it is to remind another person that they *contain multitudes.*

The poet Walt Whitman wrote these lines, which I have always loved: *Do I contradict myself? Very well then I contradict myself, (I am large, I contain multitudes.)*

We are all at risk of overidentifying with one facet of who we are, to the point that it eclipses all other facets. This makes us vulnerable to identity questions when our context changes, such as:

- The mom whose kids grow up
- The worker who loses their job or retires
- The life of the party who gets sober

If I am not X, then who am I? One of the gifts of close relationships (friends, family, intimate partners) is that these people are the keepers of our stories. When we're smacked with a life change, whether chosen or unplanned, they can remind us who we really are:

- "I loved you long before you were X and I'll love you long after."
- "That was a thing you did, not a thing you are."
- "You contain multitudes."

To love is to return another person to an experience of their expansiveness. Each of us is so much more than our worst failure and so much more than our greatest achievement. Who helps you remember that you are a diamond of many facets?

Empathy and boundaries are not mutually exclusive.

When we are kids, we ideally come to know our worth by seeing how we look in our caregiver's eyes. Our wholeness is reflected back to us. We are loved not for what we do but for who we are. As we develop what Dr. Heinz Kohut called the process of *transmuting internalization*, we become able to provide for ourselves that which our caregivers originally provided for us: a sense that we are good, worthy, whole.

Our intimate relationships reactivate the depth of longing we originally felt in childhood. That longing exists inside us. It also exists inside our partner. However, striving to love our partner unconditionally sets us up to abandon ourselves.

Your empathy may well be unconditional and limitless. But your tolerance cannot be. It's important to articulate boundaries with your intimate partner, not to be guarded, controlling, or hesitant, but so you can create conditions that allow you to love with integrity, vibrancy, truth. Tend to the space between you and your partner so you can create the conditions for love to grow.

Relational Self-Awareness Questions

Explore the following questions together with your partner:

- What helps you feel safe with me?
- When do you feel most connected to me?
- How will I know when you need space?
- What do you need in order to repair?

The quest for your "true self" or your "real self" can fuel perfectionism and abstraction.

The search for the *true* or *real* self is perfectionistic. We put a lot of pressure on ourselves to come up with the right definitions. We sometimes reach for labels to justify or legitimize our needs or desires. I want us to feel worthy as we are, to be seen just as we are. I want us to offer that to each other.

The search for the true or real self sets us up for getting stuck. If you decide that you are X, then what are you supposed to do when a desire arises for Y? Are you not allowed to pivot/adapt/grow? See what happens when you view the self as evolving, contextual, and relational.

Relational Self-Awareness Prompts

- I am able to ask for what I need when I am . . .
- I know it is time for me to pivot when . . .
- I crave situations in which . . .

Second chances demand care.

My dear friend and therapy goddess Esther Perel talks about how we have two competing needs in an intimate relationship: the need for security and the need for novelty:

- We need enough security that we can exhale and reveal ourselves but not so much security that we feel bored and flat.

- We need enough novelty that we feel alive and engaged but not so much novelty that we feel unsafe and on edge.

Imagine that you and your partner break up. Time passes. Your paths cross. The chemistry is electric and the pull is strong because you're poised at that sweet spot between familiarity and novelty. You know them: their smell, their touch, the way they like their coffee. At the same time, you do not know them: Time has passed, they've had experiences that you don't know about, and so have you. This is what I call *refinding*, and it can be seductive as hell! But it's imperative to slow down. Tread carefully. Protect your heart and theirs.

A break or a breakup is *not*, in and of itself, a poor prognostic indicator for a relationship. I know many magnificent love stories that have involved getting back together after time apart. What matters is how you meet the moment of refinding:

- Can you move with intention, not desperation?

- Can you inquire rather than assume?

- Can you be more self-reflective than impulsive?

Relational Self-Awareness Questions
Explore the following questions together with your re-found partner:

- What has changed for you?

- What has changed for me?

- What are our expectations of ourselves and each other?

Two things can be true at the same time:
1. You made an effort.
2. They feel disappointed.

- You put some effort into making dinner for your family. Nobody loved it.

- You submitted a great proposal at work. Your company went in a different direction.

- You were thoughtful and measured in giving your partner feedback. They got defensive.

- You tried out a sexy little something in the bedroom. Neither of you enjoyed it.

Wouldn't it be lovely if we lived in a world where the output was directly proportionate to the input? We'd never feel vulnerable because there would be a perfect ratio of risk to reward. Instead, we live in a world that demands that we lean into discomfort again and again. A world that demands that we invest without a guaranteed outcome. This means that we need to learn how to tolerate another person's disappointment without resorting to one of these two intimacy-blocking maneuvers:

Intimacy-Blocking Maneuver 1: Melting into a puddle of shame and self-flagellation

- "Why does this always happen to me?"

- "I can't do anything right!"

- "Nobody appreciates me."

Intimacy-Blocking Maneuver 2: Pointing the finger at the other guy

- "You should appreciate me!"
- "You're so hard to please!"
- "You never give me credit!"

I am not saying it's easy to avoid these maneuvers, but it is possible. The next time your enthusiastic effort isn't matched by someone else's enthusiastic response, you need two things:

1. **Self-compassion:** *I am proud of myself for trying. I am more than my latest action. My worth doesn't rest in others' reactions.*

2. **Levity:** *Deep sigh. Maybe next time. Jazz hands. Booty shake. Laugh at ourselves and the ridiculousness of life.*

AUGUST 18

A marriage is both a contract and a container. And a marriage is only as strong as your practices. Only as enduring as your efforts.

A marriage is a thing unto itself. A beautiful thing that demands attention and care to thrive. A fragile thing that can bruise and tear. A living thing that breathes, grows, shifts, and changes with time and circumstance. Lovers are the keepers of that messy beautiful thing. Lovers who adapt because they must. Lovers who get the opportunity, again and again, to discover what it is to be in this specific and unique chapter of their evolving story.

Behind every criticism is an unmet need.

The criticism: "You're always on your phone!" The unmet need behind it may be:

- "I'd like to connect with you."

- "I could use some help."

- "I am jealous—I'd also like to zone out a bit."

- "I'm worried you're cheating on me/bored of me/wishing you were anywhere but here. I crave reassurance that I'm who you want."

Why might it be hard for you to verbalize the unmet need? Here are a few possibilities:

- **In your Original Love Classroom, you took care of everyone else.** Identifying your own needs is now uncharted territory. You don't mean to be critical; you just don't know how to start a sentence with "I need."

- **You occupy one or more marginalized identities.** Because of your cultural identities, you've been told in ways large and small that you'll be judged (as needy/weak/angry/dangerous/bitchy) and punished for having a need. Criticism feels safer for you.

- **Your Family of Origin levied criticism like it was nothing.** Being critical doesn't register on your radar as anything besides how people talk to each other.

If any/all of these resonate, the good news is that you're blocked, not broken. Verbalizing your needs is like learning a completely new language for you. But you can do it! Just let your people know that you're challenging yourself to practice vulnerability, so they are ready to fist bump you when you expose your needs.

When you and your partner are rebuilding after a breach of trust, it's essential that you take a relational approach to the triggers that will inevitably occur.

Healing is a two-person endeavor. When the betrayed partner is triggered by a memory or a reminder, the moment must be faced as a couple. There are three paths available when the betrayed person is triggered:

- **Unhelpful Path 1:** Betrayed partner bites their tongue and doesn't tell their partner when they are triggered. This path grows resentment and loneliness, as the betrayed partner is constantly wondering *Where are you when I need you?* The injuring partner thinks things are better than they really are.

- **Unhelpful Path 2:** Betrayed partner rages when they are triggered. This path is totally understandable but unhelpful. The injuring partner can point their finger ("You're just so mad!") rather than leaning in ("I can see the pain I've caused, and I want to be with you in that pain").

- **Helpful Path 3:** Betrayed partner tells injuring partner when they are triggered. Injuring partner resists the pulls of defensiveness ("Again? I'm always in the doghouse with you!") and shame ("I am a horrible person"). Instead, they step up as an ally ("Thank you for telling me. I'm right here with you. Let's address your pain together.").

Do you know what is lovely? When someone does something for you without you even having to ask. Do you know what else is lovely? When someone does something for you because you asked.

Building an intimate partnership is a process of crafting increasingly detailed internalized mental maps of each other's preferences, tendencies, and idiosyncrasies. For example:

- How you like your coffee

- Your favorite celebrities

- Your pet peeves

- And so much more!

To love another is to learn another. What a privilege it is to know someone so well that you can anticipate their wants and needs. You know how to help them feel at ease, aroused, safe, valued . . . all because you paid attention. And because they let you in!

But learning each other is also a bit treacherous. The more you get to know your partner, the easier it is for them to assume that you know what they want/need without them having to say it out loud. We can begin to expect our partner to read our minds, putting us at risk of saying that our partner *offering* is somehow better than us *asking*.

Remember that you get more of whatever you focus on. If your partner brings you flowers, and your response to them is "You only did that because I asked you to," it will be a long time before your partner brings you more flowers. Resist the urge to create a hierarchy of how to get your needs met. Both pathways are great because getting your needs met by someone who loves you is great!

Trust is an energetic shortcut. Trust is the opposite of vigilance. Trust is a relational exhale.

Trust makes possible all of what we cherish about intimate relationships. No wonder breaches of trust break our hearts. We lose something precious, and what's lost is replaced by something exhausting:

- Checking
- Wondering
- Worrying
- Second-guessing
- Translating

The journey of rebuilding requires patience. It also requires the one who transgressed to assume a role of leadership. Let's say Partner A breaks the trust of Partner B. There are two paths this action can cause:

- **Path 1:** Partner B checks up on Partner A (e.g., surreptitiously checks their phone when they are in the shower).

- **Path 2:** Partner A offers transparency and clarity to Partner B (offers their phone, shares location information, etc.).

Path 1 fuels resentment in Partner A and compulsivity in Partner B. Path 2 offers Partner A the opportunity to stand in their integrity, witnessing themselves acting in the service of love, and offers Partner B a sense of healing. Trust tends to build far more quickly on Path 2. The more Partner B is offered truth today, the less proof they will need going forward.

Breaches of trust are game-changers but not necessarily relationship-enders. Repair requires the person who did harm to practice accountability humbly and consistently . . . and to feel proud of themselves for doing so!

Insight without behavior change lacks agency. Behavior change without insight lacks anchoring.

Insight is all about understanding our story—how we came to be who we are and why we respond to the world around us in the ways that we do. Insight makes possible pattern-recognition: "In situations like X, I tend to respond like Y because of my history of Z."

Behavior change is all about disrupting patterns. Behavior change is about saying, "Next time an X-like situation happens, I am going to instead try out this other response and see what happens." Curious data collection plants new possibilities!

Insight without behavior change is mental masturbation. It's navel-gazing. It's spinning our wheels. It's getting stuck in victim mode: "My past is my destiny." Ultimately, it's selling ourselves way too short! Behavior change without insight is a kind of self-cruelty. It's really hard to choose a new direction when we lack an understanding of how we got to where we are. Trying to be better without an understanding of our problematic patterns sets us up to fail and then get down on ourselves.

Insight and behavior change are like chocolate and peanut butter—better together!

Even when it feels crystal clear that someone "deserves" retaliation, remember that you deserve to feel at peace with your choices. Don't let the size of your pain drive the scope of your reaction.

Being betrayed or deceived is a wildly disorienting and upsetting experience. One that shakes you—body, heart, mind, and soul. You may think *Why me? How could I have missed this? How am I going to get through this?* You may feel shame, anger, sadness, and/or confusion—emotions that create a ton of intensity inside your body. Intensity that can create a strong urgency to do something. And that something might be revenge:

- Revenge that arises from a desire for the person who hurt you to experience a fraction of the hurt you feel.

- Revenge that arises from a desire for people to know "the truth" about the person who hurt you.

- Revenge that reflects a desperate desire to discharge some of the energy of your pain.

I will never ever invalidate the legitimacy and realness of your urges. But here's the issue: Healing from betrayal—a loss of choice—lies in reclaiming the power of choosing.

Revenge is reflexive, reactive. It's understandable but often unadvisable. Revenge can distract you from what you need most at a time like this: community, support, stability, focus, peace, comfort, healing, time to catch your breath. Energy and focus are profoundly compromised in the wake of betrayal. Until you rebuild these inner resources, you're better off using them to tend to yourself rather than punish others.

Finally, while your revenge will likely wreak havoc on other people, it also will likely wreak havoc on *you*. When the dust settles, you may wish you had handled yourself differently. More purposefully. More judiciously. You will need and deserve to forgive yourself for what you did when faced with the impossible.

Give yourself time and space to make choices that you can feel proud of, or at least peaceful about. Stop focusing on the punishment the other person deserves. Focus on the peace you deserve.

Saying, "I am who I am, take it or leave it" massively compromises relationship quality.

Acceptance and change exist together in an uneasy tension. Here's the classic dance:

- Partner A tells Partner B, "If you loved me, you'd accept me as I am!"

- Partner B tells Partner A, "If you loved me, you'd make this change that I want and need!"

Both are wrong. And both are right. Sometimes you and your partner are best served by exploring what troubles each of you about the other's behavior. And sometimes your partner's request for change is an invitation for you to grow.

Researcher Carol Dweck distinguished between fixed mindset students and growth mindset students:

- A fixed mindset is characterized by believing you are the way you are. Traits are traits and that's that!

- A growth mindset is characterized by believing that you can learn, train, and practice your way into greater success.

Having a growth mindset is linked to a slew of positive outcomes. Although this research has largely been focused on students, it's relevant to relationships too. High-quality relationships (rich with authenticity, closeness, safety, play, connection, etc.) require you to have a growth mindset. When your partner brings you feedback or a request to change, you need to meet the moment and see how you can grow a bit.

Instead of insisting that you are "fully baked" and therefore not interested in or able to change, choose humility and adaptability. It's very likely that whatever new mindset or habit you adopt will benefit you individually and improve the quality of your relationship.

AUGUST 26

Impostor syndrome is data, not truth.

Impostor syndrome is marked by feeling like we need to be the best. It brings a fear of failure, denial of our abilities, discounting of praise, and feelings of fear and guilt about success. We are especially vulnerable to impostor syndrome when we're in a novel context, no matter the setting (work, school, a relationship, etc.).

Nothing can change until it has been identified. To get free of impostor syndrome, start by noticing that you're experiencing it. Next, get curious about the underlying cause of the feeling—why is it coming up at this moment? Perhaps:

- You are new to something, and you're confusing novelty with incompetence.

- You have a Core Wound that relates to "not enough-ness." This Core Wound understandably gets activated when you're in a novel context, telling you that you're going to screw it all up.

- You occupy one or more marginalized identities that make you (one of) the first to do this thing/be in this role.

Finally, meet that root cause with fierce self-compassion. Insight may be enough to loosen the grip of impostor syndrome, but you may need more. Here are a few suggestions:

- **Be proud.** Instead of feeling embarrassed that you're learning something new, feel proud! How brave it is to date after divorce, learn a new skill, or begin a new job.

- **Say it out loud to a trustworthy person.** Impostor syndrome, like a mushroom, grows in the dark. Telling someone about how fake you feel can help you feel less fake.

- **Care for the little kid you once were.** The moment you realize a Core Wound is being activated, shift yourself into caregiving mode and relate to that part of you the way you'd relate to a scared kid.

AUGUST 27

Values live within you and in the spaces between you and others, illuminating how you walk your talk.

Your values are the bridge between your ideology and your behavior. You can learn more about yourself in the context of your relationships by exploring:

- Your individual values

- Your relationship values

- Your sexual values

And I hope you'll reflect on your values:

- As a person

- As a partner

- As a lover

When a couple talks together about values, they create a compass that redirects a battle of wills toward a collaborative approach to the problem they are facing. Abandon questions like, "Who screwed up?" or "Who is taking advantage of whom?" Instead, you and your partner need to focus on questions like, "How can we find a way forward that helps both of us live according to our values?" and "Remembering our shared relational values, what do we each need to do and say right now?"

Relational Self-Awareness Questions

- How do you want people to feel when they are in conversation with you? Why?

- What, for you, is the foundation of a happy intimate relationship (passion, friendship, compassion, respect, curiosity, equality, etc.)? Why?

- In a moment of frustration with a partner, how might your shared relationship values help you find common ground?

- What are your sexual values? How do you want a partner to feel during an intimate moment with you? Why?

- How do you ensure that your sexual values and your sexual behavior are aligned? How do you know when they are not aligned?

Liberation from obligation helps us access our desires. Exploration of separateness helps us access appreciation for togetherness.

When we make a commitment to an intimate relationship, we become responsible *to* another person, not *for* another person. Still, the struggle to hold the tension between *obligation* and *choice* is universal. Feeling a tension between loyalty to self and loyalty to other is not solvable. But neither is it an indication that we're doing our relationship wrong. Our individual choices have an impact on our partner, but we can be aware of that without feeling guilty about it.

At times, you will make a choice that aligns with your individual preference rather than your partner's. When you do, it can help to:

- **Find a space beyond a zero-sum mentality.** *I either choose me (selfish) or I choose you (martyr).* Binaries are too simple for complex relationships!

- **Remind yourself that choosing yourself also benefits the relationship by preventing resentment.** It's vital to feel that you are committed because you *want* to be, rather than because you "should" be.

- **Trust that choosing yourself and rejecting your partner are not the same thing.** Be explicit with your partner so you both remember this: "I adore you *and* I'm going out with my friends tonight."

There are individual differences in how long it takes to shift from upset to calm.

Research by Dr. Richard Davidson has shown that we are genetically predisposed toward being relatively quicker or slower to get upset or to move on. Moreover, we have had our particular *affective chronometry* (the time that it takes to calm down after getting upset) since we were kids. It's part of our temperament.

What does this mean for your love life? It is *not* an excuse to go full "Real Housewives of Wherever" on your partner because it's just in your DNA. You are 100 percent responsible for how you behave when you are under the influence of your strong feelings. It *does* mean that if you and you partner have different emotional timing, you need to have compassion and patience for each other. When there are differences between partners in terms of their affective chronometry, both are responsible for regulating themselves as they are having their feelings. Both are responsible for not getting stuck holding a grudge. Let's pretend:

- You are someone who, after a frustrating moment, tends to be ready five minutes later to have ice cream and watch a show.

- Your partner is someone who tends to need more time to let the internal storm quiet.

Rather than acting huffy—"Why can't you just get over it so we can have a nice night?"—you can extend some grace, remembering that your bodies experience emotions differently. You can stay calm, scoop the ice cream, and trust that they will join you when the storm passes. You can accept, not judge, this difference between the two of you. Compassion for yourself and each other goes a long way toward graciously handling difficult moments.

If you were forced to apologize when you were little, you learned to confuse accountability with control in a way that may compromise mutuality in your relationships today.

Brother steals Sister's toy. Sister screams, "Dad! He took my toy!" Dad demands, "Give your sister her toy back and tell her you're sorry." In this moment, Brother has a choice:

- **Defiance:** "No, Dad, I won't!" This will result in him being in even more trouble.

- **Submission:** "Here. Sorry." This solves the moment, but his takeaway is that *sorry* simply helps avoid more trouble.

Forced apologies keep you from learning how to bear witness to harm in the service of relational restoration. Reflect on your apology Origin Story. When you have said or done something that hurts someone you love, can you offer a heartfelt apology? If not, why not?

These questions may reveal any number of avenues of exploration for you, including how apologies were handled in your Original Love Classroom. You are hardwired for empathy, but the grown-ups may not have known how to help you tap into Empathic Attunement when your behavior was thoughtless/impulsive. If their focus was on good versus naughty behavior, your character likely was centered in the conflict, rather than the subjective experience of the person you hurt. If your caregivers lacked the skills to help you witness the impact of your behavior and instead focused on punishment, you likely need to learn how to build your apology muscle today.

You are so much more than your worst behavior.

When we haven't forgiven ourselves for transgression in our last relationship (lying, cheating, etc.), the wound festers inside us, making it really hard to establish a healthy relationship with a new partner. Even if we are not at risk of repeating that same mistake, we are at risk of sabotaging the new relationship:

- **We may struggle to accept our new partner's love.** This new kind of love can feel like a mismatch with our self-loathing.

- **We may feel suspicious of our new partner's fidelity.** That's an old-school defense mechanism known as projection.

- **We may doubt the viability of the relationship even if everything is going well.** Pessimism is the inevitable outgrowth of suppressed pain.

Forgiving yourself is not about being flippant or cavalier. It's not about minimizing the impact of your transgression. Forgiveness means understanding what was undeveloped or unhealed inside you that created the conditions for your mistake. It's about standing in the truth that you get to be *both* imperfect *and* whole. If you don't do that work, your past will continue to interfere with your present because you'll live convinced that pain is all you deserve. Your risk of reoffending is far greater if you can't bring your transgression into the light of day to be addressed, examined, and healed.

Siblings are each other's memory keepers.

Our relationships with our siblings are often the longest-lasting relationships we have. Nobody on earth carries our stories the way that our siblings do. Our brothers and sisters are our most powerful and direct link to our own history. Our siblings are our first friends, laying the foundation for how we execute aspects of closeness like cooperating, negotiating, sharing, holding our own, and giving in.

Sibling relationships can also be our deepest source of pain. Siblings do harm, deny the harm done to us, and are sometimes unable or unwilling to "grow up" their relationship with us. If this is your story, I hope you are surrounded by friends who are your "sisters from other misters" and "brothers from other mothers." I hope your *Chosen Family*—those people you deliberately keep in your life because of your mutual support and connection—witnesses you with love and grace.

Sibling relationships gift us *both* a window to the past *and* an opportunity for continued growth and discovery.

Relational Self-Awareness Questions

- In what ways did you claim your identities relative to your sibling(s)? (e.g., "They're the ___ one while I'm the ___ one")

- What do you want/need your sibling(s) to understand about your life today? Why?

- What might you need to learn about your sibling's life today? Why?

Sex is both a behavior and a gateway to some of the most powerful questions we ask as humans: *Do you value me? Are you with me? Am I okay?*

The vulnerability of sex is inescapable. The experience of being naked with another human being unlocks us, whether we intend it to or not. Even in a casual sexual encounter, we bring ourselves into the experience. We see and are seen. We feel and are felt. We make meaning. Every one of us deserves an enduring and gentle relationship with our erotic self. From that place of Sexual Self-Awareness, we learn to tolerate the complexities of the erotic without numbing out or feeling shame. We allow curiosity to guide us. We treat sexual experiences as opportunities to learn, grow, heal. Great sex begins as an inside job.

Relational Self-Awareness Questions

- What do you tend to seek in a sexual experience?
- What are the ingredients in a good/fun/rewarding sexual experience?
- To what degree do you feel permission to ask for what you want and need in a sexual experience?

"I love you, but I'm not in love with you" sometimes reflects the internalization of a highly romanticized vision of intimate relationships.

"I love you, but I'm not in love with you" is a symptom that warrants thorough assessment and thoughtful intervention. Maybe you are shut down beyond repair (I do not for a moment want to invalidate that there are many worthy reasons why relationships need to end). Maybe you internalized unrealistic expectations that love equals forever butterflies. If so, you deserve to cut yourself and your partner some much-needed slack.

Here is a question that can be helpful to fuel your self-analysis: Do you want to *want* to turn toward your partner once again? No matter what, do not plop this "love but not in love" statement on your partner's lap as if it's their problem to solve. It's not. You are half of the equation.

When families label their kids (the smart one, the athletic one, the naughty one, the creative one, etc.), they create the conditions for self-abandonment.

Perhaps it seems benign to call a kid "the smart one." A compliment, even. But there are problems. If you are the smart one:

- It means one of your siblings must not be. You are now pitted against someone you love.

- You will need to figure out how to maintain this image, fueling external motivation (saving face) rather than internal motivation (the pride of accomplishment).

- Other parts of you may become sidelined: creativity, spirit of adventure, desire to rest.

When grown-ups pigeonhole kids, kids lose access to the fullness of their lived experience. In adulthood, we may have unrealistic expectations of ourselves and others. We may struggle to grow, evolve, and let go of that which no longer serves us.

Relational Self-Awareness Questions

- What role did you need to play in your Family of Origin? Why?

- Do you seem to have the same role in your important relationships today?

- In what ways does your role in your Family of Origin limit who you are now?

SEPTEMBER 5

There's stuff in our lives that we never wanted, never asked for, and would never wish on another, that grows us nonetheless.

Spiritual bypass means using spiritual ideas to avoid feeling our uncomfortable emotions. Examples include feeling like, "everything happens for a reason," focusing solely on the positives, and figuring out how your karma/choices manifested your current reality. What I am asking you to sit with in this entry is *not* about spiritual bypass. Rather, I am asking you to rest in paradox by holding two competing truths:

1. I hate what is happening to me.

2. This experience is growing me.

It is hard to be in a "dark night of the soul," when we experience things like:

- A loved one with a new and scary diagnosis

- A flare-up of a chronic health condition

- A breakup

- A revelation of infidelity

- The death of a loved one

- Job loss

- Addiction

There are a thousand ways that life breaks our hearts into a million pieces. At first, we are 100 percent pain and 0 percent growth. With time, and tears, and support, the balance may begin to tilt, even gradually equalize. Still, I don't know if any of us ever reach 0 percent pain and 100 percent growth. I don't know if that should be the goal.

What I do know is that we get to grow on our own timeline. While growth doesn't make the pain "worthwhile," the pain (and how we cope with it) doesn't mean that the growth is forever out of reach. We don't have to hide out while we are struggling, nor do we have to have a chipper prepared statement about what our current hardship is teaching us.

When you can be real with the people in your life about the complex blend of pain and growth, you invite others to be real as well.

Stopping pain is necessary, but not sufficient.

My work with clients is about the expansion of possibilities. I want the conflictual couple to fight less, but I also want them to explore new possibilities for connection. I want the survivor of sexual trauma to experience fewer symptoms of PTSD, but I also want them to feel entitled to pleasure. Stopping the pain is the floor, but we need a higher ceiling.

Healing is a journey. In the beginning, we may not target connection, joy, and intimacy. In the beginning, we are in a triage situation, containing the fallout, preventing further damage, establishing safety. In the beginning, we simply address the pain. But as our journey continues, we need to stay open to possibilities that were unseeable during the crisis, possibilities that were unimaginable during the storm.

Relational Self-Awareness Questions

Think about a time when you were working on healing or recovering from something difficult (a breakup, a trauma, the death of a loved one, a fight with a partner, etc.).

- How did you "track your progress"? What were the indicators (crying less, smiling more, spending less time thinking about what happened, experiencing less distress when thinking about what happened, enjoying experiences more, etc.) you looked at?

- Why was that progress indicator meaningful to you?

- Was your progress indicator more about stopping the pain or reclaiming pleasure? What do you think that says about how you heal?

The nature of all systems, including family systems, is to move toward stability by any means necessary.

A healthy family system creates stability through flow, adaptation, and accommodation. People give, take, step up, and step back in ways that are empathic, attuned, dynamic. In a healthy family system, people get to grow, change, and flux without retribution or fear. People can tolerate the uncertainties of change because there is a foundation of mutual care and respect that helps change feel more exciting than threatening.

An unhealthy family system creates stability in one of two ways:

1. **By sticking individuals in narrow, rigid roles that limit growth and authentic connection:** People stuck in roles (the goof ball, the martyr, the perfect child, etc.) walk on eggshells, afraid to step out of line lest they upset the family system.

2. **By tending toward predictable unpredictability:** Roles are unclear because nobody knows who is supposed to be doing what. Needs go unmet because they aren't noticed. Kids act like parents. Parents act like kids.

If you grew up in a family that sought stability through rigidity or chaos, your healing involves nourishing the parts of you that went unseen:

- Who did your family need you to be?

- What function did your role serve?

- What did your family believe they were protecting you from by assigning you that role?

- What did that role prevent you from nurturing within yourself? How can you cultivate this now?

Healthy relationships require that we alchemize our anger into energy that clarifies and transforms.

My friend, the couples therapist Terry Real, says that we let men express two emotions: happiness and anger. As a result, anger becomes the sole pathway for emotional upset:

- Shame becomes anger.

- Sadness becomes anger.

- Fear becomes anger.

- Disappointment becomes anger.

Too many of us have suffered the collateral damage (ostracism, retaliation, or worse) of emotions that have been distorted and perverted by this binary. Although anger is endemic to the human experience, each of us has a particular relationship with anger shaped by a number of factors, including identity variables, Family of Origin experiences, and temperament. Understanding how our cultural locations shape our unique relationship with anger will help us work with it in the service of healthier relationships.

To cultivate thriving relationships, anger must be neither unleashed nor swallowed. Unleashing anger destroys trust and safety. Swallowing it destroys authenticity and connection. Rather, you must learn to be present to your anger, noticing where it lives in your body and what it is signaling. Once you can sense it with more thoughtfulness, you can make mindful choices about what to do with it next.

Relational Self-Awareness Questions

- What messages were you given about anger when you were a kid? How do those messages impact you today?

- What does anger tend to feel like in your body?

- When you feel angry, what helps you remember to pause before you respond?

One function of anger is to alert us that there has been a boundary violation.

Sometimes anger is a cover for a more tender emotion like sadness, insecurity, or shame. Sometimes anger is a messenger telling us, "Pay attention. Speak up. Draw a line." There must be a pause between the emotional alert that something is wrong and the resultant behavior—during which we choose and refine our next move:

- *Without* **that pause:** Anger expresses as an eruption, wreaking havoc and resulting in consequences for ourselves and the people around us.

- *With* **that pause:** Anger is clarifying, illuminating, constructive.

When anger is a signal that something is unfair or intolerable, the emotion threatens the status quo, which is why many of us (especially women and BIPOC and queer folk) have been shamed into silence with the message that our anger is "unattractive," "threatening," or "overly sensitive."

When you feel angry with your partner, pause so you can discern whether your anger is covering something vulnerable or signaling something inequitable. Curiosity about what is driving your anger helps you to ask for what you need from your partner. Perhaps it is a witnessing of your emotions. Perhaps it is renegotiation of boundaries, expectations, or responsibilities.

Relational Self-Awareness Questions

Think about a time when you experienced anger as a response to someone disrespecting your boundaries:

- What did your anger "say" to you about who you are as a person and what you need and deserve?

- How did you relate to the experience of anger? Did you try to stuff it down? Did you allow it to guide your next steps?

- What could you do to thank your anger for the ways it alerts you and reminds you of your worth?

SEPTEMBER 10

Endings are teachers.

It is confusing that something can both hurt us and grow us. Still, no matter how the ending came about or who is ultimately responsible for it, it opens the door to growth:

- **Endings you choose:** When you are the one who chooses to end a relationship, you are gifted the opportunity to learn about holding power with kindness. You have the chance to practice grace. You can learn to speak your truth in a way that ensures that others feel their dignity. You learn that endings are brutal even when you are sure that you need to walk away.

- **Endings you don't choose:** When you experience an ending that you didn't ask for, even fought against, you must learn about self-care. One-foot-in-front-of-the-other times like these teach you that loss is as physiological as it is psychological. Eventually, seeing how you took the next breath, and the one after that, shows you how strong you truly are.

- **Endings beyond anyone's control:** When you must say goodbye due to circumstances beyond your control, you learn lessons about persisting despite unfairness. You learn that focusing on fairness tends to be a recipe for suffering. You learn that you still get to savor the place a relationship held, even if it lasted for only a season. You learn to surrender.

Relational Self-Awareness Questions

Think about an ending. What did it teach you:

- About what you value?

- About what you need?

- About your patterns?

- About what you desire in your relationships?

- About what you tend to fear in your relationships?

SEPTEMBER 11

One person cannot do the work of two.

Let's look at a problematic yet ubiquitous cultural message that we have all internalized:

Divorce/breakup = failure, while relational longevity = success.

This message shows up in all kinds of ways. We celebrate the quantity of years together (in the form of wedding anniversaries) but pay little attention to the quality of those years. Meanwhile, people who are going through a divorce often experience the double whammy of pain from the divorce plus shame from feeling judged/ostracized. Relationship endings are confounding:

- Which relationships can be saved?
- How do you know when it's over?
- When do you keep fighting and when do you call it quits?

We crave formulas to help us know for sure that we will enjoy a long and happy relationship. This is because sitting with mystery and complexity is hard. In my work, I strive to hold deeply onto both these things at once:

- My passion for helping people acquire the tools and insights they need to create thriving relationships. These relationships feel wonderful to invest in over a lifetime.
- My humility that not every relationship can or ought to be maintained. People need and deserve to exit with their self-worth fully intact.

One thing I know to be true is that one person cannot do the work of two, even if that one person is magnificently self-aware, profoundly intuitive, and elegantly emotionally attuned. In short, love alone is not enough. Nobody can be loved out of their shame or their wounds. The best you can hope to do is partner with your beloved as they unpack and process the baggage they bring into the relationship.

SEPTEMBER 12

You may have a hard time feeling drawn to an emotionally available person because a part of you still believes you need to earn love.

Imagine you're beginning to date someone new. They are interesting, their words match their actions, they are kind and respectful, and you feel calm and engaged when you are with them. But you're finding yourself feeling "meh" about them. Keep open the possibility that you carry an old story inside of you that says:

- You should have to work to earn love.

- You need to hustle to get noticed.

- You need to struggle to get what you want.

Life may have done a very good job of getting you to believe this story. For example:

- If you are BIPOC, you've received this message innumerable times by having to work harder for your successes and prove that you've earned your opportunities.

- If you were your family's hero, showing the world that everything is okay through your hard work and achievements is simply how you roll.

- If you have a learning disability or a mental health issue, you're accustomed to things being harder for you than they are for others.

Thus, when a potential partner walks the talk, of course a part of you is skeptical. Perhaps this part of you gets even more self-abandoning: *If they are this into me, what the heck is wrong with them?* Deep breath. Hand on your heart. Talk to your potential partner about your history of having to hustle for the good stuff. You deserve their patience and understanding as you work to let love in, and they will feel flattered that they get the privilege of being among your good stuff!

Relational Self-Awareness Questions

- What if you get to keep open the possibility of flow and ease?
- What if you simply observe yourself taking each step without too much analysis but with plenty of presence?
- What if you touch, even with your little baby toe, this new belief that you can receive with ease?

SEPTEMBER 13

Brutal honesty and emotional safety cannot coexist in a relationship.

Brutal honesty is highly overrated:

- At best, brutal honesty reflects a boundary violation: the belief that I can say what I want when I want and how I want ("I'm just expressing myself!").
- At worst, brutal honesty is cruelty masquerading as a favor ("I'm just saying this to help you!").

There's no question that relationships benefit from feedback. When you share your observations about your partner *with* your partner, they can use your observations as fuel to grow, to thrive, to love you in the way you want and need to be loved.

There's also no question that sharing feedback requires skill. You must package what you say in a way that your partner can hear. This is not coddling; it's kindness. It's also practical—if your observation-sharing is primarily guided by your devotion to brutal honesty, they will hear it from a place of protection and defense rather than learning and curiosity.

Even though some say that suffering makes us stronger, we are all highly sensitive to criticism. To share feedback, we need a filter, a mental gatekeeper, that part of our brain (prefrontal cortex) that helps us think before we speak:

- *Is what I'm about to say kind?*

- *Is what I'm about to say helpful?*

- *Is what I'm about to say being fueled by a part of me that is invested in activating insecurity inside of my partner? If so, why?*

If some crazy-ass thought runs through your head, and you don't tell your partner, you're not being withholding or dishonest. You're being merciful and mature. Strong relationships rest on speaking truth with integrity and discernment. How you speak your truth matters.

SEPTEMBER 14

" . . . yes, but . . . " Two little words that hold the power to erode trust, intimacy, and authenticity in an intimate relationship.

Here are three examples of these troublesome words in action:

Partner A: "I didn't like when you raised your voice to me. It hurt my feelings."

Partner B:	"Yes, but I wouldn't have raised my voice if you hadn't thrown away the leftovers."
Partner A:	"I really want you to come visit me this weekend."
Partner B:	"Yes, but it has been a month since you've visited me."
Partner A:	"It's hard for me when your mom disciplines our son."
Partner B:	"Yes, but you should just be grateful she's helping us out."

One of the most foundational relationship skills is the ability to validate our partner's perspective. Without this skill, we are at high risk of compromising trust, intimacy, and authenticity.

In the previous scenarios, Partner B has taken Partner A's concern and deflected it. By saying, "yes, but," Partner B is guaranteeing that Partner A will stay laser-focused on their own feelings of hurt/neglect/anger and thus be unable to take in anything that comes after Partner B's "but."

The practice of reflecting our partner's words and feelings back to them is wildly underrated and deeply intimacy-promoting. Here's how I'd rewrite Partner B's responses to the three scenarios:

- "I know you don't like when I raise my voice."

- "You're wanting me to come visit. Long-distance gets tiresome, right?"

- "I hear you. I get protective of our little guy too."

There may be layers to peel back after that. But starting with validation will carry us a long way toward resolution.

What a gift it is to love someone who has a very different relationship with your body than you have.

Your partner does not have the same relationship to your body that you have. They don't judge your thighs like you do. They don't keep in the front of their minds the memory of when you looked tighter/thinner/stronger than you do today. Instead, they are grateful to be near you. Happy to touch you. Excited by the feel of your skin and the motion of your ocean far more than your body fat percentage.

What if you try seeing yourself through your partner's eyes? This question isn't metaphorical or hypothetical. Can you see you the way they see you?

- Imagine what it's like to hold you. To caress you. To snuggle you. To excite you.

- Imagine how your presence and warmth must be infinitely more satisfying and exciting than any measurement could ever be.

Even if you can hold this image only for a moment, you have shown yourself that there is another story about your body. You have seeded a new, more generous story that can disrupt your self-critical narrative. Let your partner's loving eyes become a source of respite and healing. Leverage their love, allowing it to catapult your reclamation of enough-ness. Love is miraculous like that. Their loving eyes can become your own.

Sometimes we are too distracted or tired to give our loved one what they need and deserve from us. We can be truthful about our limitations, but we also need to determine when their concerns will be the center of our attention.

Listening is the most underrated love language ever! Let's look at the distinction between *listening to respond* and *listening to understand*.

- **Listening to respond:** We take in their words and simultaneously think about what we want to say next.

- **Listening to understand:** We decenter our own perspective, feelings, and reactions and focus on understanding what our loved one is saying.

If your partner listens closely to you, it's good for *you* because:

- You flesh out your perspective.
- You feel less alone.
- You feel validated.

It's also good for *your partner* because:

- You experience them as trustworthy and present.
- They get to know you more deeply.
- They get the gift of seeing themselves as a good/kind/gentle person.

Listening closely and deeply enough to understand requires energy. If your partner is unable to give you the deep listening you need and deserve, they need to do two things:

1. **Speak their truth with love:** "What you're saying matters, and I'm aware I cannot give it the attention it deserves right now."

2. **Be proactive about scheduling a future listening session:** "How about if I zone out with an episode of my show, and then we talk for a bit?"

It's unrealistic to expect that your partner can be 100 percent available all the time for you. But your partner can consistently offer truth, kindness, and accountability.

SEPTEMBER 17

More empathy, less solution. More reflection, less explanation. More attunement, less advice.

Seeing someone you love in pain sucks. You'd give anything for a magic wand to wave and make their pain disappear. Being near someone who is hurting is wildly upsetting. In fact, we are hardwired to get upset when people around us are upset. This is called *emotional contagion*. Part of Relational Self-Awareness is getting curious—exactly what is it about that person's upset that is so hard for you? Do any of these examples resonate?

- "When I was little, my mom would disappear into her room when she was upset, so I fear abandonment. Your upset triggers an old fear."

- "I grew up in a family that told me to toughen up, so when you're upset, I do to you what was done to me. In other words, I have only one tool in my toolbox. I use it on myself, too, by the way!"

- "Like it or not, I put you on a pedestal. When you're upset, it threatens my notion of who you are/who I need you to be. I invalidate your feelings so you can stay where I put you."

- "I grew up feeling responsible to everyone for everything. When you're upset, I feel like it's my problem to fix. Isn't it?"

We tend to come by these stories honestly. However, these stories block our relational superpower of *empathy*. Empathy is presence, validation, reflecting someone back to them just as they are, without adding meaning. Being empathic means resisting the urge to say things like:

- "Everything happens for a reason."

- "God doesn't give us more than we can handle."

- "It's going to be okay."

Don't say those things. Just be near. Reflect back what you're hearing them say. Empathy, it turns out, is surprisingly simple.

SEPTEMBER 18

You do not need to wait for a crisis to ask for help.

You need and deserve help as soon as your stress load outweighs your capacity to cope. Help might mean therapy. It also might mean asking someone to run an errand for you or hold space as you talk something through. If you fear being a burden, remember that for someone who loves you, being called upon to provide support can feel like a sacred privilege.

Relational Self-Awareness Questions

- Historically, how bad do things need to be for you to feel justified asking for help?

- What are the messages you have internalized about needing help?
- Whom do you fear you've become if you ask for help?

Dominance is not strength.

If your definition of strength is domination, you cannot be intimate, connected, or relational. Here's a list of dominating behaviors that prevent connection, erode trust, and destroy relationships:

- Contempt
- Sarcasm
- Interrupting
- Gaslighting
- "What about-ism"
- Invalidation
- Defensiveness
- Escalation
- Belittling

My mentor, Dr. Mona Fishbane, talks about three kinds of power dynamics in an intimate relationship:

- **Power Over:** This is the mistaken idea that there are only two stances: winner and loser. If this is our mindset, we will do anything to keep the upper hand.

- **Power To:** This is the power to regulate ourselves. We use mindfulness, deep breathing, and self-compassion to soothe our upset insides so our words and actions are ones we can be proud of. We don't offload responsibility ("You made me act like that!"). We pause and step away, not to punish anyone else, but to calm down so we ensure our next moves align with our values and integrity.

- **Power With:** This is the power to be relational. Empowered *and* connected. Tough *and* tender. Standing up for ourselves without putting someone else down. Being hard on the issues and soft on the person.

We need and deserve leaders (of ourselves, of our families, of our businesses, of our nation) who shun Power Over because it's pathological, harmful, dangerous, and abusive. We need to commit instead to practicing Power To and Power With in order to unite, elevate, and heal.

Resist the urge to confuse wistfulness with brokenness.

You may have a host of legitimate reasons for why you're not ready to get back in the ring after a breakup. For example:

- **Grief takes time to heal.** Even if you're the one who initiated the breakup, grief is understandable and to be expected.

- **You may be craving a chapter of solitude.** Sometimes you need to be alone while you integrate the end of a love story and feel your way back into your own center.

This is all part of love's journey. But you don't need to wait to love again until all feeling for your ex-partner is gone. With time and intention, pain becomes a pang. Feeling a pang of something for your ex is very different from acting on a pang. When you feel a pang regarding a past relationship, simply notice the feeling and allow it to pass like a leaf floating down the river. No need to attach to it. No need to layer it with meaning (*This must mean I don't love my current partner*, *This must mean I am broken*, etc.). Bless your past so you can return to your present.

SEPTEMBER 21

Cultivate an intimate relationship that supports and celebrates your dreams.

Here's a relationship sequence that I worry a lot about:

- Partner A verbalizes an individual dream/hope/aspiration they have.

- Partner B rolls their eyes.

- Partner A takes their dream off the table, saying, "It's silly, I know."

This sequence is a recipe for resentment. Couples must disrupt this sequence for the sake of their separate dreams and for the health of their relationship.

It's true that individual dreams are often relationally inconvenient! One partner's dream may conflict with the other partner's dream, or an individual dream may not fit with relational goals. Couples are invited and challenged to work together to find a path beyond the simple "my dream wins" or "your dream wins." Alternative paths may include:

- **The *sequencing* of dreams:** The couple agrees to spend the next six months investing all their energy into launching Partner A's new business, and then they turn their attention to supporting Partner B's desire to travel to Paris.

- **The *layering* of dreams:** The couple agrees to make room in the budget for both Partner A's love of expensive shoes and Partner B's love of live music.

- **The *approximations* of dreams:** Although the couple cannot fully embrace Partner A's dream of moving to a house in the woods because of Partner B's caregiving responsibilities, they agree to spend two weeks in a cabin in the mountains each summer.

Intimacy invites us to forge a path founded in creativity and possibility.

Relational Self-Awareness Questions

- Are you worried that if your partner's dream comes true, you'll be left behind?

- Are you threatened by your partner's ability to dream because you've always hewed to the practical and reasonable?

- Are you resentful that you have to remain earth-bound because your partner spends the bulk of their day with their head in the clouds?

SEPTEMBER 22

Avoiding a decision means choosing the status quo.

When you don't leave a job, you are staying in that job. When you don't go out on a date, you are staying single. When you don't take a step toward ending a relationship, you are staying in it. Not making a choice *is* a choice.

Meet this awareness with a ton of self-compassion—ambivalence has a way of fueling self-criticism. I invite you to look at your decisions from a new perspective. Maybe you'll see something you haven't seen before. For instance, viewing your lack of a decision *as a decision* reminds you that you have agency. By doing nothing, you are currently using your power to hold steady to the status quo. Reframing your agency may become a first step toward a new reality.

Relational Self-Awareness Questions

- What is appealing about the status quo?
- In what ways is it working for you right now?
- What would be the first baby step toward a change in the status quo?
- How do you feel when you imagine taking that baby step? Why?

SEPTEMBER 23

Life transitions, even the happy and chosen ones, put you face-to-face with dormant pain that you may not have known existed.

Change is both thrilling and terrifying. Sometimes, changes that we think of as positive can be the most disorienting of all because of what they awaken in us. When the world around us is offering its congratulations, it can create a profound disconnect between the way we feel and the way we think we should feel. For example:

- Falling in love evokes your old struggle with trust.

- Having a baby confronts your tender spot related to dependence.

- A job promotion activates your wound around power.

Imagine that you receive a promotion. Friends, family, and colleagues congratulate and celebrate you. Your bank account reflects your accomplishment. You're supposed to be walking on sunshine. So why is your stomach suddenly in knots? Why are you tearful and edgy? Why are you flashing on childhood memories you haven't thought of in years?

While the transition feels delicious and deserved to one part of you, it feels triggering to another part of you. A promotion gives you power. In dysfunctional families, there are only two positions: powerful and powerless. If this is how you grew up, powerlessness may have felt quite familiar to you. There's an odd safety in surrendering, becoming a person that stuff happens *to*. But your new position of power means that you *make* stuff happen. Your choices impact others. To the traumatized part of you, you've become the threat, and that's confusing and confronting.

In this situation, you have an incredible opportunity to offer healing to Little You, who is sure there are only people who are hurt and people who do the hurting. You can (and will) show Little You how power can be wielded with kindness and care. But you can't begin to figure out how you want to show up as a leader until you reckon with the old tendencies that your new role awakens in you.

Don't run from the discomfort that a transition stirs within you. There's good data within that discomfort for you to attend to. There's good stuff that you can't access unless you're willing to pay attention. Your work is to hold both the challenge and the opportunity.

When your partner's infidelity is discovered or disclosed, your stability must be the top priority.

Finding out that your partner has been unfaithful is profoundly destabilizing. Infidelity is a violation of basic trust, which means that your relationship suddenly feels unsafe:

- The reality you *thought* you were living in is not the reality you are living in, so your mind is attempting to align two parallel tracks.

- You're rewinding the tape, revisiting memories in light of new information.

- You are making sense of who you thought your partner was and who you thought you were.

- Your emotions are likely running the gamut from angry to sad to confused to compassionate to envious to ashamed. Cycling among powerful feelings is exhausting. It leaves little to no bandwidth for the business of life.

It's no surprise that almost half of betrayed partners meet the clinical criteria for PTSD in the wake of discovery or disclosure. Healing takes time and intention. You need to heal. Your partner needs to heal. You will either stay together or part ways. All of this takes time. The early days and weeks must be about one thing: creating stability. For example:

- Are you drinking water?

- Are you moving your body?

- Are you eating nourishing foods?

- Do you have someone who is in your corner?
- Are you getting sleep?

There will be time for questions, exploration, accountability, decisions. Stability must come first.

Meeting someone wonderful is often an act of chance. Loving someone over time is always an act of choice.

Love is about:

- Destiny and decision
- Romance and rationality
- Allowing and acting
- Fate and free will

For some of us, choice feels confusing. Early on in a relationship, we feel smitten, and the process of falling in love feels more like trying to keep up with something that is unfolding organically. But invariably, relationship dynamics and neurophysiology change. As crushes and lust fade, love begins to feel more like an act of will. Our challenge is not to freak ourselves out when that transition occurs. "I don't feel butterflies like I did in the beginning" does not need to mean "We are doomed." Rather, this shift simply moves us from passive to active coauthors of our love story.

For others of us, love feels like a choice right from the beginning. We are hesitant and skeptical, so every date is an act of courage. We self-consciously motivate ourselves to keep stepping into the unknown.

Our challenge is not to interpret our uncertainty as an indication of our brokenness. Building an intimate relationship is wildly confronting, and we deserve to feel proud of our ability to turn toward a process that is at once intriguing and activating.

No matter our idiosyncratic relationship with romance, long-term loving is about choosing again and again to love, to communicate, to turn toward, to process, to apologize, to forgive, to learn, to grow.

SEPTEMBER 26

One of the hallmarks of a healthy relationship is having clear guardrails around conflict.

When we are young, we are little social scientists, absorbing all kinds of messages about how to handle emotions, disappointments, and misunderstandings. These messages travel with us into adulthood and shape how we meet difficult moments with our intimate partner.

Maybe you were raised in a home where you saw the grown-ups handling differences and frustrations with care and humility. If so, please tell those grown-ups thank you (and bravo from me) for offering a beautiful gift to the next generation!

Maybe you were raised in a home where you saw the grown-ups handle differences and frustrations in ways that were confusing and frightening for you. If so, your work is to reckon with your *conflict inheritance*. Get specific about what you saw and experienced. For example:

- Yelling
- Swearing
- Name-calling
- Silent treatment

Ask your partner to get specific about what they saw and experienced within their Family of Origin. Work together to create a shared understanding of what will be considered "below the belt"—that is, the behaviors that erode relational safety and trust. Commit together to the work of transforming your respective conflict inheritances. And celebrate yourselves and each other every time you give your Little Yous a new experience.

One of the most heartbreaking relational dynamics is a partner who feels ashamed instead of proud when they extend themselves to meet their partner's needs.

I invite you to be curious about the meaning you make from another person's failure to meet your expectation. When we flip-flop between trying to understand whether our partner *can't* meet our expectation/ desire/need or whether they *won't*, exhaustion sets in. Instead, see what happens when it becomes "They *aren't* making this change I have asked for." When you look at the situation this way, you might be able to move past the grief of "they can't" or the resentment of "they won't" and find yourself able to radically accept the current reality. They aren't meeting your need—now what?

The answer is massively shaped by the context: How big of a deal is it? Your initial first step will also require you to understand why this expectation or desire matters to you. If your partner isn't finding alternatives to raging at you (and is unwilling to go to therapy), you may decide this is a deal breaker. If they aren't finding opportunities to spontaneously validate your parenting, you may decide that you'll drop the resentment, remind yourself of their other awesome qualities, and prompt them to give you more affirmation. As always, be guided by self-compassion. Generosity in the service of love is essential, not shameful.

Relational Self-Awareness Questions

- Do you *need* this change to happen or has a power struggle eclipsed your request?

- Can this need be met by someone else in your life? Consider stating, "I'm going to turn elsewhere for this need, not to punish you but to unburden our relationship."

- Can you forgive this person for not making the change? If not, why not? What are you afraid of losing if you forgive?

- What does this knot remind you of? Are echoes of past hurts shaping how you experience this problem?

When an apology is offered from a place of shame and panic rather than self-reflection and remorse, what's being sought is absolution, not forgiveness.

Imagine that your partner has said or done something that hurts you, and they feel just awful about it. They feel you pulling back in self-protection, and this sends them into a panic. They are afraid of your anger and disappointment. They're afraid of you leaving. So they apologize quickly and voraciously. In this moment, a tremendous amount of relational power flows into your hands. You now hold the power to forgive your partner. Notice what it's like to hold that power:

- How do you feel in your body?

- What's it like to see your partner so unsettled, needing something so earnestly from you?

- What does it remind you of from your past?

Exploring these questions will help you hold onto *yourself* and your needs. The gravitational pull of your partner's shame might feel quite destabilizing for you. You are at risk of being taken right out of your much-needed focus on your hurt. If their shame is noisy and demanding, it will get centered. While this may feel to you like a mercy, it does not serve either of you. If you absolve them before they've had time to self-reflect, they'll miss out on the lessons that arise from sitting with themselves and their actions. They don't get to learn and they're more likely to repeat the same offense in the future.

Furthermore, in your effort to solve an uncomfortable moment by offering hasty forgiveness, you're papering over the impact that your partner's action had on you. If your hurt hasn't been witnessed, you're likely to feel resentful and guarded in the long run.

True forgiveness is about relational resolution. Ultimately you forgive your partner, but the process is all about the "we."

To criticize your partner's body is to reveal your own beliefs, fears, and expectations.

When you fall in love with someone, you fall in love with the body they are living in at that moment in time. You are not promised this as their forever body.

The thoughts, feelings, and attachments you have about your partner's body offer you a superhighway into your own interior! We all have internalized messages that make certain aspects of bodies more or less valuable/desirable/beautiful. While the types of bodies that are elevated may vary from culture to culture, we cannot escape how we have been socialized to understand or perceive beauty.

We are not in charge of our thoughts, but we are in charge of what we *do* with our thoughts. Specifically, we do *not* need to say out loud/invest energy into every thought in our head. Instead, we can:

- **Name the critical thought we are having about our partner's body.** Acknowledge that the thought largely reflects internalized messages.

- **Connect emotionally to that thought.** Perhaps we feel sad that cultural messages lead us to hold our partner in any less than the warmest regards.

- **Choose a different thought.** There are certainly things about our partner other than looks that we adore about them. Choose one that appreciates our partner's health, smile, generosity, or playfulness.

Relational Self-Awareness Questions

- What does a change in your partner's body evoke in you emotionally? Why?

- When was another time in your life when you felt this way?

- What do you fear you partner's changing body says about you? In other words, in what ways do you feel your partner's body is a reflection of yourself?

Relationships are about *both* giving *and* receiving help.

A lot of us have learned to ignore, deny, and suppress our suffering. We only ask for help when we're in a clear and obvious crisis. We wait until we are up against the wall, unable to keep ourselves together for one more second. This pattern has an Origin Story:

- Maybe you inherited cultural messages that equate needing help with weakness, so you formed an identity that people like you can't have needs.

- Maybe you once needed help that didn't arrive, and you swore to never let yourself experience that again.

- Maybe you saw someone use dependence as a means to control others.

Whatever the root cause might be, you now divide the world into two camps: the ones who need help and the ones who provide it. After you've spent so many years identifying as a helper, it becomes terrifying to receive. Being cared for feels wholly disconnected to who you have known yourself to be . . . but allowing yourself to be cared for is wholly necessary for intimacy. Look for opportunities to allow someone to help you and celebrate the courage it takes to try a new relational role.

If you struggle with letting other people care for you, remember how much pleasure there is in being "of service."

The day of my daughter's junior year homecoming dance was one of my favorite kinds of days—my whole day was focused on her.

- We ran last-minute errands to ensure that she had everything she needed for the day.

- I was the jewelry polisher, the granola bar grabber, the flatiron fixer, the head of hydration, and the photographer.

- For a long while, my job was just to sit in her room while she readied herself. Holding space. Present. (Mostly) quiet. Offering opinions when asked and a steady stream of affirmations.

I wasn't taking care of her. I wasn't managing her. I was at her service. What a delightful relational dance! This care-through-service dynamic offers joy in both roles. The server gets to feel productive, helpful, and necessary. The servee gets to feel tended, cherished, and valued. However, being served can also induce tougher feelings:

- **Guilt:** *Are they really okay with this?*

- **Shame:** *Am I worth this level of attention?*

- **Fear:** *What price will I pay for letting myself receive this care?*

Any tender feelings that arise warrant your attention because they hold the power to block you from savoring the experience. If you find yourself struggling with the role of servee, try to remember that the other person is getting the pleasure and honor of being the server:

- They get to stop thinking about their own troubles for a while and place their focus solely on someone else.

- They get to feel powerful. They are making things happen that make the other person feel good.

- They get to feel proud of themselves. Of their patience, their attention to detail, their generosity.

Talk about a win/win! Intimacy needs two people to participate. Let yourself accept being served.

OCTOBER 2

The more your loved one shows you contrition, the more you can look at them with eyes of love.

I once ran out of gas on the way to drop my daughter off at school. She had to walk the rest of the way while I called roadside assistance. Not my finest hour! One of my first thoughts was that I didn't want to tell my husband that this happened. But then I got curious about the urge to cover my tracks. I recognized this urge as a Core Wound of mine that conflates my mistakes with my worth. I put my hand on my heart and took some deep breaths. I reminded myself that I get to be imperfect and loved, that I am a masterpiece and a work in progress. Having forgiven myself, I could report the facts to him without needing either punishment or absolution. And because I owned my mistake, he handled it with a shrug and a smile, just the way I hoped he would.

This is how we all need and deserve to have our mistakes handled, right? My worst-case scenario was that he'd say, "You should have known better," which would have felt cruel *and* would have matched the invalidating, unhelpful stuff I had been telling myself. I vastly reduced the chances of hearing that from him by telling my story openly and without defensiveness.

When we own our humanity, we are at less risk of feeling attacked or criticized by the people around us.

Be the kind of partner who strives to do the kind of things that put a smile on your partner's face. That is not subjugation. That is not being a sucker. That is being relational, and it ought to be a source of pride.

In individualistic cultures, putting yourself first is seen as normal, strong, and desirable. Prioritizing someone else is seen as weak, needy, and desperate. Especially for those of us who grew up in highly individualistic cultures (e.g., those dominant across North America and Europe), accommodating someone else's needs or wants can feel like a loss rather than a source of pride.

However, being in an intimate partnership requires two people to become a "we." Becoming a "we" means both partners:

- Create a shared vision for the future
- Highlight shared values that guide decision-making
- Respect each other's differences
- Honor each other's unique needs and wants
- Cultivate positivity, play, and joy
- Modify their own behavior based on what is best for the relationship

Let's focus on that last one. Modifying your behavior based on what is best for the relationship can feel tricky, even risky. However, one of the hallmarks of a healthy relationship is that you can be generous and self-sacrificing:

- Without worrying that it will be used against you down the road
- Without it becoming an expectation or a relationship rule
- Knowing full well that your partner will do the same for you

Relational Self-Awareness Questions
When you do something for your partner, do you worry that:

- It will be used against you down the road?
- It will become an expectation or a relationship rule?
- Your partner would not do the same for you?

Which of the above most resonates for you? What does that worry remind you of? Have you had that experience before? In this relationship? In a prior relationship? In your Family of Origin? What do you want your partner to understand about this fear?

OCTOBER 4

If you and your partner are recovering from a betrayal, having fun together is fuel, not forgiveness.

Trust rebuilds by doing the hard emotional work together. The partner who did harm practices healthy boundaries, demonstrates remorse, and stays calm in the face of the hurt partner's upset. The hurt partner stretches a little, asks questions (instead of attacking), expresses sadness (instead of rage), and practices lots of self-care (instead of self-destruction).

Trust also rebuilds by having fun together. Having dates, traveling, laughing, making love. These experiences help reset a hypervigilant nervous system and remind both partners that the hard stuff is worth it.

Sometimes the hurt partner is afraid to have fun for fear it will convey to the one who did harm that the hard stuff is over. But two things can be true at once:

1. We need and deserve positive experiences together.

2. We are still in a process of rebuilding.

Delight and diligence must coexist. The hurt partner may need to say out loud, "I want to make love, but it doesn't mean I've fully forgiven you." The one who has done harm may need to say out loud, "I appreciate you letting me hold you. I know we're not out of the woods." Moment by moment and day by day, rebuilding trust is possible for couples who are willing to have courageous conversations and create moments of levity and play.

OCTOBER 5

Marry your friend.

Research shows that the happiest marriages have a deep and abiding friendship at their core. Because passions ebb and flow, chemistry is far too fickle a beast to carry a lifelong commitment. While chemistry is necessary but not sufficient, friendship is a beautiful bedrock.

Here's what a foundation of friendship looks like to me:

•   Mutual admiration

- Being able to hold each other in warm regard
- Being able to trust that you're traveling in the same direction
- Delighting in each other's achievements
- Appreciating each other's perspectives as additive rather than threatening
- .Cutting each other slack
- Meeting each other's low or cranky moods with gentleness, not judgment

Marry someone who has your back. Someone whose back is easy for you to have. Marry someone who brags on you. And someone you love being proud of. Marry someone who lightens your load. And someone you feel delighted to care for in return. Marry your friend.

OCTOBER 6

In the best of worlds, we get to meet our parents again and again because they, and our relationship to our childhood, continue to evolve.

Dr. Mona Fishbane, one of my beloved mentors, encourages us to view our parents as our grandparents' children. Through that lens, we can catch glimpses of a parent's resilience: how they were deprived, what they endured, what they overcame, and the emotional/relational tools they could not have developed before they were tasked with raising us. This perspective shows us how two things can be true at the same time:

1. Your parents did the best they could do when you were little.
2. You didn't get what you needed when you were little.

Holding both truths is essential for our health. Let's look at what happens when we overlook one truth or the other:

- If you focus solely on how bad your parent had it, you're at risk of stuffing your feelings, invalidating your needs, and getting walked on in your relationships.

- If you focus solely on how you didn't get what you needed when you were little, you're at risk of creating an emotional cutoff from them, and you're at risk of asking others to heal an emotional wound they didn't create.

> In some cases, emotional cutoffs between adult kids
> and their parents are necessary for self-preservation.

We are all works in progress. A parent who can talk humbly to their adult kid about how they weren't able to be who the adult kid needed them to be is some of the realest and most beautiful stuff ever! It doesn't "make up for" early pain, but witnessing is healing.

OCTOBER 7

Remember not to confuse something that is private with something that is shameful.

With trust comes disclosure, and trust is earned with time and experience. As you get to know someone, there will be things you wait to share. You are not hiding or keeping stuff from this person you are getting to know. Do not shroud in shame those stories or facts that are still private for you. Let them just be private, not because they are shameful, but because the relationship is not yet ready to hold them.

When you decide to disclose, you deserve to be told by the other person, "Thank you for trusting me with something private" (a response that will reinforce the ever-growing trust between you), not "You should have told me sooner!" (a response that indicates you've done something bad/wrong/shameful). When it comes to opening up to someone you love, you get to take the time you need to cultivate trust and security with that person. Trust that your heart will help you know when you're feeling safe enough to share a tender part of your story with them.

> It's important to note that people need informed consent—for example, you may need to know about each other's sexual health status or any other facts that could put your partner in danger in any way.

OCTOBER 8

There is no "right" or "best" pathway to become a couple, but it is worth examining your biases and preferences around how to fall in love.

Some people catch their love interest's eye across a crowded bar. Others meet while getting their sweat on at the gym. Some people get set up on a date by a mutual friend. Lots (and lots) of people swipe right. And some of us are friends . . . who become lovers. Recent research compared different pathways for falling in love and found that the friends-to-lovers pathway to romance is "prevalent, preferred, and overlooked by science." Fascinating, right?

Todd and I were good friends for many months who drank some beer and then kissed a little and then went back to friends and then maybe kissed some more. I remember that I was so caught between fear and faith:

- **Fear:** I remember how scared I was to date him, in part because I didn't want to risk losing our friendship. But it was more than that—I was afraid that something might be off or doomed about a relationship that began as a friendship. That something wasn't "right" with our chemistry.

- **Faith:** I knew that I felt safe with him, comfortable around him, seen by him, valued by him. I knew I loved his humor and his ambition. I'm glad I chose faith over fear.

It makes sense to me that science overlooks the friends-first path. It doesn't fit with our collective, romanticized, meet-cute, butterflies-in-the-tummy sense of how love begins. I love that (some) researchers believe what they see instead of seeing what they believe.

Let's celebrate all of the love stories. The ones that sizzle with early chemistry and the ones that build with a slow burn. The ones that take off like a flash and the ones that marinate into something rich and delectable.

What are your biases and preferences when it comes to how relationships begin?

OCTOBER 9

Making a heartfelt apology is a key relationship skill.

We hurt people who matter to us. It's such an unfortunate and inevitable reality. Being willing to offer a heartfelt apology helps. The problem is that few of us learned how to do this in our Family of Origin. And we sure as heck don't see it modeled in our culture. Making a heartfelt apology is a key relationship skill. Here's how to do it:

- **Take responsibility:** "I did X."

- **Name the impact:** "My action hurt you."

- **Bear witness:** "Tell me how you're feeling."

- **Offer to repair:** "I wonder if this would help."

- **Avoid *if*:** "I'm sorry if I hurt you."

- **Avoid *but*:** "But I didn't mean it."

- **Avoid passive voice:** "Sorry you were offended."

- **Avoid cross-complaining:** "You did Y."

Research shows that the most important ingredient in an apology is acknowledgment of responsibility. This one can be tough. Some of us get blocked because we slip into a shame spiral. Some of us focus on how we wouldn't have done our bad thing if they hadn't done their bad thing. Maybe we believe we wouldn't feel hurt if the tables were turned—this belief blocks our repair as well.

Would it be different if you knew that owning your hurtful behavior helps? Standing in accountability helps heal the rift between you and the person you love. Far from being a sign of weakness, taking responsibility takes strength. It sets the other person up to begin their forgiveness work *and* gives you the opportunity to witness yourself standing in your integrity.

OCTOBER 10

Marriage involves becoming a member of your partner's family.

Marriage takes you more deeply into another family system: new traditions, new responsibilities, new loyalties. Here are a few thoughts about joining your partner's Family of Origin:

- **Remember that you have a set of patterns and tendencies that are uniquely yours.** You are shaped by your personality and your history. Do you tend to jump in with both feet? Do you tend to hang back and observe the scene for a while?

- **Your partner's family system has its own idiosyncrasies around welcoming someone new.** Do they tend to fling the doors wide open and turn newcomers into insiders right away? Are they wary of outsiders, perhaps because self-protection has been essential to their family's survival?

- **It's very different to be the first newcomer versus the sixth.** Your partner's family may be slow to warm up simply because this is their first rodeo.

- **What you focus on will amplify.** Look for moments of sweetness and ease as you get to know these people, rather than scanning for evidence that you're being scrutinized, rejected, or marginalized.

- **Expect these relationships to deepen over time.** The fifth Thanksgiving, tenth Sunday dinner, or twentieth family party will feel different from the first few.

Be careful not to take personally that which might be a systemic dynamic. Remember that it will take time to form bonds and rapport with this new family of yours. Be gentle with yourself and celebrate the small wins along the way.

OCTOBER 11

Marriage involves integrating your partner into your family.

Let's look at what it's like to help your partner get to know *your* Family of Origin. Many of the statements in yesterday's entry hold true. I would also add:

- **Be a "cultural ambassador."** It's lovely to ask your partner how you can be of assistance while they are introduced and integrated into your family system. Do they want you to stay close by and help grease the wheels? Are they okay being turned loose to get to know your people however feels best?

- **Your partner doesn't have the same history with your Family of Origin that you have.** See what it's like to experience your family through your partner's eyes. They might bring far more generosity and levity to the experience than you are able to bring. See this as an opportunity, not a threat!

The bottom line is that it can be pretty special to watch the people you love learning to love each other! As those connections deepen, your connection with your partner may deepen as well.

OCTOBER 12

Interrupting someone is a boundary violation of sorts, causing a rift in understanding, connection, and trust.

Interrupting is a common relational behavior, and how we perceive it and react to it depends on context. Research by Dr. Katherine Hilton has shown that people can be lumped broadly into two categories:

- **High intensity speakers:** These folks are uncomfortable with moments of silence in conversation and consider talking at the same time a sign of engagement.

- **Low intensity speakers:** These folks find simultaneous chatter to be rude and prefer people to speak one at a time in conversation.

Your relationship with interruption depends on which team you're on. If you're a high intensity speaker, you likely don't mind being interrupted, so long as the other person is agreeing with you and amplifying what you're saying. If you're a low intensity speaker, even an "agreeable interruption" feels rude to you. But people in both groups likely agree that when the interrupter is changing the topic or raising their voice, it sucks.

I've seen many conflicts escalate when people interrupt each other. I've also seen conflicts head down gnarly side streets when people fight about what counts as interrupting. Perceptions of and reactions to interruptions are somewhat idiosyncratic, so couples must create ground rules. Maybe in your partner's mind, they are showing their enthusiasm and empathy when they jump in. But if you tell your partner it feels rude to you, then your partner's work is to practice letting their face show their investment in what you're saying, rather than their voice.

If your partner agrees to stop interrupting, I encourage you to be mindful about how long you hold the floor. Your partner may interrupt because they feel you are going on a bit too long and not leaving space for their perspective or questions. I don't want to put a time limit/word count, but it's important to attune yourself to your listener:

- How engaged do they look?

- How much space are you making for them?

- What's driving you to talk right now?

- What are you afraid might happen if you give your partner the floor?

How we manage the process of a conversation can build or erode trust. If we agree to stop interrupting, we must also agree to share responsibility to ensure everyone is heard.

Love's irony: Something may feel (to you) like an expression of loving protection while at the very same time feeling (to them) like undermining or a lack of faith.

I told Todd that I had created a silly game to be played during a summer vacation with my extended family. The goal was for the kids in the family to get to know the men (dads, uncles, and grandpa) in the family a little better:

Todd: "This plan is doomed."

Alexandra: "Thanks for the vote of confidence!"

We headed out for a walk and worked it through:

Todd: "There's just no guarantee that your family members will receive your game the way you intend them to, and I don't want you to get hurt. I am a lawyer—I get paid to look around corners."

Alexandra: "Thanks for your concern. I'm feeling good about it. I will share the game with love and release the outcome!"

Our work is to create a marriage that allows us to be who we are. I don't want Todd to bite his tongue even though his perspective has the power to hurt my feelings at times. He doesn't want me to squelch my vision of family fun, even when my ideas sometimes crash and burn.

I want the realists of the world to remember to:

- **Own your concern when you express it.** "I am feeling concerned…"

- **Verbalize the intent.** "I know you're trying to create a fun experience…"
- **Bonus points for explicit praise:** "I love your creativity."

I want the dreamers of the world to remember:

- **Other people's concerns are their concerns.** What you do with their concerns is up to you. Be accountable.
- **You can hold two things at once.** Their worry and your willingness to take a risk.
- **Bonus points for explicit praise:** "I love your desire to protect me from harm."

When the realist and the dreamer can come together in this way, they can replace their extremes (risk-aversion and impulsivity) with the harmonious traits of groundedness and creativity.

Commitment transitions, like moving in together, activate anxiety. This is inevitable and must be approached as a team.

Moving in together is big! You are taking a step into a deeper sense of commitment, which is lovely and terrifying at the very same time. When you cohabit, you get the yummy stuff like sharing a bed, waking up together, and enjoying life's ordinary moments. But you have to be ready to deal with the emotional activation that emerges when two lives become increasingly entwined. Even in a happy and healthy relationship, domesticity is a trigger for misunderstanding, frustration, and mismatched expectations! For example:

- When you do the dishes while your partner checks their email, you are at risk of getting flooded with images of your "worst-case scenario": the disappearing woman.

- When you go longer than usual without making love, you are at risk of getting scared that you're becoming that dreaded "sexless couple" that articles have warned you about.

Make it a practice to notice when those fear-loaded stories begin to creep in so you can stop catastrophizing and meet the moment. Talk with your partner about your fear without making your fear your partner's fault. Talk together about the routines and agreements that work for you both. By acknowledging that the commitment or lifestyle change you've made together has significantly shifted things around, you can approach challenges with compassion, lightness, and team spirit rather than blame and shame.

Our wounds and our gifts are often next-door neighbors.

It's a beautiful and complicated truth that our gifts are often forged in the fire of our wounds. For example:

- Your passion for advocacy is rooted in your childhood experience of being bullied.

- Your deep empathy is born of your experience of feeling misunderstood.

- Your ambition is rooted in your childhood efforts to excel; this was your effort to manage a Family of Origin that felt out of control.

- Your artistic talent began as a need to create a fantasy world that allowed you to escape a painful reality.

- Your social justice work emerges from your experiences of racism, homophobia, sexism, antisemitism, or ableism.

- Your excellence in hosting and creating welcoming spaces offers solace to the lonely kid you once were.

It's awe-inspiring that we can become now what we needed then. When we become aware that this duality is part of our story, it can make us feel strong and proud. We can feel the heartbeat of our resilience. When someone else sees it and says "Wow!" it can feel really affirming.

But there's a deeper layer we sometimes miss. When we realize that a gift/talent is compensatory—that is, an effort to heal or make up for something—we may turn against it, believing it somehow counts less. Let's commit to never minimizing our gifts. If anything, gifts with tender Origin Stories warrant even more celebration. They are the reward for saving ourselves.

OCTOBER 16

If your Family of Origin confused your behavior with your character, you may have grown into an adult who is prone to defensiveness.

Defensiveness is a common (and problematic) Coping Strategy that may reflect any number of Origin Stories. For example, if the grown-ups in your Family of Origin confused your behavior with your character, your tendency toward defensiveness as an adult makes so much sense. It is not an excuse, but it is a context.

When a grown-up talks to a kid about their less-than-desired behavior as *behavior*, it sounds like this:

- "You got so mad at your brother, didn't you?"
- "You really didn't want to go to grandma's house to visit, did you?"
- "You are really raising your voice right now, aren't you?"

By using impermanent, descriptive words, the grown-up is conveying that this behavior is just a behavior. In contrast, when a grown-up talks to a kid about their less-than-desired behavior as *character*, it sounds like this:

- "You are such an angry person."
- "You are so stubborn."
- "You are impossible."

By using permanent, identity-based words, the grown-up conveys that the behavior is *who* this kid is.

We all need and deserve the opportunity to define ourselves, be seen as more than our unsavory moments, and have the ability to develop, grow, change, evolve. If you didn't have that growing up, it's no wonder that conflict with an intimate partner feels immensely threatening. You are terrified that your partner will squish you down with a label you cannot climb out from under. Rather than protesting a misunderstanding with someone you love, you are fighting a battle for self-definition, for sovereignty. Try to remember this the next time you work through a knot with your partner. Can you offer Little You compassion, even when you've made a mistake?

Consent is a series of verbal and nonverbal feedback loops that ensure safety, connection, and pleasure.

Consent involves far more than "no means no." No is the basement, the bare minimum. A commitment to not violate is miles away from a desire to please. My favorite analogy for the new model of consent is that sex is like jazz improv. Musicians create something beautiful by tuning into each other and flowing together in a moment-by-moment way. Similarly, the greatest sexual experiences require that we attune ourselves to our partner so we can play in a present-focused and responsive way.

Relational Self-Awareness Questions

- Who taught you about consent?
- What did they teach you?
- How do you ensure consent in your sexual experiences today?

Holding your partner in warm regard fosters intimacy. Putting them on a pedestal erodes it.

There's a world of difference between *admiration* and *idealization*. The basic difference is this:

- **Your admiration of your partner is about *them*.** You are seeing (and admiring) their talents, beauty, courage, kindness, ambition.

- **Your idealization of your partner is about *you*.** It is inherently comparative. As you elevate your partner, you denigrate yourself.

Admiration is relational. Admiration fuels intimacy because it is a feeling predicated upon intersubjectivity: *I see you. I witness you. I hold onto myself while celebrating you. Your love of me feels thrilling, not threatening.*

Idealization, on the other hand, is self-referential. A hall of mirrors. Idealization erodes intimacy—if you have your partner high on a pedestal, you can't reach them. Your perception of their perfection only serves to highlight your awareness of your defects. Rather than celebrating your partner, the arc of emotion bends back to you, and you feel shrunken in their presence. Intimacy cannot occur because you are too busy picking yourself apart to connect with them. Worse yet, if your partner is on a pedestal, you are at risk of punishing them for their accomplishments, seeing these as slights against you or evidence that they will leave you. This dynamic primes you to search for signs of their disinterest.

Loving someone will shine a spotlight on what needs to be healed. Treat the idealization of a partner as a symptom, pointing you toward the need to heal a story of your inadequacy in the service of love.

OCTOBER 19

One of the most loving questions we can ask is "How can I support you right now?"

I love questions. But this is the questioniest question of them all! Let's explore why. When someone you love is hurting, you feel a stir of emotions too. Emotions are contagious like that. Plus, emotions are bodily states. The sequence ends up like this:

1. Someone you love is upset.

2. You feel upset.

3. Your upset acts like a signal.

4. You leap into action in response to this internal signal.

That last step can get you into trouble. Action mode (problem-solving, validation, comfort, distraction, follow-up questions, etc.) arises from a loving place inside of you. Your offers are made with the best of intentions. But here's the gut punch: These actions also contain an element of arrogance and projection. Each of these actions assumes that you know what is needed.

Further, any/all of these actions may also be an extension of your own discomfort sitting with your loved one's upset. You may be attempting to soothe their hurt in an attempt, in part, to regulate your own upset. The question "How can I support you right now?" helps us by:

- Slowing us down

- Putting power and autonomy into the upset person's hands

- Freeing us of the responsibility of mind-reading

- Inviting us to the intimate act of building a bridge between two people

OCTOBER 20

Normalize going to couples therapy.

Romantic myths say that an intimate relationship should happen naturally. Real-world love shows that most of us enter intimate partnership without having learned the skills and tools we need. Romantic myths say that if love is right, it's easy. Real-world love shows that there is great healing potential in the messy work of loving and being loved. Romantic myths say that we should never hurt or be hurt in an intimate relationship. Real-world love shows that an intimate relationship will activate old patterns and old pain. We need and deserve time and space to discern between what was then and what is now.

Listening to these romantic myths can make it hard for couples to advocate for their relationship by seeking couples therapy. Asking for help can feel tantamount to admitting defeat. But seeking couples therapy is a sign of strength, not weakness. It reflects the depth of your investment, not your brokenness. Couples who seek therapy deserve to feel proud, not ashamed. When you go to couples therapy, you are saying to yourselves and each other that this relationship is worthy of investment.

OCTOBER 21

Your body is yours. You cannot invite someone into a space that does not belong to you.

Maybe you were never told that your body belongs to you. Maybe you thought it was yours until it was mistreated, and now there's distance between you and your sacred earthly home. Be assured that reclamation is always possible. The connection you have with yourself may be disrupted, but it cannot be destroyed. Being able to truly enjoy sexual connection with another person begins with an ability to enjoy connection to yourself:

- Can you listen to your body?
- Can you be patient with your body?
- Can you be curious about how pleasure builds inside of you?

Sometimes people say something like, "I don't have a trauma history. Why do I feel so disconnected from my body?" If you have been raised in the feminine, all you have to do is look at how society holds women's bodies in collective contempt. How we feel entitled to comment on and regulate them. How we judge them endlessly.

Layer in the fact that sex education and pleasure don't go together. Add in mainstream porn, which makes sex look more like a performance than an expression of self. This perfect storm of factors makes it understandable to feel like your sexual self belongs to everyone but you. If this is an area of healing for you, go slowly and be sweet to yourself.

OCTOBER 22

Your primary trusting relationship is the one you have with yourself.

Research by Dr. Susan Johnson has shown that what distinguishes couples who are able to recover from infidelity from those who are not is the degree to which the person who breached trust is willing to remain attentive, open, and responsive to the pain of the one who has been betrayed. But it isn't easy:

- To stay steady in the fact of your partner's rage
- To be accountable and review the sequence of events
- To tolerate the shame that arises when you're confronted with the impact of your choices

Relational witnessing is the only thing that stands a chance of healing relational pain. But the betrayed partner needs something more: a trusting relationship with themselves. One that allows them to say to themselves, *I am exploring the potential for healing. I don't know where this will go. But I know I am worthy and whole no matter what. I promise not to get self-critical if this bold experiment does not work.*

To even have a chance at rebuilding trust, the "offending" partner must bring patience and an open heart, while the betrayed partner must bring courage and self-compassion. That's the stuff of relational resilience.

OCTOBER 23

"Sometimes, when we're lying together, I look at her and I feel dizzy with the realization that here is another distinct person from me, who has memories, origins, thoughts, feelings that are different from my own. That tension between familiarity and mystery meshes something strong between us."

—Barack Obama

This is my all-time favorite quote about love. I reference it in nearly every talk I give. Intimacy is about occupying a Both/And space:

- Both familiarity and mystery
- Both comfort and surprise
- Both known and unknown
- Both confident and humble

You will never have your partner all figured out. Whatever you think you know reflects only this moment. They are a moving target, ever-changing across time and space. So are you. If you think you're done learning about your partner, it might be time for a self-awareness gut check. What purpose might that story serve for you? Does it keep you safe? Does it allow you to pull back or disengage?

Leaning in is far from a risk-free endeavor, so your hesitance to dive in is understandable. Peeling back another layer means shaking up the homeostasis of your relationship. The side effect of seeing your partner with fresh eyes is letting yourself be seen anew as well. I don't care if you've been together for decades, the fear that says *If you really saw me, you couldn't love me* is ever-present. When it comes to intimacy, risk and reward are inextricably bound.

OCTOBER 24

If you have only ever solved stuff on your own, you will treat a "we problem" like a "me problem."

A man and a woman are in the early stages of dating:

- Something happens—a disappointment or a misunderstanding.
- She raises the problem.
- He ends the relationship saying, "I can't give you what you want."
- She's left with a fear of attracting only emotionally unavailable men.

> I've given this scenario in gendered terms,
> but this doesn't mean it's the only way it happens.

Freeze on that moment of disappointment/misunderstanding. That moment is a *relational* dilemma. A two-person problem. Both people need to roll up their sleeves and ask themselves:

- *What old stories are getting activated in me?*
- *What am I afraid of?*
- *Who does my partner remind me of in this moment?*

If your Family of Origin left you to figure stuff out alone, you will tend to make unilateral decisions in inherently relational dilemmas. Why? Because you're inexperienced at sitting in discomfort *with* another person. This is how you survived being left alone with big feelings when you were young—you are simply doing what you've always done. So you decide something like, "They're too demanding," and dream about finding someone you have yet to disappoint.

Insight into how the past shapes the present is the first step toward breaking old cycles and creating space for a new, richer connection.

OCTOBER 25

If you cannot allow yourself to feel deeply, you will forever deem your partner's emotions to be overreactions.

If you've spent a lifetime priding yourself on being logical, you will likely judge your partner for being emotional. If you've spent a lifetime soothing yourself, you will feel contemptuous of your partner's need for comfort. If you've spent a lifetime "sucking it up," you will criticize your partner's requests for change.

When a couple gets caught in a pattern, having different versions of the same fight over and over that leaves each partner feeling misunderstood and unheard, polarization is inevitably in the mix. You judge them as too emotional. They judge you as too shut down. Round and round you go, the chasm between you growing with each iteration.

Healing begins by peeling back the layers of what your partner's emotionality evokes in you. From there, avenues for insight open. As it turns out:

- **A part of you might feel jealous that they allow their strong feelings.** That which we envy, we hold in contempt.

- **A part of you might feel scared that their strong feelings mean they will leave you.** That which frightens us, we seek to control.

- **A part of you might feel lonely when they are mad/sad.** That which threatens us, we seek to fix.

Your reactions to your partner are direct pathways to your Core Wounds, but only if you're willing to let go of your judgment of them and explore the landscape of your interior. That stuff is uncomfortable and disturbing. But your reward for this discomfort is that you get to feel braver and more whole. Your partner's reward for your discomfort is getting to feel safer in your presence. Everyone wins!

Gaslighting is defensiveness with the volume turned all the way up.

The term *gaslighting* originates from a 1944 movie about a man trying to drive his wife crazy to steal her inheritance. He alters the gaslights in their home, and when she says, "Is it darker in here?" he says, "Nope."

Gaslighting is a conscious and systematic distorting of reality, denying facts or feelings to get someone to question their memory, perception, or sanity. Gaslighting takes "You're wrong" and turns it into:

- "You're making it up."
- "That's not what happened."
- "You're confused/sick/crazy."

If you feel that your partner is gaslighting you:

- Stay focused on the facts, not the feelings.
- Use "I" statements to help you stand in your reality and help your partner hear your reality.
- Consider couples therapy so you have another source of data.
- Evaluate the viability of the relationship.

In 2022, there was a 1,740 percent increase in internet searches for this term—no wonder Merriam-Webster declared it the word of the year. What the dictionary didn't say, however, is that disagreeing is not the same as gaslighting.

Our pain can be big, and we want the other person to recognize/see/validate it. Our partner feels the same way. That conflict can feel truly crazy-making: "Why can't you see it the way I see it?"

It's so painful when someone cannot or will not stand in our shoes. Neither partner deserves to be left alone in their pain. You must learn to hold your partner's pain alongside your own so both of you can stand shoulder to shoulder, looking together at this messy and painful situation.

OCTOBER 27

Love is a skill.

I've been teaching people how to love for a very long time . . . except I don't really teach them so much as *remind* them:

- How to reconnect with love
- How to move with love, not against it
- How to be skilled, aware, present
- How to be truthful and brave in love

We are not starting from scratch. We already are love. Made of it. Built from it. Full of it. Love is who we are, and learning about love is a journey of remembrance and reclamation.

Relational Self-Awareness Prompts

- Love is . . .
- What helps me love bravely is . . .
- What I want to remember about love is . . .
- When I was little, I learned that love . . .
- What I know to be true about love is . . .
- I am most loving when I . . .

OCTOBER 28

You need and deserve to feel deeply connected to your you-est you.

We can become disconnected from ourselves for all kinds of reasons:

- Investing so much in productivity that we don't invest enough in inner listening
- Investing so much in pleasing others that we don't recognize the sound of our own voice

- Investing so much in survival that we lose track of joy

- Investing so much in work that we stop prioritizing movement and healthy eating

- Investing so much in achievement/striving that we fail to honor our enough-ness right here right now

There are so many more. What are your exit doors from connection to yourself?

> We must acknowledge that connection with self is far easier when people have adequate social safety nets: living wages, compassionate work settings, reverence for the care economy, reproductive rights, protection from violence and oppression based on identity variables.

Relational Self-Awareness Prompts

- I lose myself . . .

- I find myself . . .

- I'm the one who . . .

- I am my favorite me when . . .

OCTOBER 29

Although it may feel paradoxical at first glance, we are stronger and braver when we can tolerate ambivalence.

Many of us have internalized the unhealthy belief that certainty equals strength. Culturally, we tend to idealize clarity, definitiveness, and surety, and we hold contempt for ambivalence, flux, and contradiction. However, essential aspects of emotional resilience include:

- The ability to tolerate complexity
- The ability to shift perspective in light of new information
- The ability to hold contradictory truths within ourselves and within our relationships

During an emotionally charged conversation with Todd, part of me feels wise and clear, wanting to give him the benefit of the doubt and work together toward common ground. Another part of me feels stubborn and stuck, wanting to stay within my narrow perspective and push him away.

The more I can make space for this internal multiplicity, the savvier I can be about how I respond. I must hold onto the Both/And, rather than labeling one feeling "right" and one feeling "wrong" or stuffing one feeling and acting on the other. I find it helpful to say it out loud: "Part of me is ready to connect, and part of me feels so stuck." This helps Todd understand me more deeply. It helps me feel less flustered and more present.

Relational Self-Awareness Prompts

- I feel both ____ and ____.
- I want both ____ and ____.
- My relationship is both ____ and ____.

OCTOBER 30

In a moment of frustration, when you can remember that your partner is your ally, not

your adversary, you can stop fighting against your partner and start fighting for connection.

So often we experience conflict with our partner as a zero-sum proposition:

- Either you win or your partner wins.
- Either you are right or your partner is right.
- Either you are being reasonable or your partner is being reasonable.

Framing conflict in this way is the inevitable result of an individualistic, hyper-competitive culture that prioritizes production/accomplishment/outcome/doing over sustainability/collaboration/process/being. We are all socialized this way, like it or not. So of course we are at risk of viewing conflict as a battle instead of an opportunity.

Zero-sum sounds like:

- "You aren't here when I need you!"
- "You don't understand me!"
- "You're not putting any effort into our relationship!"

The process of learning how to be deeply and abidingly relational is subversive. It requires unlearning and reimagining what we have been taught and what we have learned about success. It requires humility and a willingness to be confused.

Relationality sounds like:

- "I'm feeling disconnected. Can we talk?"
- "I feel like we're talking past each other. Do you feel like we're on different pages?"
- "I would love for us to figure out how to prioritize our relationship a bit more. I love feeling cherished by you."

Zero-sum is low vulnerability and high blame. Relationality is high vulnerability and low blame. When we fight together for connection, love and intimacy win.

It is uncomfortable to look at past choices we made because we didn't know then what we know now.

On the journey of Relational Self-Awareness, we name, perhaps for the first time, experiences of being mistreated, misunderstood, misled. We also look at our own past choices, many made from a place of reactivity, defensiveness, and an absence of awareness. Knowing how these choices hurt us, and hurt people around us, is why we need to go ever so slowly with our emotional work. Peel back a layer. Have a cry. Hand on the heart. Send self-compassion. Let it sit. Peel back another layer.

You have your whole life to figure you out. What a blessing and a mercy that is. We learn to repair and pivot instead of digging in and doubling down.

No matter where you are on your journey, I want to remind you to be gentle with yourself as you work on your healing. You deserve nothing less than your steady self-compassion.

When one of your parents talks negatively to you about your other parent, it's a boundary violation.

Triangulation is the term for bringing a third person (in this example, you) into a dynamic between two other people (in this example, your parents). Triangulation typically happens when parents are in an unhappy marriage or going through a divorce, and a child (even an adult child) is enlisted as a sounding board, ally, or pseudo-therapist in one parent's relationship problem with the other parent.

> "Other parent" can also refer to a stepparent
> or other attachment figure/grown-up.
>
> Note that this is different from one parent protecting
> their child from another parent who presents a real danger.

Let's examine this more closely. First, what may fuel a parent's urge to vent to their kids?

- **Loneliness:** A parent may be poorly resourced in terms of friends. But you cannot be your parent's therapist.

- **Fear:** A parent may be afraid of losing their kid to the other parent. But you are not a chess piece.

- **Trust:** A parent might be worried about outsiders knowing the family's "dirty laundry," so a kid is a safe place to vent. But you are not your parent's vault.

- **Anger:** A parent may be justified in their rage and hurt, so much so that trashing the other to their kid feels obvious. But you are not the judge or the jury.

I want to validate that you deserve a relationship with each parent that exists separately from your parents' relationship with each other. Healthy boundaries with your Family of Origin build the bandwidth and capacity you need to nourish your intimate relationship.

Ending or redirecting a conversation can be an act of love.

Triangulation brings a third person into a conflicted dynamic between two others. But triangulation can get disrupted, such as when you say to your parent something like, "I love you, and . . .

- . . . I'm not able to participate in a conversation about my other parent."

- . . . your concerns are valid, but you'll need to bring them to someone else."

- . . . it's very painful for me to be pulled into your relationship problems like this."

- . . . I need to change the topic."

Clarity is not cruelty. In fact, disrupting triangulation protects all of you from the detrimental internal and relational impact of poor boundaries.

If you've been your parent's pseudo-therapist for a long time, change will be hard. For them and for you. Your parent might be skilled at sucking you back in while you are still learning to stand in your power. Catching and redirecting the conversation will get easier with practice.

If you refuse to participate in triangulation, you still get to participate in validation:

- You can remind your parent how strong/brave/kind/resourceful they are.

- You can remind them that they have survived 100 percent of their bad days.

- You can offer to help them connect with a therapist/book/podcast/support group.
- You can offer giggles, snacks, happy reminiscing, time together.

When you lift the weight of triangulation off the relationship, you create space for a different experience of your parent—and for them to have a different experience of you.

Even if you "have the right" to go where you want, when you want, your relationship will be much stronger and healthier if you: Ask rather than announce. Coordinate rather than command. Decide together rather than declare.

Whether I am talking with my 22-year-old college students in class or my 52-year-old couples in therapy, one issue transcends all other relationship challenges: navigating time together and time apart.

I believe that each of us has a "relative set point" for how much couple time versus solo time we need. Having a strong need for couple time isn't better than having a strong need for solo time (or vice versa), but differences between partners' set points can definitely be a source of tension. There is also the difference in *how* couples make their plans. Do you ask your partner if it's okay to go out with friends or plan a solo trip? Or do you announce it?

What are your associations with the idea of *asking* your partner before you make solo plans? For some people, this approach evokes in them feelings of powerlessness, loss of agency, being "one-down" in the relationship. It feels like a child getting permission from a parent.

What are your associations with the idea of *announcing* to your partner that you're making solo plans? For some people, this approach feels powerful and confident. It feels like they are ensuring they can't be mistreated or taken advantage of.

At the heart of an intimate relationship is ongoing willingness to check in, collaborate, and co-create a vision of a day/week/month/lifetime. Therefore, an ask is not to ensure that you have permission, but rather to ensure that you convey to your partner that you are aware that your individual choices affect them (and vice versa).

An ask sounds less like, "May I please have dinner with my friends on Thursday?"

It sounds more like, "I'd like to head out for dinner with my friends on Thursday. How does that sound to you?"

Rather than a burden, asking can be viewed as a sacred responsibility. Rather than a constraint to freedom, asking can be viewed as a way of solidifying the bond between you. Asking provides each of you the freedom to express your individuality through solo plans, adventures, and hobbies.

NOVEMBER 4

We reduce polarization by seeking the nuggets of reasonableness in the other person's position.

Our culture's investment in the creation of binaries makes polarization inevitable:

- Masculine/feminine
- Good/bad

- Thinking/feeling
- White/Black
- Weak/strong
- Independent/dependent

Unsurprisingly, polarization is a common "presenting problem" when couples come to therapy. Couples move from polarization to collaboration by recognizing that perspective creates perception, by standing where their partner is standing and by working to view the problem through their partner's eyes.

Relational Self-Awareness Prompts

- What I understand about my partner's perspective is . . .
- If I were my partner, I can imagine feeling . . .
- What must be difficult for my partner is . . .

NOVEMBER 5

Dating is risky and requires tolerance of the unknown.

We cannot be 100 percent certain about all the variables in dating. This can feel quite confronting to those of us who relish our illusions of control. Forward motion in a relationship requires someone to step out onto a limb and invite the other to cross over into something more. The tightening in the chest you might feel in this moment reflects that a risk is being taken. If you are the one taking a step by expressing your interest, and the other person isn't ready, willing, or interested, you are going to stand at a crossroads when it comes to your reaction and path forward from there:

- Path 1 is disappointment: *I'm bummed about the outcome.*
  - "What a bummer that I won't get to kiss those lips."
  - "How frustrating that what I had hoped for isn't going to happen."
- Path 2 is shame: *I'm a fool for having tried.*
  - "What a fool I am for thinking I had a chance."
  - "How embarrassing that I imagined myself worthy of affection."

On Path 1, you will need some time and some self-care, but your relationship with yourself remains intact. Path 2 means abandoning yourself and allowing the other person's response to determine your sense of self.

If you catch yourself heading down Path 2, course correct by reminding yourself that Path 1 exists. After all, shame does a good job of convincing us that it's our only option. Affirm that the situation sucks but celebrate the courage it takes to do something as hard and brave as proclaiming your interest.

NOVEMBER 6

If you've spent a lifetime in people-pleasing mode, You're going to feel salty when someone says no to your request.

What's harder for you: being the helper or the helpee? I am infinitely more comfortable being the helper, and I suspect I'm far from alone. When I began writing books, I quickly realized that publishing takes a village. Over the years, I have needed to put myself out there and ask all kinds of people for all kinds of stuff. Which means that I have heard all kinds of no. Polite nos. Kind nos. Clear nos.

Early on, I noticed that my response to hearing no was anger. I did not feel angry that their no meant I would not get the thing I wanted from them. Instead, I felt angry about the apparent clarity and ease with which they said no.

That which we judge or protest in someone else usually holds a key to our own inner world. For much of my life, I have felt profoundly obliged to accommodate every request that is made of me. In part, this is a wonderful and aligned expression of me. I love to be of service. In part, saying *yes* keeps me from sitting with the discomfort that accompanies disappointing someone else. Historically, disappointing someone else has felt more painful for me than stretching myself too thin.

Other people's nos were wonderful teachers, pointing me toward an area in need of healing. I am making good progress. In fact, I recently said no to something, and my publicist replied, "Good job on saying no!" She knows that I am a people-pleaser in recovery and that affirmation helps.

NOVEMBER 7

When you ask but do not receive, be careful not to confuse disappointment with shame.

When faced with your partner's *no*, there are two options:

- **Stay with *disappointment*.** Direct your negative emotion outward—not at the other person but at the limitation/boundary/ refusal itself.

- **Slip into *shame*.** Direct your negative emotion inward, personalizing the situation as a reflection of yourself. (*If I was more ___, they would say yes.*)

Do you feel the difference? Resist the urge to blame or shame anyone involved in the situation—you *or* the other person. Instead, simply acknowledge your displeasure with the denial.

If asking is historically hard for you, it can be tempting to say in response to their no, "Are you kidding me? Do you have *any* idea how much self-talk/shadow boxing/Beyoncé-listening I had to do to get brave enough to ask? The least you can do is say yes!" But your courage does not obligate anyone to make a certain decision.

However, your bravery in asking stands regardless of the outcome—their no does not obliterate your courage! Be proud that you advocated for your own needs. You get to ride that courage like a horse into your next bold ask.

We cannot will someone else into a more expanded/healed/relational version of themselves. Their no may reflect that they have reached the outer limit of their relationality. You might be able to see all the ways that leaning into your ask would be good for them. Nevertheless, stay humble about the limits of your control. Maybe even feel a little grateful that it's not all up to you!

NOVEMBER 8

We are stronger, smarter, kinder when we honor the wisdom of our bodies.

Many of us live our lives from the neck up:

- We think our way into solutions.

- We set our schedules based largely on the needs/demands of those around us

- We make choices based on "shoulds."

- We run our emotions through a filter of whether they are "rational" or "make sense."

Sound familiar? Some of us come by this tendency through very understandable conditions. Perhaps our Original Love Classroom was not versed in the language of emotions. Perhaps the grown-ups ruled with an iron fist, outlining clear expectations for who and how we needed to be. Since then, life may have reinforced our push-through-at-all-cost mode. External affirmation like good grades, athletic success, or career accomplishments can keep us on the hamster wheel of hustling.

Old habits are hard to break, until something has to give. At that point, what used to be previously tenable but tiring becomes impossible. Crisis, loss, and fear are both painful and clarifying. Sometimes they help us lose the illusion of who we thought we needed to be, of what we thought mattered most. Sometimes they get us back to basics:

- Sleep

- Breath

- Ease

- Rest

- Boundaries

- Movement

- Solitude

- Nourishment

These things sustain us in ways that dollars, praise, likes, and follows never can. Moreover, they set us up for success in the relationships that matter most to us.

When your partner raises a concern with you, and you respond by asking, "Can I reflect back what I'm hearing you say?" you do two powerful things at once: You witness your partner's experience *and* you stave off your defensiveness.

Recently, Todd let me know that I had done something that hurt his feelings. I felt an awful flip-flop of perspectives: ashamed of myself for what I had done and mad at him for being hurt by what I had done. (Do you know that flippy-floppy place? It's no fun!) With it came a rush of urgency: to explain myself, to counter his narrative (and attempt to change his emotional response), to cry, to flee.

As these urges swirled inside me, I knew I was at a fork in the road. I could give in to those urges or I could reach for him. So I practiced a "move" that I've taught to thousands of people.

Alexandra: "Can I reflect back what I'm hearing you say?"
Todd: "Sure."

I talked him through what I had just heard him say. That move did two things at once:

1. It provided Todd with a much-needed witnessing of his experience. Witnessing soothes hurt.

2. It provided me with something I could do instead of defend/ explain/cry/flee. Something that bought us time while my body calmed down. Something that didn't require much cleverness (because we lose IQ points when we are upset or panicked).

Something that focused my attention where it needed to be in that moment: on *him*. By hearing him back, I simply couldn't get lost in my shame or the outrage disguising it.

That move saved us.

Difficult moments demand skillful responses. Having a measured response at the ready is loving, not contrived. It may feel awkward, but in relationships, effectiveness matters more than effortlessness.

To love someone across time is to become intimate with the landscape of their fragility.

To love someone is to be granted access to their inner chamber. You become the bearer of their history. You learn the story behind each scar. You also have a front row seat to every one of your partner's humiliations. You see all of their stumbles. You are there for the illnesses, the freak outs, the surrendered dreams. When your partner gets frustrated with life, you are likely their safe place to vent.

It is also very likely that their ability to love you exactly the way you want to be loved may be limited by the pain of their past. A past you weren't even there for! So frustrating.

Your partner's work is to become more and more savvy at frustration tolerance and wound management. Your work is to resist the urge to say what you could say:

- "You're just like your mom/dad."

- "I tried to warn you."

- "You're still stuck on that?!"

Knowing what you know about your partner gives you a unique ability to hurt them in their most tender places. Don't do it. Use your power to remind them that they are so much more than their old pain.

The journey to sexual self-confidence starts with fierce self-compassion.

We talk a lot about how we internalize shame and silencing messages about sex. But there's a confusing undercurrent that needs to be addressed: the number of well-meaning messages that encourage us to break free from sexual shame by being sexually bold. Mindlessly internalizing this opposite set of messages about how we "should" be can create a new variation on an old theme. It carries the same risk as the shaming, silencing messages: disconnection from self. Under this new paradigm, sex becomes a performance, an attempt to offload shame by proving your prowess.

If you crave more confidence in the bedroom, practice fierce self-compassion and listen to your body. Remember that being sexually self-confident is not about how much you can handle or how "extreme" you can be. Rather, it is about your ability to stay present in your body and connected to a partner. It's about being, not doing.

There is beauty in the "re": Reimagine. Rediscover. Remember.

Please stop viewing your life as linear. Straight lines create entirely too much pressure. It's high time we celebrate curves of all sorts. Paths that wind. Detours. Side streets. Circles, cycles, patterns. You can pack so much more humanity into the nooks and crannies found within a curvy line.

For example, take the pressure off yourself and your partner that you must have hard conversations the "right way" the first time (whatever the hell that means). Drop the illusion that a proper conversation must move from A to B to C. You cannot possibly be expected to have your facts lined up and your words all perfect, and your partner can't either. Try for a bit, then pause. Step away and REcover. Shower. Breathe. Sleep. Dance. Come back and REvisit.

When you circle back, you're a bit different and so is your partner. Pay attention to what feels different on the "re" and celebrate your fresh takes. When couples tell me that they have the same conversation "over and over," it can mean they are legitimately stuck. But more often, couples feel this way because they're priming themselves to see the sameness rather than any evolution. Focusing on the theme will make us miss the variation. Noticing the changes and progress brings us closer to each other.

Relational Self-Awareness Questions

- Which "re" words feel especially important to you right now? Why?

- Which "re" words aggravate you? Why?

- Which "re" word would you add to this list?

For some of us, the greatest challenge of intimate partnership is allowing ourselves to receive.

It can feel great when someone does something especially for us. But for those of us who are not comfortable on the receiving end, it can cause us to be unsure when our partner decides to give. For example:

- Your partner agrees to a move in support of your career.

- Your partner cancels plans so they can take care of you when you're sick.

- Your partner stands up for you in a dispute with your family.

In these moments, can you choose gratitude over guilt, or do you attempt to rationalize that it's okay to receive because you did something for them last time? What might be blocking your ability to lean into someone's care/protection/accommodation? For example:

- **Your Family of Origin kept score.** Allowing yourself to receive was dangerous because it would be used against you later.

- **You raised yourself because the grown-ups were lost in their own pain/addiction/illness.** Letting others do things for you is a muscle you never learned to flex.

- **In a previous relationship, ledgers equaled love.** You were constantly reminded of what the other person had done for you.

- **Gender role socialization taught you that you are in charge of providing.** In your mind, providers shouldn't have needs.

- **Gender role socialization taught you that you were a caregiver.** In your mind, you shouldn't need care, or you shouldn't have dreams or ambitions that require other people to adjust.

Intimacy requires a steady flow of *both* giving *and* receiving. When you notice guilt blocking your gratitude, you are gifted a massive opportunity to heal something inside of you. The beneficiary of your internal work is your partner! When you do your work, you can shine on them. When you can shine on them, you reduce the chances of later resentment. People become resentful when they feel unseen. Let goodness in, commit to seeing and supporting one another, and it will create a positive feedback loop between you and your partner.

A strong intimate partnership is nurtured by two people who are willing to walk the talk.

Great relationships don't happen by accident or chance. They are forged. They are cared for. They are forever works in progress. Great relationships happen when two people commit to:

- Choosing each other again and again
- Being willing to have the hard conversations
- Cultivating an atmosphere of pleasure and play
- Practicing self-compassion so they can offer gentleness to their partner
- Living as an intimate ally of their partner's Core Wounds and triggers
- Talking about their differences (gender, cultural, personality, etc.) with curiosity instead of judgment
- Accepting the inevitable changes that come with time
- Respecting vulnerability as the foundation of intimacy
- Honoring their relationship dynamic as highly responsive to what's going on within and between partners and therefore worthy of care
- Learning their partner more deeply every day

Let's normalize taking multiple conversations to work through relationship challenges. Build on brief-but-collaborative conversations, rather than striving for comprehensive discussions that leave you both exhausted.

When Todd and I were young parents, we'd take our kids to a party, and if the kids were having fun, we'd stay longer than we planned. Then, they were still having fun, so we'd stay even longer. Then one (or both) would melt down, and we'd rush out in a swirl of discouragement, tears, and sweat, berating ourselves for not having left sooner, promising ourselves we'd do it differently next time.

There's an art to leaving while it's still good. This parenting wisdom also applies to moving through difficult conversations with our partner:

- Especially the emotionally tender ones
- Especially the ones that have no easy answers (also known as most of them)
- Especially the ones that touch old wounds or fresh hurts

Leave something on the table. End the conversation while it's still good. Let this conversation settle so new perspectives can bubble up. Let your brain and your heart rest. Get yourself a snack. In all likelihood, you have covered more ground than you think you have; wrap up (for now) while you're still on the same team.

The challenges that couples face are deep, multifaceted, nuanced, and are therefore worthy of more than one conversation. Remember:

- Ending a conversation doesn't need to mean ending your time together. Pause the conversation and watch a show. Or bake bread. Or whatever.

- Breaking something big up into smaller conversations is a sign of respect, not an avoidance strategy.

- Persisting through exhaustion sets you up to say things you might regret or to take a more extreme stance than you'd take if you were feeling fresh.

- When you end before you get flooded and cranky, celebrate like crazy. You're relational rock stars!

NOVEMBER 16

We call them relationship dynamics, not relationship statics.

It's a relational myth to think that love is two people who feel exactly the same about each other all of the time: the same level of commitment, the same frequency of sexual contact, the same amount of time together and time apart. We are shaped by infinite forces, seen and unseen. So why do we get so uncomfortable with the inevitable attentional imbalances that accompany love? I think it's because the imbalance stirs up some very uncomfortable feelings that lead to some very uncomfortable stories about ourselves and each other.

> This is all a matter of degrees. I'm not talking about significant or consistent relational imbalances in attention, affection, or commitment.

If you sense that you're more into your partner than they are into you, you may start to feel:

- **Dependent:** You want more of them and you're waiting for their availability.

- **Afraid:** They may judge you for being needy and clingy.

- **Vulnerable:** You wonder how they might use their power over you.

Those are some emotionally charged knots! They likely have old roots tied to negative experiences—anything from feeling socially left out in junior high, to feeling unseen as a minority, to internalized gendered stories about "needy women" or "p*ssy-whipped men."

And if you feel like your partner is more into you than you are into them, you may start to feel:

- **Anxious:** Maybe something is wrong with them. How can they be so sure of this?

- **Smothered:** Maybe they are relying too much on you?

- **Critical:** If they're so into you, are you actually just settling?

It often appears that one person is leading the pursuit of intimacy and the other is following. This isn't necessarily a bad thing. But it can sure kick up a lot of emotional dust. Getting clear on the story you attach to your relationship dynamic will guide your next steps.

Relational Self-Awareness Questions

- What Origin Story gets kicked up when you're in either of these positions?

- How might you experience an imbalance of interest/affection/enthusiasm if you viewed it as inevitable or normal, rather than pathological?

"We'll figure it out": what a magnificent way to say "I love you."

When someone we love is worried, we instinctively want them to worry less. But *how* we get them from worried to relaxed matters. So often, we say things like:

- "It's not a big deal" or "That won't happen," which invalidates the person's worry.
- "You're being a worry wart" or "Don't be silly," which leaves the person feeling bad/wrong/weak for being worried.

Even though we may say these things with the best intentions, neither of those paths is effective. The person is still worried, but now they are alone in their worry—a worse state of affairs, for sure. Invalidation and judgment deprive a worrying person of a potent resource: connection.

When you are worried, it feels better to draw close to someone who feels emotionally safe and trustworthy . . . even though the objective circumstance is no different! You essentially "borrow" their calmer nervous system for a little while. This is called *co-regulation*. It's not needy; it's necessary. Humans have been doing it for thousands of years. We are wholly dependent on it when we're babies, but we never fully outgrow the need to be connected to people we love when we're worried.

> "We'll figure it out" can also be used as a delay tactic.
> That is *not* the context I'm talking about here.

Relational Self-Awareness Questions

- How do you feel when someone you love says, "We'll figure it out"? Why?

- How do you feel when you say this to someone else? Why?

- Was this something you heard when you were a kid? From whom? In what settings?

To offer forgiveness in the absence of accountability is to abandon the self.

In a sustainable relationship, forgiveness is not a moment but a process. One that involves deep relational interplay. Your partner's ability to step into accountability invites you to step into a measure of acceptance.

Acceptance does not mean that what happened was okay. Rather, acceptance means that you are working to remember that there is more to your partner than the lousy thing they did. That there is more to you than the hurt you feel.

Forgiveness cannot be demanded. It can only be invited. If the one who did harm is seeking forgiveness, they can set the stage with their:

- Apology

- Acknowledgment

- Remorse

- Care

The one who did harm must not ask for a plan ("What will it take to forgive me?") or a promise ("When do you think you will be able to forgive me?"). In seeking certainty, the one who has done harm is asking the one who has been harmed to carry not only their own pain but also their partner's redemption. That's simply too much. Instead, the one who has done harm must engage in reflection. Take a journey inward. Approach and examine the unattended pain that fuels impulsivity. It seems paradoxical that a self-focused process holds the potential to offer healing, security, and protection to someone else. But intimacy is made possible by self-awareness.

Please remember that if you are the one who has been harmed, you are under no obligation to forgive, now or ever. You may need time to discern whether forgiveness is possible and whether forgiving is a loving act toward yourself. You will need to spend lots of time observing your partner to discern whether they are capable of the kind of empathy that makes repair possible.

If your relationship ends in the wake of a betrayal, the person who has been hurt may opt to forgive nonetheless. Liberating yourself from the heaviness of resentment is a gift to yourself. Forgiving the past is also a gift to your future partner because it frees you up to love them for what they are offering, rather than loving them to the degree they promise to be different from your ex.

Our urge to control something outside ourselves points us in the direction of something unhealed inside ourselves.

Intimate relationships evoke very strong feelings and needs in us. Feelings of entitlement and insecurity are part of the human condition. What matters is how those feelings get handled when they arise.

There's a world of difference between a feeling and an action. People who are abusive act out their entitlement and insecurity by controlling their partner's behavior. In a healthy intimate relationship, we notice the urge to control and say to our partner:

- "I'm having a reaction to what you're doing."
- "Something isn't sitting well with me."
- "Can we talk about this together?"

An urge to control another person arises from an unhealed source. This is neither a justification nor a rationalization of controlling behavior. Instead, exploring the relational truth beneath the control impulse allows both partners to feel whole, heard, and safe.

NOVEMBER 20

None of us can be understood outside of our context.

We are the sum total of our experiences. Each of us has a lineage, existing as part of a larger tapestry that includes:

- Family
- Ancestry
- Community
- Culture

Manifested in story, language, myths, foods, gestures, music, art, clothing, ritual, traditions, holidays, and more, culture is how we express our connection to context. In an intimate partnership, each partner's work is to contextualize the other.

In the coming weeks, you will likely be moving through holidays and attending family gatherings. If you are partnered, I invite and challenge you to keep your partner contextualized. Resist the urge to judge their relationship to holiday traditions. Whether your families celebrate the same holidays or not, see what happens when you situate yourself alongside your partner, curiously exploring their relationship to the holidays.

Relational Self-Awareness Questions
Exploring these questions together with your partner:

- What was this day/holiday season like for you when you were little?

- Can you tell me a story about this holiday?

- What foods, music, and activities were special to you on this holiday?

- What was difficult for you about this holiday?

- If I had been with you when you were little, what would I have thought about your family's celebration? Why?

- Do you have photos of yourself and your family celebrating? May I see some?

NOVEMBER 21

You are a unique individual and you are inextricably bound to everything and everyone.

We put too much pressure on ourselves to find "the real me." This idea of a fixed, separate, rock-solid self has never landed for me—instead, I believe we come to know ourselves via our connections to others. We are not separate from our contexts. We are inseparable from everything around us. As spiritual folks say, we are the wave *and* the ocean. We continue to know ourselves through our experiences. Therefore, we are never "done." And we don't ever have to be!

What if the true self is less about a fixed identity and more about a state of being? What if the true self is simply the state of having moment-to-moment access to our interior? Access to our inner experience allows us to:

- Savor the goodness around and within us
- State our needs/wants/preferences
- Sense when it is time to step away from an interaction

While intimacy is undoubtedly the experience of deep connection with someone else, it is also a wonderful way to access our true self.

Relational Self-Awareness Prompts

- The setting where I feel most present is . . .
- I feel most present when I am with . . .
- It is easiest for me to savor when I am with . . .
- It is easiest for me to savor when I feel . . .

NOVEMBER 22

Sexual healing occurs when sex is: Less duty and more celebration. Less script and more improv. Less performance and more expression.

Less pressure and more flow. Less outcome-focused and more process-centered.

Sex exposes our bodies and our emotions, creating fear that we will be humiliated, disappointing, hurt, or hurtful. We focus on performance (how we look, how we sound, how long we last, etc.) as a defense against these terribly vulnerable feelings. When we worry about performing, we're lost in our heads, watching ourselves from a third person perspective rather than being in our bodies. (William Masters and Virginia Johnson called this *spectatoring*.) When we focus only on getting it "right," we miss out on feeling good, connected, and present.

Relational Self-Awareness Questions

- What thoughts take you out of the moment during sex?
- What thoughts help you cultivate joy during sex?
- What do you want your partner to understand about your sexual self?

NOVEMBER 23

We underestimate how confronting it can be to let ourselves be admired by someone we deeply admire.

Admiring someone is pretty easy. *Receiving* the admiration of someone we admire can be surprisingly complicated. For example:

- You had a crush one someone you had deemed out of reach. You lamented the pain of this unrequited love until you became aware that this person actually had feelings for you. All of a sudden, you're freaking out and can't bring yourself to make a move.

- You fangirled/fanboyed over someone in the professional realm; now that person wants to collaborate with you, and you have no ideas for how to go about it.

Situations like these require what I call the *swoon-slay dialectic*. *Dialectic* refers to holding the tension of two competing truths without foreclosing on either. In other words, a Both/And. You can *both* swoon (feel dizzy in the presence of the other's brilliance/beauty) *and* slay (hold onto your own magnificence and power). Your swoon doesn't negate your slay. Also, you can slay while feeling a bit swoony!

When you quiet your inner critic long enough to step into the expanded realm of mutual admiration, you get to witness yourself being brave. Hanging in there with the swoon-slay dialectic is not easy! Sometimes we blow the whole thing up to avoid the immense discomfort of emerging from underneath the familiar stories about our inadequacy and inferiority. Resisting self-sabotage in this scenario is a major accomplishment and should be celebrated like mad. Persisting in an uncomfortable situation, even one that is a "dream come true," is a major feat!

Can you let yourself see in you what this person sees in you? Can you quiet the story of your not-enough-ness to step into something more expansive?

NOVEMBER 24

Some folks are so talented at guilt-tripping that they'll have you not just apologizing

but second-guessing all your life choices and ways of being in this world.

Have you ever been the recipient of top-notch guilt trips like these?

- "Well, I just waited here all day for you to call."
- "How could you say something like that after all I've done for you?"
- "So nice of you to tell them before telling me."

A guilt trip is like a sneak attack. An all-blame-no-vulnerability tactic. The person giving the guilt trip gets to hold steady while the other person spins. This is an ineffective means of communication, perpetuating a power dynamic and preventing real communication between two people.

Let's rework the above examples to align with Relational Self-Awareness:

- "When you didn't call me, I felt hurt and sad. Can you help me understand what kept you from reaching out?"
- "That comment you made really hurt my feelings. Can you please let me know when we can talk about it?"
- "When you told them your news before you told me, I felt let down and disappointed. Can you please help me understand your decision-making process?"

Far more inviting of closeness and connection, right? The next time someone tries to give you a guilt trip, instead of getting salty or shame-y, here's how you could respond instead:

- "It sounds like you're really disappointed/sad/hurt/mad. Do I have that right?"

- "Can you tell me more about how you're feeling?"
- "It sounds like you are confused about my choices. Would you like to hear a bit more about what I was thinking?"

When you try one of these alternative responses, make sure you give yourself a pat on the back. Change isn't easy! You cannot prevent someone from giving you a guilt trip, but a commitment to modeling healthy relationship habits can be contagious to those around you.

You are not a machine. Nor are you a mystery to be unlocked. And you are certainly not a problem to be solved.

There's no such thing as "figuring out" your sexuality. You can't make a list of capital-T Truths that capture the essence of your sexual self. Your sexuality is profoundly contextual, shaped by multiple forces within you and in the space between you and your partner. Context shapes how you experience the present moment, including:

- Mood
- Stress level
- Body image
- Sense of safety
- Energy level
- Health status

Around you, context includes:

- Relationship tone

- Temperature of the room
- Time of day
- Who else is around
- Schedule
- Partner's mood

Ever wondered why something may feel amazing during one sexual experience and the same thing feels not so great in the next one? It's because all these previously mentioned forces affect attraction, desire, arousal, and orgasm. But when you and your partner honor the power of context, it helps you shift from good/bad/right/wrong labels to a collaborative approach that helps each of you create a sexual vibe that feels safe, exciting, and connecting.

NOVEMBER 26

Perhaps the opposite of ambivalence is not certainty but patience.

Relational Ambivalence is common. It's also painful.

"Why can't I figure out what I want?" Uncertainty is stressful and emotionally taxing. And it can affect your sense of self-esteem.

I invite you to remember that if you are in a relationship and you are not making a decision to leave, you are choosing to stay. For now. For today.

> As in all these entries, this does not apply to abusive relationships, in which decision-making is shaped by risk, safety, and consequence.

See what happens if you reframe your decision to stay in a relationship as:

- **A choice:** Your agency is evidenced by the fact you remain in the relationship. This reframe can help you remember that you're a protagonist in the story of your life.

- **An act of patience:** Patience is a grace you can offer yourself. A grace that is important for either ultimate outcome, whether you're leaning toward staying or going.

The process from confused to clear will always teach you something, whether you end up deciding that the relationship must end or whether you decide to invest more.

Relational Self-Awareness Questions

- What happens inside of you when you reframe this decision to stay? What do you feel in your body? Where do you feel it?

- What stories do you attach to patience? Where do those stories come from?

- How would you describe someone who is patient? If your answer is critical (e.g., "People who are patient are weak/self-abandoning/ suckers"), check in with yourself. Whose voice is behind those words?

NOVEMBER 27

What a skill it is to learn the difference between reactively retreating and intentionally pausing.

We can dream of a day when our patience is infinite, our perspective expansive, our empathy ceaseless. Until that time, we need a set of skills to minimize the fallout of our humanness. Even when our default setting is calm and open-minded, we get reactive for all kinds of reasons. When we get reactive, we say stuff that is unkind and one-sided. We say it louder than necessary. We walk away.

Attachment research shows us that one of the most painful things we can experience is not being able to reach for someone we love. Did you experience disconnection like this while growing up? Perhaps a grown-up who stormed off, drove away, or locked themselves alone in a room? If you did, pause and wrap your arms around yourself. That kid you once were must have felt terrified in those moments. Unfortunately, the grown-up you are today is at risk of doing this as a grown-up. (Yes, we sometimes repeat even the painful stuff we experienced.) You are also at risk of feeling awful if/when your partner retreats when they are upset.

Let's talk about *reactive retreats* versus *intentional pauses*.

A reactive retreat includes:

- No announcement/preview
- Huffing, stomping, walking away
- No plan for reengagement
- An impact on the other person: desperation, confusion, fear

An intentional pause includes:

- An indicating announcement, like, "I love us too much to keep talking" or "I don't want to say something I'll regret"
- Eye contact, stepping away gently
- A plan for reengagement, such as "I'm going for a walk—let's talk in an hour"
- An impact on the other person: disappointment, calm, acceptance

Moods happen. Reactions follow. Some stuff is not in your control. What is in your control is how you handle yourself when you get moody and reactive. Creating an intentional pause is an act of self-care and an act of love as well. It assures your partner/kid/friend that you are stepping away but not for good. That you are taking space in the service of the relationship. That you are responsible for restarting the conversation when you have found your way back to center.

NOVEMBER 28

Jealousy in an intimate relationship arises in response to a real or perceived threat of losing someone who matters tremendously to us.

Jealousy is a teacher. First, though, it is a flashing warning light. Rather than acting on or against it right away, pause:

- **Don't push jealousy away because you equate it with weakness.** If you do this, you lose out on the lessons and possibilities for healing.

- **Don't act out, becoming critical, controlling, or accusatory.** If you do this, you lose out on the opportunity to talk with your partner about insecurity in a way that deepens intimacy.

- **Don't shut down.** Numbing out doesn't serve you and it doesn't help your relationship.

Instead, turn your attention inward. Listen. Feel. Imagine jealousy is a troubled kid who needs some tender loving care. Your feeling of jealousy is a piece of data that warrants your investigation:

- **Has a Core Wound of yours been triggered?** If so, then self-compassion and reparenting yourself is the order of the day.

- **Do you and your partner need to clarify a relational boundary?** If so, try to frame the conversation about shared relationship values and agreements.

- **Does your partner have a history of boundary violations (with you or other partners)?** If so, you will feel safer if and as your partner can talk with you about what they've learned from their past and the commitments they make that help them stay in their integrity.

It's no fun to feel jealous, but it's infinitely easier when you know you can face it as a team.

Self-soothing is an essential relationship skill—a job that you cannot hire out.

Partner A suggests to Partner B that they make love. Partner B politely declines, citing exhaustion. Partner A, feeling rebuffed and hurt, spends the next several hours sulking.

If Partner A gets into the habit of relying on Partner B's affirmation (via their sexual availability) to regulate their emotions, the stage is set for Partner B to become resentful. Partner B will begin to feel like there's no room for their experience, that all the relational oxygen is taken up focusing on Partner A's needs and fears. Partner B can reassure Partner A, "I'm committed and I'm attracted to you," and that reassurance might help Partner A feel connected. But Partner B's words cannot override Partner A's internalized story of their own worthlessness. Instead:

- Partner A needs to do the introspective work of naming the story (e.g., "I'm ugly/worthless/replaceable") that gets activated when Partner B isn't in the mood for sex.

- Partner A needs to connect with the feelings (shame, embarrassment, etc.) attached to that story.

- Partner A needs to meet that story with another story: "Based on my history, I'm at risk of spiraling in moments like this. But I'm okay. We're okay."

- Partner A might also need a self-care practice (music, a shower, journaling, meditation, etc.) to slow down the shame spiral.

With their emotions a bit more regulated, Partner A can reach for Partner B, not for soothing, but for connection: "I'm disappointed, but I'm okay. How about we watch a show together instead?" When Partner A self-regulates, Partner B is more likely to offer words of reassurance from a place of desire, not obligation: "You know I love that sweet body of yours, and I'm gonna for sure get after it tomorrow."

The love of another is not enough on its own to heal feelings of worthlessness. Rather, we must cultivate a sense of worth for ourselves. This is no easy feat, but the journey toward a more enduring sense of self-compassion is worthwhile, both for ourselves and for our relationships.

NOVEMBER 30

Women's sexual pleasure threatens the status quo . . . and that is a very good thing indeed.

Unlike every other part of our bodies, the clitoris has one purpose and one purpose only: pleasure. Zero "effs" to give about anything else. Is it any coincidence, then, that the history of the clitoris is much like the history of women's oppression? That which ought to be celebrated and revered has instead been held in contempt. Until very recently, the clitoris was omitted from medical anatomy textbooks. You know that if something is being rendered invisible, it must really hold the power to threaten the status quo.

Because pleasure is predicated upon autonomy, systems of oppression have attempted to regulate, control, and silence women's sexuality for thousands of years. Women's sexual liberation is subversive.

Let us envision and work toward a world without sexual trauma, sexual assault, and sex trafficking.

Let us envision a world with comprehensive sex education and reproductive rights.

Let us envision a world where women can be unapologetic about the pursuit of pleasure.

DECEMBER 1

The antidote to worry is present-moment focus.

As a child, I kept a heart-shaped wooden box next to my bed. Inside were five tiny worry dolls. Before bed, I would tell a worry to each of those dolls—they were supposed to carry the worries while I slept. Worry was my original Coping Strategy.

Worrying is part of living. It's the understandable side effect of our inability to control outcomes and perfectly protect the ones we love. Let's reflect on how you worry:

- What are the subjects you generally worry about?

- What do you feel in your body when you worry?

Next, consider whether you can transform your worry into a problem that you can actually do something about.

- If so, write it down and work on a plan.

- If not, get focused on the present moment. Deep breathing. Dance party. Distraction.

Finally, share your worries with someone you trust can help. Just be careful of these two pitfalls:

- Resist the urge to judge them for not worrying about what you're worrying about. (I've done this with Todd, but only about 1,237 times.)

- Let your trusted person know whether you want advice or witnessing. Either is legit!

It is unhelpful to label someone "overly sensitive" and far more helpful to explore how feedback is being given.

Are you too sensitive or is your partner too rough? The answer: *yes.* When your partner is the giver of the feedback, the onus is on them to approach you in a way that maximizes your chances of being receptive and minimizes your chances of being defensive—and you know, "too sensitive." How can they give feedback in a healthy way?

- **Go Meta:** "Please let me know when you're available for some feedback" or "I have something I'd like to talk with you about. When is a good time?"

- **Tell the story but drop the interpretation:** "Here's what happened. Here's how I felt about it."

- **Be generous with the context:** "I suspect we're both struggling because it's a hectic time" or "I know you probably didn't intend to hurt me."

- **Be relational:** "I want us to figure this out together."

Let's say your partner gives you all this and a bag of chips, but you're still raw as hell. Why might that be?

- **When someone we love is upset with us, it's excruciating.** As humans, we have an evolved fear of getting kicked out of the tribe. Your fear just means you're real.

- **If you grew up in a family of divorce, you learned that conflict can end relationships.** Your experience taught you to have a large reaction to relationship distress.

The way forward together is to find a space beyond right/wrong. In this space, you can figure out how to communicate disappointment in a way that enlists the other as an ally.

When you manage your stress, you nurture your relationships.

It's not that we're bad at managing stress. It's that stress has a gnarly way of taking us out of connection. Stress is all-consuming, narrowing our field of vision. Stress taps our reserves, making it hard to stay present with the people we love. Stress shifts us:

- From expansive to narrow

- From curious to quick-tempered

- From emotionally attuned to frozen or numb

I often say that if a society truly wanted to promote healthy intimate relationships and healthy family systems, that society must provide robust social safety nets and fair wages, be diligently anti-racist, promote reproductive justice . . . and so on. The absence of equity, care, and support is wildly stressful. It's very hard to regulate your nervous system when you're stretched thin or one paycheck from disaster.

Further, when your nervous system is chronically and/or acutely dysregulated, it's very hard to cultivate intimacy with another person. Might you be more motivated to do things that ease your stress and quiet your nervous system if you remind yourself that it's good for your relationship?

This is not a guilt trip. (After all, you likely didn't create a lot of the stuff you're stressed about.) Instead, this is an invitation. Obviously, you deserve rest, play, creative time, deep breaths, movement, and time off for your own sake. But some of us got confused early in our lives—we think that being alive and being stressed out are kind of the same thing.

If your partner/friend/kid gives you the feedback that you're distracted or grouchy, consider that you might have needed that feedback to check in about your stress level. Can you consider what you might be able to take off your plate? Can you consider what tasks might warrant a B-minus rather than an A-plus? Can you ask your body what would feel good and then give that to yourself? After all, that body has done a lot for you.

Stress compromises our capacity to listen deeply to and connect deeply with the people we love. While there's no denying the overwhelm of our busy lives in this modern age, opening a conversation about the stress we're feeling, with our partner and within ourselves, will create a whole new set of possibilities for how we can manage it.

Let's resist the urge to label actions (our own or someone else's) as the "right" or "wrong" thing to do.

Certain language can hurt our relationships:

- "I can't believe you did that."

- "It's your fault."

- "Blame me for that."

- "You should have known better."

Language like this moves the conversation from curious to critical, from collaborative to adversarial. These are "crystal ball" phrases, implying that there is a parallel world where we know with certainty that outcomes would have been different if people's choices were different. (We do not/cannot know this.) Words/phrases like these amplify defensiveness. Instead of being curious and collaborative, people become more worried about covering their booties than looking together at a problem. Fear of getting stuck "holding the bag" keeps them from feeling and expressing empathy.

Even when the intent behind these words is pure ("I love you," "I am protective of you," "I am worried about you," etc.), the impact is that the other person feels invalidated, unseen, unsupported. What can you say instead?

- "Are you available for feedback?"

- "If I knew then what I know now, I would have . . . "

- "It is hard for me to see you. . ."

- "I worry that. . ."
- "Can you help me understand X?"

You may feel afraid that banning these crystal ball phrases from your vocabulary will keep people from taking responsibility for hurtful or thoughtless behavior. But I think you'll be pleasantly surprised. It's actually much easier to take responsibility when the atmosphere is one of grace and space.

> As with everything I recommend, this does not apply to situations of abuse. Abusive behavior *is* wrong, and abusive behavior is always the fault of the one who is being abusive.

Relational Self-Awareness Questions

- What might happen when you ban binary words (good/bad, right/wrong, mistake/right answer, guilty/innocent, should/should not, etc.) from your relational vocabulary?
- What are other ways you can express your concerns without using that language?

DECEMBER 5

Love is built and nourished in small, sweet moments.

Romantic myths teach us that love lives in:

- The grand gestures
- The sweeping declarations
- The emotional climaxes

That's what movies, song lyrics, and social media tell us, right? If it's not magical and epic, it doesn't count. If it doesn't take your breath away, it doesn't matter. But research by the Gottman Institute has found that thriving intimate relationships are often built upon small things, helping us move from the land of romantic fairy tales to the realm of real-world love stories.

Thank goodness! We don't have to be adrenaline junkies. We don't have to bust our booties to create peak moments and then languish in no man's land until we can create the next peak moment. We can savor nuances between nothingness and magnificence, such as:

- Sweetness

- Kindness

- Curiosity

- Silliness

- Thoughtfulness

- Exploration

- Rest

- Play

- Ritual

Each of these is a small but meaningful deposit into the relational bank account. Microdoses of warm experiences that become a cushion where we can land softly in the more difficult moments.

I'm here for the grand gestures. But I know (thanks to the Gottmans) not to give those gestures more weight than the ordinary ones. Let's just make sure we remember to savor the little stuff too.

Even the most attentive partner cannot love you out of your shame.

Shame is a dreadful gremlin that sits on our shoulder, whispering in our ear that we are not enough. When we are in the throes of shame, we cannot also be in the depths of connection.

A loving partner can offer you comfort and nearness, but this part of your healing journey is about your relationship with you. Your partner can tell you you're great and that they don't see you the way you see you. The worst-case scenario? You'll turn it back onto them, leaving them feeling confused and unseen. The best-case scenario? You let their words in enough to solve the moment, but you'll be back at the mercy of shame the very next time something sets you off.

If you are kicking up relational dust because you've been swallowed up by a shame-y story, your partner's love cannot fix that for you. When it comes to shame, you ultimately must reckon with yourself. It's less about becoming immune to ever feeling shame and much more about getting wise to yourself.

Relational Self-Awareness Questions

- If you imagine shame as a gremlin on your shoulder, what does it whisper to you?

- How do you know when shame has crept in? Is it a sensation in your body? Is it a thought pattern?

- What kind of relational dust does your shame tend to kick up? If you're experiencing shame and a partner/friend/relative attempts to validate you or connect with you, how might your shame distort their words?

If you were a parentified child, intimacy can feel to you like a loss of control.

Parentified child: A kid (usually, but not necessarily, the oldest) "recruited" by the family system to take care of the adults.

A parentified child may:

- Provide validation, affirmation, and advice to a parent who feels lonely in their marriage
- Serve as a parent's confidant, maybe even keeping a secret from the other parent
- Referee conflict and negotiate "peace treaties" between parents

There are confusing "benefits" that come with the parentified child role. You feel special, powerful, necessary. You feel a pseudo-sense of being in control. Then you grow up, fall in love, and experience a sneaky suspicion that your notions of intimacy are perhaps not so healthy and tenable.

Intimacy is about mutuality. Mutuality requires trust and surrender. Surrender for a parentified child is anathema because what feels good/normal/right is vigilance and caretaking.

If this lands for you, awareness is your first step. Your parentified child was necessary back then, but that part of you gets to rest now. Your empowered adult self gets to co-create an intimate relationship on a foundation of interdependence.

Accommodating someone else does not necessarily mean that you've abandoned yourself.

Intimate partnerships are full of relational collaborations. Some of these are *extraordinary:* Are we exclusive? Where should we live? Will your brother live with us until he's back on his feet?

So many, however, are *ordinary.*

Here's one from my marriage: I was cozied up on the couch with my laptop, and the back door was open so I could enjoy the crisp evening air. Todd came into the room and began to close the door. I said, "Wait! Please keep it open!" This is a power struggle because only one of us could get our way. One of us would *define* what happened next, while one of us would *defer.*

Round 2,298,983 in this marriage went to the lady—the door remained open. Ten minutes later, we experienced another power struggle in which I deferred to his preference.

Our intimacy work is to meet these define-and-defer moments with grace and gratitude:

- Todd chose to let it go and move along. Keeping the door open when he prefers it to be closed is part of the price he pays for loving and being loved by me.

- I expressed my thanks. Thanking him for accommodating me keeps him from building up resentment, and it helps me internalize the good feelings that arise from knowing that he made an effort to care for me. I don't need to be on the lookout for a way to "return the favor" or "even the score," but it's good for our relationship that I make sure to deeply acknowledge the fact that he accommodated rather than escalated . . . which he could have done, right?

Resist the urge to turn every micro-decision into a statement about self/identity/commitment/power. Intimacy asks us to practice the sacred art of letting stuff go.

DECEMBER 9

A relationship becomes a weird little world unto itself.

The best part of building a life with someone is creating a weird little world for two, out of things like:

- Humor that feels connective, not hurtful

- Traditions that are founded upon restoration, not obligation

- Unwritten rules that ensure intimacy, not dominion

Your relationship doesn't have to make sense to anyone else. It does need to make sense to the two of you. Things like inside jokes, idiosyncratic rituals, even a mission statement, can encapsulate for the couple, in a way entirely their own, what they are about:

- What do we stand for?

- What are our shared values?

- What's our motto?

A mission statement both reflects and reinforces the "container" that is the relationship. The container is what helps each partner feel safe enough to let their freak flag fly.

Adulting is hard! Being able to get weird/raw/silly with each other is essential. Being playful cushions us against the daily grind. When we are with our partners, what we want most of all is to be able to let down. To exhale. To take off the mask.

Relational Self-Awareness Questions

- In what ways did you see the grown-ups in your family celebrate their weirdness when you were little? What was that like for you? If they struggled to celebrate their weirdness, why might that be?

- If you are partnered, how do you and your partner celebrate your weirdness?

- If you are single, how do you want to celebrate your weirdness in your next relationship?

DECEMBER 10

So many fights can be avoided by courageously asking for what we need instead of being critical when we haven't gotten it.

When our partner intuits what we need (comfort, a pep talk, a helping hand, etc.), we likely feel seen, supported, and valued. I think we also like when our partner gives us what we need without us needing to ask—it allows us to bypass the vulnerability of asking. When you need to ask for what you need, you are suddenly (and uncomfortably) face-to-face with:

- The fact that you are not a self-contained unit—you have needs!

- The risk that your partner may not give you what you need

- The fear that your partner may judge you for your need

- The loss of the fairy tale that love means perfect attunement

It is wholly reasonable to ask your partner to be more perceptive, more effusive, more engaged. But it is also wholly reasonable to reflect a bit on the discomfort of the ask. Challenge yourself to consider the possibility that it's easier to focus on what they aren't giving instead of focusing on what it's like to need.

Relational Self-Awareness Questions

- What is difficult for you about "the ask"?
- When is another time in your life that you have feared or dreaded "the ask"?
- When your partner doesn't give you what you want/need before you have to ask, what feeling arises in you?
- Does that feeling remind you of anything from your past?

DECEMBER 11

When you're trying to assess the health of your intimate relationship, make sure you take a longitudinal view, not just a snapshot.

How are we? Sometimes we're led to assess the health of our intimate relationship because we're unsure whether to invest more or move on. But status updates are a good idea even for those who simply want to continue coauthoring their love story. Your relationship is a work in progress, so assessing the "state of our union" makes sense. First, though, you must get clear on the difference between rumination and reflection.

- **Rumination:** This is replaying the past or future-tripping about what may come next. It feels like stuckness. Its focus is on fear, blame, self-doubt.

- **Reflection**: This is reviewing the past in order to guide choices in the present that build toward a co-created vision of the future. It feels like collaboration. Its focus is on purpose, learning, growth.

Your goal? Less rumination, more reflection. Ideally, check in about how the space between the two of you feels, celebrating what is working and tweaking what isn't, so you can get back to the business of living and loving.

Second, remember that your relationship can't be captured in one moment, one day, or one week. Look for changes over time: trends, patterns, cycles. If you're reflecting on how you and your partner manage conflict, examine more than just your most recent fight. Think about how the texture and tone of your conflicts has changed over time:

- Do each of you tend to get less disconnected/angry/escalated than you used to?

- Are you able to repair more quickly and easily?

- Are you doing things a bit differently that keep you from careening off the guard rails? If so, what are those things? Why do they help?

Don't let a snapshot represent the full story. You and your relationship are too complex for that. Love is more complex than that.

Regret may simply indicate that you have yet to glean the lessons from the experience.

Regret indicates stuckness. You may be stuck because you haven't fully mined the lesson that is available from the experience you're reflecting back on. See what opens up for you when you shift from "I regret that happened" to "What do I want/need to learn from that experience?" You're not letting yourself off the hook; you're creating a space for learning.

The regretful memory may never fully stop feeling painful. But a pang is still preferable to an ache. You move from ache to pang by integrating the memory into the larger story of who you are, where you've been, where you're going. The meaning-making process adjusts the emotional heat to a temperature that is more tolerable, helping you see that all of life's experiences can serve your growth and healing if you use regret to fuel introspection.

Relational Self-Awareness Questions

Think about a time in the past that makes you feel regret:

- What did that experience teach you about yourself?

- What do you know now that you didn't know then?

- What feeling do you want to have about this experience instead of regret?

- If a dear friend was in your shoes, what would you want for them?

- What will you do differently if/when you are in a similar situation in the future?

DECEMBER 13

What if you are right on time?

Psychologist Dr. Bernice Neugarten found that we anchor ourselves on a social clock as much as a biological clock. We feel better when we deem that we are "on time," and we feel anxious when we sense we are "off time." Where do we get these time frames? We compare ourselves to our peer group and the folks around us, including people we see on social media. This "time" is especially important to us when it comes to life milestones like:

- Sexual initiation/experience
- Finishing school
- Getting married
- Having a baby
- Buying a home
- Retiring from our career

We are profoundly relational creatures who crave belonging. But we get confused about what belonging really means. We confuse belonging with sameness. We also try to quiet our anxiety by striving for normalcy. (Whatever that is.) We want to do things "the right way" so we feel happy/successful/at ease. We want our relationships to be "on time" because the risk of loss is so great. Remember that your path, as a person and as a partner, gets to unfold with its own rhythm.

Relational Self-Awareness Questions

- In what realm(s) do you feel insecure about your timing?
- What alternative story is available to you? In other words, what is beautiful/just right about your path?
- What might be different for you if you believed you were right on time?

The next time you're having a hard time, try replacing "I am not okay" with "I am feeling deeply."

Pain is one of life's inevitabilities. Things happen that we wish wouldn't happen; as a result, we hurt. But all too often when we are hurting, we add another layer to our experience of pain: a story about our pain. This story tends to be profoundly unhelpful, as seen in these common examples:

- "Other people have it worse."
- "I shouldn't feel this way."
- "I am not okay."

When we conflate our pain with brokenness (e.g., *Something is wrong with me*), we end up adding fear and shame to an already intense internal state. In doing so, we make it even harder to reach out and ask for support.

Start to notice when you are adding suffering to your pain. Then, instead of saying, "I am not okay," say, "I am feeling deeply." Do you feel how this change in language creates a shift from self-criticism to self-compassion? Anything criticism does, compassion can do better!

Marriage requires you to be both clear-eyed and starry-eyed.

Like all institutions, the institution of marriage is imperfect. It is a work in progress. For those considering or participating in marriage, I want to encourage you to get comfortable being *both* clear-eyed *and* starry-eyed:

- **Clear-eyed:** We marry for love, yes, but also for matters that are decidedly unromantic: health insurance, immigration status, tax benefits, family needs. A marriage is a contract that requires constant negotiation of everything from coordinating schedules to squaring bank statements to folding laundry. Be clear-eyed about the many unglamorous realities of marriage.

- **Starry-eyed:** A marriage is a wonder—a commitment to one person across time! Todd and I celebrated a recent wedding anniversary by attending a local outdoor concert and slow-dancing barefoot on the grass. I felt my tummy flip as his arms tightened around me, a squeeze I've breathed into for over a quarter of a century, and a squeeze that conveys how much I matter to this one soul. Moments of swoon make the pragmatic ones worth it!

If you are someone who wants to say "I do," I hope that your eyes are both clear and starry. I hope that when you look into the eyes of your beloved, theirs are clear and starry too. Being clear-eyed and starry-eyed creates the internal and relational capacity to hold both the contract and the wonder at once.

DECEMBER 16

Self-abandonment is breaking up with yourself to save the relationship.

Have you ever had the awful sense of standing at a crossroads, required to choose between yourself and your partner? Self-abandonment includes:

386

- Letting go of passions, hobbies, interests
- Saying things like, "I'm fine," "Whatever you want," "Just go ahead"
- Feeling confusion, numbness, flatness

Self-abandonment is a symptom indicating that our relationship dynamic is off-track. When one or both partners sacrifice the "me" for the sake of the "we," it reveals that the dynamic has become win/lose. Resources are viewed like pie: The bigger the piece I get, the smaller the piece you get. Partners feel like they are on opposing teams: I am fighting for me and you are fighting for you.

In a thriving intimate partnership, there is no need to self-abandon. We commit ourselves to keeping some "me" in the "we."

Relational Self-Awareness Questions

- What have you given up for the sake of the relationship?
- What do you want your partner to understand about the price of that sacrifice?
- How can you take back some "me" to strengthen the "we"?

Infidelity shatters a relationship. Two people, standing amid the wreckage, ask, "What, if anything, is to be built from these broken pieces?"

Infidelity is a crisis. A turning point. There's no undoing, no "business as usual." But there is a *next*.

Next might be that the relationship ends. If that is the case, both the one who cheated and the one who was hurt will still need to heal. This painful chapter must be woven into the larger tapestry of their life stories.

Next might be that the couple explores building something from the shattering. Together. Slowly. Surrounded by wise guides and allies. It's accountability meeting curiosity. It's remorse meeting grace.

Because stigmatized stories end up shrouded in secrecy and shame, we don't often get to hear stories of rebuilding. I am adamant about naming the courage it takes to consider rebuilding because our culture so often judges those (especially women) who opt to stay. But we can name courage without obligating anyone to mend and without elevating repair above release.

Authenticity is about savoring alignment. Authenticity is a process of learning to recognize friction between what we're saying and how we're feeling. Authenticity is a commitment to course correction.

Because we are infinitely relational, we are forever scanning the scene for who we need to be to stay safe, to win favor, to fit with cultural notions of how we are expected to behave. Because we come to know ourselves in the context of our relationships, there's no need to pursue the quest for the "true self." Instead, intimacy invites us to reimagine the notion of *authenticity*.

Authenticity isn't a personality trait. Authenticity is a skill, a practice, a way of being. It's a commitment to consistently checking for any gap that may exist between how our insides feel and what our outsides show.

Healing is not about deciding *I'm going to be authentic from now on.* Rather, healing is about learning how misalignment feels inside our bodies. We must learn how our insides signal a breach between how we're feeling/what we need and what we're showing/asking for.

Authenticity isn't about having no filter, then shrugging our shoulders and exclaiming, "I'm being authentic!" Authenticity is about cultivating spaces where we are surrounded by people who cheer when we slow down, check in, and share what feels real and alive within us.

Relational Self-Awareness Questions

- To what degree do you see the self as relational versus essential?

- What happens inside you when you think of authenticity as a process instead of a personality trait?

- How do you know when you are out of alignment? How does your body cue you?

- In which relationships is it easiest for you to practice authenticity? Why?

DECEMBER 19

You inhabit a space between your inheritance and your legacy.

Your Family of Origin passed on to you a million formative lessons. For example:

- How to love and be loved

- How to deal with frustration

- How to approach differences

- How to handle loss

Those lessons are your inheritance: the sum total of the dynamics you observed and absorbed as you were growing up. You never asked for this inheritance, but you received it nonetheless. Your work is to hold fast to the lessons that serve you well. Love those lessons, live those lessons, and forge them into your legacy.

Your legacy is what you share with the world, how you live today. Fight like hell to heal so that you can shed that which lives within you but does not serve you or your relationships. It's beautiful to outgrow old dysfunction, but it can also feel lonely. And it can be challenging to hold a space of compassion with those who embody dysfunction but don't see what you see. If you are heading into days filled with family time:

- Can you allow yourself to be different from those who raised you?

- Can you hold awareness of your growth with more gentleness than bitterness?

- Can you give yourself permission to step away when you feel yourself slipping back into old patterns?

DECEMBER 20

What is your favorite compliment to receive? Why?

This is my favorite question to ask my family and friends. It opens so many avenues for connection. It gives shy or less vocal people their moment in the sun. It even creates a conversational bridge between kids/adolescents and adults. When I ask this question, I make careful note of the answers I receive—knowing more clearly how someone likes to be seen/valued helps me love them more strategically.

Some people have a hard time coming up with an answer to this question. Why?

- **Some of us had a Family of Origin that didn't do compliments.** As a result, the whole realm of praise feels like a foreign land.

- **Some of us have been in a chaotic/traumatic/abusive relationship.** Any kind of feedback, even positive feedback, may have been treacherous and used for harm. Our adaptation was to fly beneath the radar, avoiding being seen at all.

If you have a hard time answering this question, what might help you step into the vulnerability of letting yourself be seen by others? Could you open that door a little? Could you start by complimenting yourself quietly while nobody else is around?

So, just between us, what is the best compliment someone can give you? Why? Being seen and celebrated for the qualities we are most proud of can bring us close to the people we love. It starts by recognizing those qualities in ourselves!

DECEMBER 21

You and your partner will stand again and again at decision points that require asking three questions:

What do I need? What do you need? What do we need?

The last question—*What do we need?*—exists because building an intimate relationship creates a third entity: *we.* The process of working together to make choices that nourish and strengthen the "we" affirms for both partners why they are here, investing and building together.

Sometimes these decision points are easy: "This issue matters more to you than to me. Doing it your way is fine with me!" But it's often much trickier than that, isn't it? The decision point may be evoking our entire history of giving and taking, demanding and surrendering, asking and offering . . . including our history before we met our partner. When this happens, use self-reflection to help you sift the past from the present.

Relational Self-Awareness Questions

- How were decisions made in your Family of Origin? Collaboratively? Top-down? Angrily? Gently?

- How much did your Family of Origin allow you to weigh in on family decisions? What was that like for you?

- What do you want your partner to remember when you face a decision together?

- What do you want to remember when you and your partner face a decision?

DECEMBER 22

The more deeply you understand your family lineage, the more liberated you are to create an intimate partnership based on choice, not conditioning.

Your lineage has a profound impact on your expectations and beliefs. You can evolve beyond your ancestry, but it will require you to courageously turn toward your family tree with open eyes and an open heart.

What if you viewed this holiday season as an opportunity to better understand your Original Love Classroom? I'm not talking about calling people out or working through sensitive issues. I'm talking about ethnography. Deep curiosity about contexts that shaped your elders, and therefore you.

Here are 10 curious (and hopefully non-controversial) questions to ask the older folks in your family:

1. What major world events shaped you when you were young? How?

2. What were your favorite foods when you were little?

3. Who was your best friend when you were little? What did you like to do together?

4. Describe the home you grew up in. Did you have a favorite room in that home?

5. When you were little, what did you want to be when you grew up? Why?

6. How was dating different when you were a young adult versus today?

7. How was marriage different when you were young versus today?

8. What's your favorite memory of your parents?

9. What did you and your siblings like to do together?

10. How did your family celebrate your birthday when you were little?

Ask. For help. For clarification. For support. When silence fills the space between you and your partner, there is no room for closeness.

When we make the courageous choice to ask our partner for something, it is incumbent upon us to be mindful of *how* we ask:

- Ask without accusing

- Ask without embedding blame

- Ask without assassinating the other person's character

Still, for the sake of your relationship, ask. When we go without help, or support, or clarification, we create the conditions for resentment to take root. Where resentment thrives, intimacy cannot. Biting your tongue may be an effort to keep the peace, but you likely feel far from peaceful.

How does biting your tongue show up for you?

- Do you close the cupboard doors a little too hard?

- Does your tone become terse?

- Does a story creep in (e.g., *I'm all alone here*)?

Treat those as the symptoms of the underlying problem: your unmet need. Amid the wrapping paper and the appetizers and the family dynamics, there is a lot to do and manage. Therefore, the holidays can be a great time to practice asking for what you need.

Love exists in cycles of connection, disconnection, and repair.

Love is alive, dynamic, ever-changing. Our work is to move with the currents, not against them. But this, like so much in life, is easier said than done. When we are connected to our partner, it feels hard to remember that there is any other way to be besides vibing off each other and appreciating the ease. But then we hit a bump (because there's always a bump), and it can feel so jarring. *How are we here again? Where did all those good vibes go?*

When I have couples in therapy who are planning a vacation, I gently remind them that a change of location can bring a boost of yummy closeness, which can lure us into a belief that we're done with all the yucky stuff. This belief makes a moment of irritation or impatience feel all the more startling and hurtful when it inevitably happens. But by anticipating this together, the couple is better able to meet the moment of tension with calm instead of panic.

By naming what's happening, we slow down the fearful stories that can threaten to overtake us—that we can't do anything right, that there's something wrong with us. Accepting the challenging moment empowers us to work with it instead of resisting it, judging it, or blaming someone for it.

Relational Self-Awareness Questions

- Which phase of the conflict cycle tends to be the biggest struggle for you? Savoring the calm? Tolerating the rupture? Leaning into the repair?

- Why is that phase of the cycle toughest for you? Think about your Family of Origin, personality, and gender role socialization.

There's an ocean of difference between being the only one who initiates relationship talk and being the only one who is ready, willing, or able to engage in relationship talk.

Couples tend to have patterns of initiation: who tends to initiate sex, who tends to take the lead on social plans, who tends to raise relationship concerns. Why a particular partner takes the lead in any given domain is determined by lots of factors: gender, temperament, love language, Family of Origin dynamics. The best-case scenario is for couples to feel a sense of overall relational reciprocity because each partner assesses relational health and quality of connection within their respective "zones of genius." Sure, your roles are differentiated, but there is a sense of appreciation for what each of you is keeping an eye on. Appreciation might sound like this:

- "I know you initiate sex more often than I do. In my worst moments, I feel pressured. In my best moments, I feel grateful that you value our erotic connection."

- "I know that you initiate relationship talk more than I do. In my worst moments, I feel scared of disappointing you. In my best moments, I feel lucky to have a partner who makes sure we don't get disconnected from each other."

For some couples, the assumption is that if you're the one who is always initiating relationship talk, it's because your partner can't measure up in terms of capacity for relationship talk. That's not necessarily the case. In a perfect world, you'd both initiate relationship talk. But one person may not be able to for various reasons (capacity, temperament, etc.). The issue isn't all about who initiates, it's about willingness. You may need to be okay with initiating as long as you have faith the other will show up for the conversation.

When one partner changes their behavior, it begins to change the entire relational dance, but changing relational choreography between the two of you will take time. If you have been the only partner practicing Relational Self-Awareness and now your partner is trying to show up in a more relational way, you both will feel a bit confused and disoriented. Your partner will likely feel this uncertainty even more—you have been learning, but they are new to the practice of turning inward. That's okay! There is a difference between frustration with something new (clunky) and a complete disregard for any change at all (contemptuous):

- **Clunky:** "I'm trying. Please be patient because this is a new language for me."
- **Contemptuous:** "This is lame and I disregard all of it!"

The former indicates that you both need to keep practicing. The latter indicates you likely need a couples therapist or more intensive support.

Taking care of your half of the equation, your part of the dance, will create the conditions for your partner to do the same. But it does not guarantee they will, at least not right away. Your love and effort may not be enough to convince them to meet you even partway. Be gentle with yourself if this is the case. Be sad, but not self-critical.

DECEMBER 26

Talk about agreements, not compromises.

When I am working with a couple that is at a crossroads, I invite us to drop the language of *compromise* and opt instead for the language of *agreements*.

Transaction is woven into the word *compromise*. We get focused on what each of us is getting and giving up. Using this language, we risk forgetting that love is about celebrating each other's expansion. Further, compromise reinforces a power dynamic. Power dynamics are inevitable in a relationship, but when we bump into them, we are better off expanding the conversation to ensure that both partners feel seen, heard, and understood.

In contrast, when we create an *agreement*, we meet up in a space of mutuality and care. The process is active on both of our parts. Agreements help us anchor on what we value as individuals and as a couple. Agreements are more likely to leave both of us feeling proud and grateful and reduce the chance of future resentment.

Making decisions as a couple is inevitable, imperfect, and stressful. But the framing matters. So make agreements, not compromises.

DECEMBER 27

Do not confuse patience with foolishness.

Patience is not foolishness. Giving someone time to heal, to get clear, to feel ready for a next step toward commitment is brave.

I am *not* talking about making excuses for patterns of neglect, abuse, or deceit. I am talking about sticking around to see whether someone is able to shift their part of an unhealthy or upsetting dynamic. Holding steady while someone figures out whether they are as ready for you as you are ready for them. Not indefinitely, but for now.

The one practicing patience is at risk of telling themselves a story that says *I am a fool to stay.* The emotion attached to that story is shame. There is courage in steadiness, in staying the course, in holding tight. The steady light of someone's patience can be a force for healing. You can support your patience by:

- **Asking your partner to express appreciation for your patience:** Tell them how much you love it (and how much it helps) when they notice you trying hard to hold space with love and calm.

- **Noticing signs of progress:** Our collective default setting is to confirm our fears, so put the work in to notice evidence of progress in the direction of your hopes instead.

- **Scheduling check-ins:** Ideally, your partner will take the lead on sharing updates with you, knowing that their feedback will help you hold steady. Desiring occasional updates doesn't equal pressure! It's ensuring that your process is a relational one.

Patience isn't easy, but it also isn't foolish. Because our wounds tend to be relational, our healing needs to be as well. When partners commit to Relational Self-Awareness, an intimate partnership can be a powerful crucible for transformation and evolution.

DECEMBER 28

Resentment is relational data.

Resentment is defined by Merriam-Webster as "a feeling of indignant displeasure or persistent ill will at something regarded as a wrong, insult, or injury." It is a complex emotion, an alchemical mix of feelings we'd rather avoid than experience:

- Disappointment
- Disgust

- Anger

- Fear

Resentment and blame are next-door neighbors. If you are feeling resentment, you will quickly (and maybe unconsciously) point your finger at the person/job/situation that is "causing" your resentment.

Consider a different stance. See what happens when you view resentment as an indicator light blinking on your car's dashboard. An alert. A cue. A piece of data. Your resentment lets you know that something is amiss between you and your partner.

- A boundary is off.

- An expectation is unclear.

- Agreements need to be reimagined.

Instead of blaming your partner for your resentment, think about resentment as a two-person situation. One that you can approach your partner to puzzle through with you. You might say something like, "I'm finding myself feeling resentful. This resentment is making me feel short-tempered/devalued/exhausted. It's not pleasant for me, and it's not good for us. Can we work together to combat this feeling so I can feel more at ease and we can feel more connected?"

Relational Self-Awareness Questions

- When you conjure up the feeling of resentment, where does it live in your body?

- What does it feel like?

- If it could talk, what would it say?

- Does your resentment have a color? A shape? A name?

Stress perpetuates itself. But so does progress.

Stress is highly contagious. When you are struggling, it affects your partner, not because the two of you are codependent but because you are coregulated. As social creatures, our nervous systems key off each other, especially in an intimate relationship:

- How you are doing affects your partner.

- How your partner is doing affects you.

Work stress is pretty much inevitable, and research indicates that it doesn't stay at work. It comes home. Home to your partner. Home to your family. Far from a guilt trip, this is an invitation to reflect and adjust. Although work stress is an inevitable occurrence, it is not an unaddressable problem:

- I want you to practice stress management because you deserve to feel calm and grounded on the inside.

- But I also want you to practice stress management because the quality of your relationship rests, in part, on how well you manage your own stress.

The same, obviously, is true in terms of your partner managing their stress, for their sake and yours! We must bravely and gently take responsibility for the energy we bring into our relationships.

When our romantic relationships bridge cultural differences, as they so often do, we are gifted the opportunity to view the world through the eyes of another.

One of the most beautiful and significant features of the modern landscape of love is that nearly 20 percent of new marriages bridge a racial and/or ethnic difference. (This number would be much higher if it included love across differences in areas like education, socioeconomic status, ability, and religion.) All love stories are layered, but intercultural love stories have degrees of complexity that grant opportunities and nuances that are above and beyond:

- Individual histories
- Couple dynamics
- Family system dynamics
- Cultural history and legacy

It can be scary to talk about differences. It can be especially scary to talk about cultural differences, knowing that they have historically led to judgment, power struggles, exclusion, and violence. Our hesitation is understandable! But engaging with each other while blind to the cultural differences present in our partnership results in three relational missteps:

1. **We deny the existence of that aspect of self or other.** In effect, we're saying to those identities, "There is no space for you here." How much more transformative love is when all our parts have a seat at the table!

2. **We lose the opportunity to advocate for each other.** Because difference and power are so entwined, partners move through the world with different experiences of privilege and marginalization. Partners with privilege have a responsibility to bear witness to their partner's experiences of microaggressions and systemic oppression.

3. **We cut ourselves off from the richness of experiencing the world through the eyes of another.** I can't think of a more powerful pathway to wisdom, compassion, and love than saying to our beloved, "Tell me how this moment looks and feels through the lens of *your* life story."

If your love story is one that bridges cultural differences, proceed with awareness and relish the richness. Use your differences as gateways to ever greater curiosity and compassion.

DECEMBER 31

Instead of resolutions, let's welcome the new year with reflections, declarations, and blessings.

As you prepare to transition into a new year, may you do so with the gentleness and grace you deserve. Take some time for reflection, integration, and declaration.

Relational Self-Awareness Prompts

- What I want to leave behind is . . .

- What I want to choose instead is . . .

- What I embrace about myself is . . .

- What I will strive to cultivate in others is . . .
- My blessing for myself is . . .
- My blessing for the people around me is . . .
- My blessing for my community is . . .

GLOSSARY

Both/And: Borrowed from the therapeutic approach Dialectical Behavior Therapy, a Both/And is a "space" where two seemingly competing truths must both be "held" at the same time. When you can allow both truths to coexist, shying away from simplistic answers and instead tolerating complexity and nuance, you build emotional agility and resilience and create healing. For example:

- I am *both* insecure *and* brave.

- My partner is *both* devoted *and* forgetful.

- Our relationship is *both* strong *and* evolving.

Chosen Family: Those people you deliberately keep in your life because of your mutual support and connection; this is a term commonly, but not exclusively, used in the queer community.

Coping Strategy: Your Coping Strategies are "where you go" when you get upset. Said another way, your Coping Strategies are what you learned to do to make your too-big feelings feel manageable. The field of somatic (brain- and body-based) psychotherapy has taught us that our Coping Strategies can be classified according to the *Four Fs*: Fight (get loud and critical), Flight (retreat and leave), Freeze (go numb and shut down), and Fawn (placate and accommodate). Our Coping Strategies tend to be adaptive when we are kids and block intimacy once we become grown-ups. For example:

- People-pleasing

- Numbing out with drugs and alcohol

- Demanding perfection or overworking

- Needing to be needed
- Being hyper-independent
- Leaving before we can be left

Core Wounds: Our Core Wounds are the hurt left by an experience or a dynamic we had to deal with when we were too young to understand, control, or change it. Core Wounds stem from experiences that are too much for us to handle, that happen too soon in our lives, and/or that we're left to deal with all alone. For example:

- *I am not a priority.*
- *I am not protected.*
- *I don't belong.*
- *I am not worthy.*

Discernment: Discernment is the ability to assess a situation and select a response that best serves you and the relationship.

Empathic Attunement: Empathic attunement is the ability to "tune into" what someone else is feeling and to be curious about why they might be feeling that way. To practice empathic attunement, we must soothe our own emotional reactions so we can listen carefully to our partner's words and notice their facial expressions and body language. Empathic attunement is a sophisticated and powerful relational skill, one that helps us more deeply understand our partner and that helps our partner feel comforted and understood.

Family of Origin: Your Family of Origin is made up of the people you grew up with. Contrast your Family of Origin with your Family of Creation (the family you made when you grew up) or your Chosen Family (those people who became your family by choice) (*see also* Chosen Family).

Going Meta: This phrase conveys that you and another person are going "up a level"—asking someone if they are available for feedback, as opposed to just giving the feedback. Going Meta is "talking about talking."

Ghostbusters: Couples who are committed to working together (again and again) to explore how pain from the past is compromising connection and ease in the present.

Golden Equation of Love: My Stuff + Your Stuff = Our Stuff. The Golden Equation of Love helps couples avoid the pitfalls of blame and shame by viewing their relationship as a system. Each partner has a unique profile of strengths and Growing Edges, and relationship dynamics and problems reflect individual vulnerabilities that have been activated and that play out in the space between them.

Growing Edge: Your Growing Edge is something that you are working on trying to improve upon or master in your life today. A Growing Edge might be a skill like offering a heartfelt apology, a practice like choosing rest over hyper-productivity, or a mindset shift like accepting that you are imperfect.

Little You: Little You is your inner child. This is the young part of you that gets activated during difficult moments, for example with your partner.

Origin Story: The experiences you went through that shaped your current relationship to relationships. In this book, we mostly talk about the Origin Story that helps you understand your Core Wounds and your Growing Edge, but your talents, passions, and superpowers all have Origin Stories as well (*see also* Core Wounds, Growing Edge).

Original Love Classroom: Your Original Love Classroom is the household and environment you grew up in. When you were little, you were a mini social scientist, taking in all kinds of messages (implicitly and explicitly) about who you were allowed to be and who you needed to be. You also made a lot of observations in your Original Love Classroom about gender dynamics, how differences were handled, and how repairs were made. The lessons you learned in your Original Love Classroom shape how you experience your intimate relationship today.

Pace Discrepancy: A Pace Discrepancy is when one partner is more ready to take the next step in a commitment sequence than the other partner. Pace Discrepancies are common, even within committed loving relationships. Pace Discrepancies offer an opportunity for the couple to face the difference in readiness as a team instead of slipping into a cycle of pressure and withdrawal.

Relational Ambivalence: Relational Ambivalence is a feeling of stuckness, of feeling unsure whether you should stay in a relationship or end it.

Relational Self-Awareness: An ongoing curious and compassionate relationship we each have with ourselves. By helping us take responsibility for how we "show up" in our relationships, Relational Self-Awareness provides the foundation for thriving intimate relationships.

Sexual Self-Awareness: An ongoing curious and compassionate relationship that you cultivate with your sexual self. The process of developing Sexual Self-Awareness includes understanding how your early experiences and cultural conditioning shape how you think and feel about sex, knowing and articulating your sexual boundaries, and creating erotic experiences that feel joyful and nourishing. For more on Sexual Self-Awareness, please refer to my second book, *Taking Sexy Back*.

THEMES BY DATE

Healing from the Past

January 1, 4, 5, 10, 22, 29
February 21, 25
March 1, 2, 4, 13, 23
April 11, 19
May 2, 5, 10, 14
June 1, 5, 17, 23
July 10
August 7, 30
September 4, 7, 10
October 6, 16
November 1, 2, 20
December 7, 19

Practicing Self-Compassion

January 11, 13, 16, 18, 30
March 9, 14, 25
April 1, 20
May 6, 11, 16
June 21, 25
July 5, 19, 24, 29
August 9, 13, 15, 17, 23, 26, 31
September 6, 12, 15, 29
October 2, 7, 15, 28, 31
November 8, 21, 23
December 4, 6, 18, 20, 31

Honoring Your Feelings

January 9, 14, 21, 25
February 2, 3, 4, 12, 13
March 6, 21, 24
April 15, 23
May 8, 19, 24, 27
June 2
July 25, 27
August 29
September 8, 9, 13, 18, 30
October 26, 29,
November 7, 13, 17, 29
December 1, 3, 12, 14, 28

Understanding Relationship Dynamics

January 2, 17, 20, 31
February 14, 15, 23
March 7, 8, 11, 12, 22, 27
April 8, 17, 22, 25
May 13, 17, 20, 31
June 4, 18, 29, 30
July 3, 11, 13, 15, 22
August 1, 3
September 11, 17, 27
October 18, 23, 25, 27, 30
November 9, 16, 24
December 9, 11, 24, 30

Getting Your Needs Met

January 3, 8, 12, 24, 28
February 1, 10, 16, 18, 26
March 5, 19, 30
April 2, 6, 7, 12, 30
May 12, 22, 28
June 22, 28
July 4, 6, 8, 21
August 8, 12, 14, 19, 21, 28
September 21
October 1, 3, 12, 19
November 3, 6
December 8, 16, 21, 23, 26

Transforming Conflict

January 6, 19, 27
February 8, 11, 27
March 17, 20, 28, 31
April 4, 26, 29
May 15, 18, 21, 23, 29
June 7, 11, 14
July 9, 12, 18, 20, 28, 30
August 6, 11, 25
September 14, 16, 19, 26, 28
October 9, 13, 20
November 4, 15, 18, 27
December 2, 10, 25

Addressing Relationship Problems

February 24
March 15, 29
April 3, 18, 24
May 7, 26
June 9, 26
August 2, 5, 16, 20, 22, 24, 27
September 3, 5, 22, 24
October 4, 22
November 26, 28
December 17, 27, 29

Developing Sexual Self-Awareness

February 5, 7, 9, 19
April 9, 14, 27
May 1, 3, 9, 25
June 6, 10, 12, 15
July 1, 2, 16, 31
August 4, 10
September 2
October 17, 21
November 11, 22, 25, 30

Navigating Love's Stages

January 7, 15, 23, 26
February 6, 17, 20, 22, 28
March 3, 10, 16, 18, 26
April 5, 10, 13, 16, 21, 28
May 4, 30
June 3, 8, 13, 16, 19, 20, 24, 27
July 7, 14, 17, 23, 26
August 18
September 1, 20, 23, 25
October 5, 8, 10, 11, 14, 24
November 5, 10, 12, 14, 19
December 5, 13, 15, 22

ADDITIONAL RESOURCES

FIND A THERAPIST

- The Gottman Institute
- International Centre for Excellence in Emotionally Focused Therapy (ICEEFT): Dr. Sue M. Johnson
- American Association for Marriage and Family Therapy (AAMFT)
- American Association of Sexuality Educators, Counselors, and Therapists (AASECT)
- Therapist.com

CRISIS SUPPORT

- National Sexual Assault Hotline (RAINN): www.rainn.org
- Domestic Violence Aid, Resources and Help Lines: https://ncadv. org/resources
- National Suicide Prevention Lifeline: Call 988 or visit https: //988lifeline.org

CONNECT WITH DR. SOLOMON

- Dr. Solomon's website: https://dralexandrasolomon.com/
- Dr. Solomon's weekly podcast *Reimagining Love*: Listen on major podcast platforms

- Dr. Solomon's e-courses:
  - *Intimate Relationships 101: Building Relational and Sexual Self-Awareness*
  - *Can I Trust You Again?: Rebuilding After Betrayal or Deceit*
  - *Loving Bravely: Helping Clients who are Single, Dating, and Single Again*
- Dr. Solomon's other books:
  - *Loving Bravely: Twenty Lessons of Self-Discovery to Help You Get the Love You Want*
  - *Taking Sexy Back: How to Own Your Sexuality and Create the Relationships You Want*

REFERENCES

[1] Kristin Neff, *Self-Compassion: The Proven Power of Being Kind to Yourself* (New York: William Morrow Paperbacks, 2015).

[2] Raymond C. Rosen, "Prevalence and Risk Factors of Sexual Dysfunction in Men and Women," *Current Psychiatry Reports* 2, no. 3 (2000): 189–195.

[3] National Center for Injury Prevention and Control, Division of Violence Prevention, "Fast Facts: Preventing Sexual Violence," *Centers for Disease Control and Prevention*, June 22, 2022, https://www.cdc.gov/violenceprevention/sexualviolence/fastfact.html#:~: text=Sexual%20violence%20is%20common.&text=One%20in%204%20women%20 and,harassment%20in%20a%20public%20place

[4] Wendy Maltz, *The Sexual Healing Journey: A Guide for Survivors of Sexual Abuse*, 3rd ed. (New York: William Morrow, 2013).

[5] Laurie Mintz, *Becoming Cliterate: Why Orgasm Equality Matters—And How to Get It* (San Francisco: HarperOne, 2017).

[6] Ximena B. Arriaga, Madoka Kumashiro, Eli J. Finkel, Laura E. VanderDrift, and Laura B. Luchies, "Filling the Void: Bolstering Attachment Security in Committed Relationships," *Social Psychological and Personality Science* 5, no. 4 (2014): 398–406.

[7] Richard V. Reeves and Ember Smith, "The Male College Crisis Is Not Just in Enrollment, but Completion," *The Brookings Institution*, October 8, 2021, https://www.brookings .edu/blog/up-front/2021/10/08/the-male-college-crisis-is-not-just-in-enrollment-but-completion/.

[8] Aimee Picchi, "More Women Are Now Outearning Their Husbands—and Emotions Can Be Big," *USA Today*, March 3, 2020, https://www.usatoday.com/story/money/2020/03/03 /gender-wage-gap-more-women-out-earning-husbands/4933666002/.

[9] Andrew Christensen and Neil S. Jacobson, *Reconcilable Differences* (New York: Guilford Press, 2000).

[10] Pauline Boss, "Ambiguous Loss," 2023, https://www.ambiguousloss.com/.

[11] C. J. Eubanks Fleming and Alexis T. Franzese, "Should I Stay or Should I Go? Evaluating Intimate Relationship Outcomes During the 2020 Pandemic Shutdown," *Couple and Family Psychology: Research and Practice* 10, no. 3 (2021): 158–167.

[12] Terry Real, *Us: Getting Past You and Me to Build a More Loving Relationship* (New York: Rodale, 2022)

[13] Ibram X. Kendi, *How to Be an Antiracist* (New York: One World, 2019)

[14] Shirley P. Glass, *Not "Just Friends": Rebuilding Trust and Recovering Your Sanity After Infidelity* (New York: Atria, 2002).

[15] Francesca Donner, "The Housework Men and Women Do, and Why," *The New York Times*, February 12, 2020, https://www.nytimes.com/2020/02/12/us/the-household-work-men-and-women-do-and-why.html.

[16] John M. Gottman, Catherine Swanson, and James Murray, "The Mathematics of Marital Conflict: Dynamic Mathematical Nonlinear Modeling of Newlywed Marital Interaction," *Journal of Family Psychology* 13, no. 1 (1999): 3–19.

[17] Lori A. Brotto, *Better Sex Through Mindfulness: How Women Can Cultivate Desire* (Vancouver: Greystone Books, 2018).

[18] Jill S. Huppert, William A. Volck, Rudy G. Ellis III, Marianne C. Bernard, Debra L. Herbenick, and Paula J. Adams Hillard, "College Men Lack Basic Knowledge About Gynecology," *Journal of Pediatric and Adolescent Gynecology* 24, no. 2, e47 (2011).

[19] "A No-Holds-Barred Conversation with Expert Iyanla Vanzant," *The Oprah Winfrey Show*, season 25, episode 86, aired February 16, 2011.

[20] Jeffrey A. Hall, "How Many Hours Does it Take to Make a Friend?" *Journal of Social and Personal Relationships* 36, no. 4 (2019): 1278–1296.

[21] Audre Lorde, *Sister Outsider: Essays and Speeches* (Toronto: Crossing Press, 2007).

[22] "The SIECUS State Profiles 2019/2020," *Sexuality Information and Education Council of the United States (SIECUS)*, https://siecus.org/state-profiles-2019-2020/.

[23] "Sex and HIV Education," *Guttmacher Institute*, February 1, 2023, https://www.guttmacher.org/state-policy/explore/sex-and-hiv-education.

[24] John M. Gottman and Nan Silver, *The Seven Principles for Making Marriage Work: A Practical Guide from the Country's Foremost Relationship Expert* (New York: Harmony, 2015).

[25] Leslie S. Greenberg and Rhonda N. Goldman, "Emotion-focused couples therapy: The dynamics of emotion, love, and power," In A. S. Gurman (Ed.), *Clinical Casebook of Couple Therapy.* (pp. 255–280). Guilford Press.

[26] "Fundamental Attribution Error," *Wikipedia*, https://en.wikipedia.org/wiki/Fundamental _attribution_error

[27] Walt Whitman, *Leaves of Grass: The Original 1855 Edition* (Mineola: Dover Publications, 2007).

[28] Heinz Kohut, *How Does Analysis Cure?*, eds. Arnold Goldberg and Paul E. Stepansky (The University of Chicago Press, 1984).

[29] Esther Perel, *Mating in Captivity: Reconciling the Erotic and the Domestic* (New York: HarperCollins, 2006)

[30] Carol S. Dweck, *Mindset: The New Psychology of Success.* (New York: Random House, 2006).

[31] Richard J. Davidson, "Comment: Affective Chronometry Has Come of Age," *Emotion Review* 7, no. 4 (2015): 368–370.

[32] Daniel J. Siegel, *Mindsight: The New Science of Personal Transformation* (New York: Bantam Books, 2010). Adapted from Dan Siegel's "River of Integration" concept.

[33] Mona D. Fishbane, "Facilitating Relational Empowerment in Couple Therapy," *Family Process* 50, no. 3 (2011): 337–352

[34] Lydia G. Roos, Victoria O'Connor, Amy Canevello, and Jeanette Marie Bennett, "Post-Traumatic Stress and Psychological Health Following Infidelity in Unmarried Young Adults," *Stress and Health* 35, no. 4 (2019): 468–479.

[35] Danu A. Stinson, Jessica J. Cameron, and Lisa B. Hoplock, "The Friends-to-Lovers Pathway to Romance: Prevalent, Preferred, and Overlooked by Science," *Social Psychological and Personality Science* 13, no. 2 (2022): 562–571.

36 Roy J. Lewicki, Beth Polin, and Robert B. Lount Jr., (2016). "An Exploration of the Structure of Effective Apologies," *Negotiation and Conflict Management Research* 9, no. 2 (2016): 177–196.

37 Katherine Hilton, "What Does an Interruption Sound Like?" (PhD diss., Stanford University, 2018), https://searchworks.stanford.edu/view/12742076.

38 Judy A. Makinen and Susan M. Johnson, "Resolving Attachment Injuries in Couples Using Emotionally Focused Therapy: Steps Toward Forgiveness and Reconciliation," *Journal of Consulting and Clinical Psychology* 74, no. 6 (2006): 1055–1064.

39 "It's No Trick; Merriam-Webster Says 'Gaslighting' Is the Word of the Year," *National Public Radio*, November, 28, 2022, https://www.npr.org/2022/11/28/1139384432/its-no-trick-merriam-webster-says-gaslighting-is-the-word-of-the-year.

40 William H. Masters, and Virginia E. Johnson, *Human Sexual Inadequacy* (Boston: Little, Brown, 1970).

41 Gottman, Swanson, and Murray, "The Mathematics," 3–19.

42 Bernice L. Neugarten, "Adaptation and the Life Cycle," *The Counseling Psychologist* 6, no. 1 (1976): 16–20.

44 "Resentment," *Merriam-Webster*, https://www.merriam-webster.com/dictionary/resentment.

45 A.W. Geiger and Gretchen Livingston, "8 Facts About Love and Marriage in America," *Pew Research Center*, February 13, 2019, https://www.pewresearch.org/fact-tank/2019/02/13/8-facts-about-love-and-marriage/.

ACKNOWLEDGMENTS

Writing a book is a Both/And. It is both a solo venture and a team sport. I want to thank Team RSA. I am blessed beyond measure to be in the trenches with the most dynamic and brilliant young women. Elizabeth Vogt, you are my podcast producer, assistant, thought partner, and ally. I am forever grateful that we took a chance on each other. Megan Gaumond Oval, you are simply the best Emotional Support Megan a girl could ever ask for! Sam Hardy, you are such a bright light in this world.

I want to thank the hundreds of thousands of people around the world who follow my work on Instagram. This diverse community asks me thoughtful questions, shares incisive feedback, and serves as my steady muse as I continue to develop the framework of Relational Self-Awareness.

Thank you to Kate Sample, Chelsea Thompson, and the incredible team at PESI. I love being in partnership with you, and I look forward to continuing to grow and collaborate together. Jill Marsal, I am lucky to have you as my literary agent. Dana Kaye, my ride-or-die, I love working with you and your team at Kaye Publicity (Hailey, Ellie, Kaitlyn, Nicole, and Julia). Thank you also to all the advisers who keep AHS Global Media afloat: Colleen Keith, Mary Chan, Danelle Cloutier, Katie Pagacz, Julie Pcsck, Kim Padgitt, Stephen Breimer, and Mark Turner. Thank you to Vienna Pharaon for teaching me how to use Instagram all those years ago, and to Mark Groves for generously sharing my writing time after time. I love being on this journey with you both!

Finally, thank you to my family and friends for your belief in me and your love for me. My relationships with you are my foundation, my source, and my inspiration.

ABOUT THE AUTHOR

Alexandra H. Solomon, PhD, is one of the most trusted voices in the world of relationships, and her work on relational self-awareness has reached millions of people around the world. Dr. Solomon is a licensed clinical psychologist at The Family Institute at Northwestern University, and she is on faculty in the School of Education and Social Policy at Northwestern University, where she teaches the internationally renowned course *Building Loving and Lasting Relationships: Marriage 101*. In addition to writing articles and chapters for leading academic journals and books in the field of marriage and family, she is the author of two best-selling books, *Loving Bravely* and *Taking Sexy Back*. Dr. Solomon regularly presents to diverse groups that include the United States Military Academy at West Point and Microsoft, and she is frequently asked to talk about relationships with media outlets like *The Today Show*, *O Magazine*, *The Atlantic*, *Vogue*, and *Scientific American*. She is the host of the weekly podcast *Reimagining Love*.